Brides *of the* MULTITUDE

PROSTITUTION IN THE OLD WEST

By Jeremy Agnew

WESTERN REFLECTIONS PUBLISHING COMPANY®

Lake City, CO

ISBN 978-1-932738-49-0

Library of Congress Control Number: 2008928264

Cover and book design: Laurie Goralka Design
Cover photo: Courtesy of P. David Smith

First Edition

Printed in the United States

Western Reflections Publishing Company®
P.O. Box 1149, 951 N. Highway 149
Lake City, CO 81235
1-800-993-4490
westref@montrose.net
www.westernreflectionspub.com

DEDICATION

For Glenn,
who had a passion for the history
of the Old West – and never let the facts
get in the way of a good story!

ACKNOWLEDGEMENT

Many thanks to P. David Smith for his support in making this book a reality.

CONTENTS

INTRODUCTION

*T*he purchase of the Louisiana Territory from France in 1803 by President Thomas Jefferson added a vast, unexplored land of more than 900,000 square miles to the existing United States. The Treaty of Gualadupe Hidalgo that ended the war with Mexico in 1848 added another 500,000 square miles. These huge additions of vast, empty land initially contained only a few white people, but the western-most limit of the frontier continually changed as civilization expanded inexorably through it across the continent towards the Pacific Ocean. What took place during those years of settlement is a vital and lasting part of our heritage, and the West of today still contains reflections of this American experience.

The period of rapid westerly expansion that lasted from approximately 1840 to 1900 embraced fur-trapping and the Indian Wars, immigration and settlement of the new land, westward expansion of the railroads, the rise and fall of the great cattle drives, and the discoveries of gold and silver in the Western mountains. Westward growth was also promoted by the Homestead Act, signed into law by President Abraham Lincoln in May of 1862. Under this act, any family had the right to homestead up to 160 acres of public land.

The movement of settlers into the West created the largest mass migration experienced in the history of the United States. Between 1860 and 1870, a million people poured into the region and, by 1880, were joined by another two-and-a-half million. Because heavy manual labor was a necessary force in settling the West, the early years of homesteading, mining, railroading, and cattle-raising produced a society that was dominated by young, single men. The Civil War and subsequent fluctuations in the country's economy cast many men adrift to seek their way in the world; therefore, many of the players in the drama of the developing West were enticed by stories of a life of independence and a place to make a new start. Some followed the magical lure of the frontier that promised potential fortunes in gold mining, cattle, and railroading. Others followed the romanticized image of the West of men braving nature and the elements, creating a new life for themselves while forging a frontier out of the wilderness.

The rapid expansion of the western frontier created cultural upheaval and social limbo. Married men often left their wives behind while they pursued their dreams of wealth and fortune in the West. They left with the promise that they would return with the legendary pot of gold or would send for their families as soon as they struck it rich. Wives, sweethearts and other civilizing influences were mostly left back East or in towns such as St. Joseph and Independence, Missouri, which were the jumping-off places for the westward journey.

Mining was one of the important factors in development of the West. Periodic fevered stampedes to the gold fields and silver lodes of the Rocky Mountains and the Sierra Nevada Mountains of California attracted huge influxes of unattached young men between 1850 and 1900. Many mining settlements, cattle towns, and railroad construction camps of the developing West boomed in a carnival-like atmosphere. Law and order were often left behind, and vice of all types flourished. In some of the larger mining towns, such as Bodie, Deadwood, and Leadville, murder and mayhem frequently prevailed. In this unrestricted atmosphere many previous social restraints were left behind, and men did things that they would have never dreamed of doing while under the influence of wife and home.

Of the few leisure occupations that were available to this young male society, the three most popular were drinking, gambling, and womanizing. Therefore, the rise of prostitution in the West was fueled by a vast pool of single men and a decided lack of women[1]. Just as men were lured by the touted riches of the West, so were the ladies of untroubled virtue; however, their target was the easy money to be made by catering to the men's needs for companionship and sex.

While gambling, drinking, and prostitution were indeed a part of life in the Old West, it is important to realize that upright, law-abiding, church-going citizens outnumbered prostitutes and despera-does[2]. Some men did not drink or smoke, and some never looked at women other than their wives. These upright citizens generally ignored the shootings, shouts, and shrieks that carried through the night from those who caroused in the red light district. They continued to quietly build civilized towns and make homes, raise children, and build a life for their families.

As well as being eyed by ladies of easy virtue who were out to make a fast dollar, the vast collection of young, single, eligible men was looked upon as a reservoir of potential husbands by unmarried young women. Many women headed west with the sole intention of getting married as soon as possible. Most of them did[3].

The marriage market was brisk in many frontier towns. Women who hired maids complained that the help only stayed a matter of weeks before they left to marry. Women looking for maids or servants often hired girls who were not particularly good-looking in the hopes that they wouldn't marry as fast. These employers usually found that beauty was not necessarily a prerequisite for marriage to lonely men, and often even the homeliest girls remained single for only a few months. The same problem existed in many communities that hired unmarried, female school teachers. Their pupils often had a succession of different teachers during the school year.

By the time 1900 arrived, the rush to lands west of the Great Plains had slowed. The arrival of wives and families spurred the establishment of churches, schools, and law and order. This resulted in a settling influence and the establishment of the social graces. Gambling, drinking, and prostitution, which had earlier been accepted as part of frontier life, was now publicly frowned on, and the story in the chapters that follow about the women of easy virtue in the Wild West came to a close.

PART I

The Women

Chapter 1

VICTORIAN ATTITUDES

"Her virtue was sold,
for an old man's gold."
(couplet from a popular Victorian music hall ballad)

*P*rostitution in the second half of the Nineteenth Century was influenced by the presumed superiority of Victorian men over women and the resulting role forced on women by Victorian society. These factors also played important parts in contemporary attitudes towards prostitution and in why women became prostitutes.

Prostitution has been referred to as the "world's oldest profession." The exchange of sexual services by women in return for tangible rewards from men has existed at least as far back as recorded history. Prostitution is described in early Greek and Roman writings, and one of Western society's earliest historical records, the Bible, describes it as an existing contemporary fact. In Roman times, prostitution was treated as a necessary institution to preserve marriage by allowing sexual release to men who could not otherwise obtain it.

Prostitution is promiscuous and impersonal, and involves only superficial social contact between the participants. The word "prostitute" is derived from the Latin word *prostitutus*, which means "to set forth in public" or "to expose publicly." Used as a verb, the common English usage of "prostitute" means to sell promiscuous sexual services. The word is also applied as a noun to a woman who sells herself for sexual purposes[1.]

Prostitution has been, and still is, primarily a female occupation. Although there are male prostitutes, some serving a female clientele (gigolos) and some catering to male homosexuals, females selling sexual services have always vastly outnumbered men doing the same. The two primary conditions for female prostitution are a population that is predominantly male and a shortage of willing female sexual partners. This was the situation that existed in much of the early West.

Though prostitution has existed through the ages, the rise and spread of visible commercial prostitution in the United States coincided with nineteenth century urbanization and the growth of the Industrial Revolution. Prior to that time the population was primarily a rural, agricultural population composed of the family unit and a social structure that did not readily lend itself to prostitution. Illicit sex on the farm was more on the order of a quick roll in the hay than an organized commercial transaction.

The change from a primarily agrarian society to an urban, industrialized society in the 1800s resulted in the massive relocation of a rural population that hoped to find work in the developing cities. Young untrained and unskilled women flooded the large cities and, unable to compete in the growing labor pool, often could not find employment. As jobs became increasingly difficult to find, many women turned to prostitution as their only way to make enough money to survive, thus making prostitution in the urban areas increasingly widespread.

Opinions about prostitution in the emerging West ran the gamut from it was "a corrupter of the morals of young, single men" to it was "an outlet for fun and relaxation for hardworking miners and cowboys." Whatever the social ramifications have been, prostitution has always been a sexual liaison. From the Victorian viewpoint, prostitution was a sexual liaison that was for sale, a type of sex that was publicly condemned. Public opinion of the late Nineteenth Century was that prostitution was a social evil that should be eradicated in order to bring society back to its Puritan ideal. In fact, prostitution was commonly called "*The* Social Evil." However, the private reality was that many men, both married and single, visited prostitutes.

Sooner or later prostitution in most towns in the West became technically illegal, and the law considered prostitutes to be criminals. Practically speaking, however, prostitution was generally tolerated and was looked upon a necessary evil that had a crude value to society. Prostitution was considered to be a readily available outlet for men who had no other release for sexual tensions, thereby hopefully reducing the incidence of rape, molestation, and other sex-related crimes. Although prostitutes were accepted in the early West, because there was a lack

The morning shift at the Mary McKinney Mine in Anaconda, Colorado, was typical of the active young men in the West who sought relaxation with girls and drink after work.
(Glenn Kinnaman Colorado and Western History Collection.)

of available women, they were later viewed as leading men astray and destroying the sanctity of marriage.

To fully understand prostitution on the Western Frontier, it is first necessary to look at Victorian attitudes towards women and sex. The word "sex" is used here in its widest sense to include not just the physical act of reproduction, but also the psychological differences between the genders, the social status of women in the mid- to late 1800s, Victorian morality, and contemporary attitudes that existed towards women.

The time period from 1840 to 1900 corresponds roughly to the Victorian era. Correctly speaking, the term "Victorian" refers to the time period between 1837 and 1901, when the English monarch Victoria was on the throne. The word "Victorian" is also used here in the broader sense to designate the characteristic moral and social climate that existed during the last half of the Nineteenth Century.

Victorian sexuality was a combination of repression, obsession, hypocrisy, prudery, and permissiveness. This curious collection of attitudes resulted in what, by today's standards, could be considered an unenlightened attitude towards sex, procreation, and, by association, the human body itself. In the mainstream "public" Victorian view, sex was considered to be a base form of male expression that had to be given

Though the existence of gambling was often publicly denied, saloons such as this one in Leadville, Colorado, in the 1880s did plenty of business.
(Courtesy Denver Public Library, Western History Collection, X-6363)

periodic release in order to prevent dire consequences. Sex was viewed as a bestial obsession that had to be accepted and tolerated by women; and it was considered to be one of the unfortunate flaws in the male character, along with others, such as drinking and gambling. Nineteenth century medical writers solemnly declared that anything sexual was strictly a male function, and women were led to believe that they had no sex drive. Medical opinion held that women wanted to marry in order to have children and not for physical and emotional reasons. Many Victorian men valued women primarily for their reproductive function.

As well as a public denial of sexuality, the Victorian era included a public denial of vice in general, such as drinking, gambling, and similar activities — including prostitution. This was carried to the extent of pretending that these vices did not exist, even though their occurrence was common knowledge. This was a era when public respectability had to be maintained, and these activities were considered to be subjects unsuitable for public exposure and discussion.

The Victorian double standard created sexual repression, yet many activities that were publicly condemned (and especially those that involved women) were often actively practiced in private. While the official attitude of society was one of purity and decency, the incidence of private indulgence in pornography, prostitution, and some expressions of unusual sexual behavior were higher than might be expected. This apparent paradox of one type of behavior and morality for public consumption and another set of values for private behavior was not a Victorian invention. History is full of examples of sexual hypocrisy.

One rather amusing example of hypocritical Victorian behavior is revealed by an early settler on the Northwest coast. He described the habit of the local Indian women of bathing naked in ocean tide pools next to the beaches. His narrative condemned this nude bathing as an absolutely disgusting practice and exhibition of vulgarity. From reading his description, however, the author had obviously watched the women very closely indeed, in order to be able to report every "disgusting" aspect in great detail.

As another example, titillation could be obtained under the pretense of serious scientific inquiry. Popular attractions were the so-called "anatomical museums," which displayed glass jars of diseased and malformed organs. Displays of items dealing with reproduction were particularly popular, because this was such a clandestine subject. Museums in the East, such as New York's impressively-named Natural Anatomical Museum and Academy of Natural Science, displayed figures of naked men and women, along with diagrams and models of reproductive organs, and examples of "sexual oddities."

✿ VICTORIAN WOMEN ✿

In the Victorian world, feminine purity was the foundation of the social structure. Women were supposed to provide social and moral stability through the characteristics of "goodness" and "purity." One contemporary gauge of a Victorian woman's morality was her ability to cook, sew, and keep a neat, clean house. A dirty house was considered to be the sign of a fallen woman.

Women were supposed to remain occupied with domestic duties within the home and not seek careers. One authority went so far as to propose the idea that a woman who tried to educate herself would find that she took on male characteristics, among which her reproductive organs would shrivel, resulting in sterility and a growth of facial hair.

As a part of a society that encouraged male dominance, women were considered to be inferior to men, both mentally and physically.

One example was an established medical belief that the female respiratory system was different from that of a male. Hence, women were more subject to breathing difficulties. In fact, there was some truth to the observation, but instead of an inherent biological difference, the real cause was women's corsets. They were so tightly-laced to produce the ideal Victorian hourglass figure that they inhibited expansion of the rib cage and sometimes made it difficult to breathe.

Corsets were also blamed for other ailments. As viewed by one self-styled authority, tight corsets increased upward blood flow to a woman's head and put pressure on her nervous system, thereby causing personality changes. Another "expert" theorized that the tight lacing of corsets created downwards pressure and increased blood flow to the "lower organs," thus endangering a woman's morals. In reality, the result was often a prolapsed uterus caused by excessive pressure on a woman's insides. One critic went so far as to offer the opinion that tightly-laced corsets could lead virtuous women into a life of prostitution.

Physicians of the era promoted the idea that females were inherently frail, and that their biology made them prone to insanity, mental exhaustion, and other debilitating "nervous" afflictions. Medical opinion

The traditional "wasp-waisted" Victorian figure was achieved by tightly-laced corsets, which some reformers denounced as immoral.

(Glenn Kinnaman Colorado and Western History Collection.)

also held that women had more delicate systems than men and were subject to more physical complaints than their male counterparts. Man's nature was theorized to be governed by his brain. With perverse logic (because virtuous women were supposed to be non-sexual) a woman's nature was theorized to be determined by her reproductive organs.

Even the excessive reading of romance novels by women was thought to disturb the nerves and induce nervous hysteria. "Hysteria" was a vague medical term derived from the Greek name for the womb. According to authoritative medical opinion, hysteria was a common female disease that manifested itself in fainting spells, insomnia, shortness of breath, fits of laughing, weeping, screaming, morbid fears, and an inability to speak.

A further opinion of a woman's frailty was perpetuated in the Victorian attitude towards menstruation. Rather than being accepted as an unpleasant, but unalterable, fact of life, Victorian women were taught to view "the curse" or "the poorlies" with repugnance, and were encouraged to take to their sick-beds while wallowing in self-disgust. This viewpoint was amplified by male attitudes, which perpetuated the myth and used this time of the month as an excuse to continue to suppress women as social, political, and business equals. Manufacturers of patent medicines capitalized on this attitude by stating that menstruation was a serious illness that required regular doses of various proprietary elixirs.

The Victorian attitude towards the human body was one of almost pathological modesty. This was an era when "proper ladies" should never be naked, except perhaps for bathing. Even then, many women managed the somewhat inconvenient feat of washing all over while wearing a nightgown or shift. At night, long flannel nightgowns reached the floor at the bottom and the neck at the top, with never a hint of anything else between. For the purposes of procreation, the middle of many nightgowns had a strategically placed opening that was just large enough to allow the discreet consummation of the sex act without the humiliation and embarrassment of undressing.

Doctors in the Victorian era had a difficult time in diagnosing female illnesses because often the physical examination of female patients had to be carried out through their clothing or included the use of a doll as a surrogate patient to point out where an ailment was. Childbirth was usually attended only by female midwives. If a doctor were present, he might have to perform the delivery by feel while the patient was totally covered by a sheet or blanket.

The words "naked" or "nude" never entered into the vocabulary of proper Victorian ladies, or even their thoughts. Many married couples rarely or never saw each other naked. Some women were so repressed that they dressed and undressed in a darkened closet so as to never reveal their bodies — even to themselves. Whalebone corsets, hoop skirts, thick cotton stockings, voluminous petticoats, bustles, and floor-length dresses hid and protected everything underneath from view. Women's bodies were so covered up that the momentary sight of a woman's ankle revealed under a flowing skirt might be enough to cause a gentleman great embarrassment, though it was certainly of great interest. To the proper Victorian gentleman, today's miniskirts, bikinis, shorts, and bra-less fashions, would be fantasies beyond even his wildest imagination.

Attitudes towards modesty were so extreme that legs on furniture, such as chair legs, were referred to a " limb," because "leg" was not considered an appropriate word for polite company. Piano legs might have a ruffled skirt placed on them so that their "limbs" were not exposed to public view. It was considered highly indelicate to offer a lady a "leg" of chicken. Instead she was offered the white meat. Chicken "breasts" were called "bosoms."

Some of this silliness rose beyond the sublime to reach the ridiculous. For example, some Victorian residents of Colorado Springs, Colorado, were so shocked at the naughty implication in the name of Son-of-a-Gun Hill, a steep section of the cog railroad that ran up nearby Pikes Peak, that they actually spelled the name "Sun-of-a-Gun" to give it more propriety.

While some modern scholars of Victoriana are prone to dismiss such anecdotes as fable, enough stories have been handed down from people born in the late Victorian era to authenticate them.[2] It should be noted, however, that these are extreme examples of Victorian prudery. Evidence exists in women's literature and diaries that many Victorian women and their husbands enjoyed uninhibited sexuality. Much of the Victorian literature that recounts prudish stories reflects the view of what male writers and contemporary society thought that women should do and feel, rather than what they actually did.

Another piece of evidence that contradicts the idea of universal prudery is the existence of many examples of written Victorian pornography. In addition, highly-explicit erotic photographs of nude women — and men — started to appear in the 1850s, soon after the widespread use of the camera and photographic plates that could be developed with relative ease.[3]

Women of the Victorian age held a place that was subservient to men. Liberality and equality for women, particularly in the East, was virtually unheard of. The first political entity in the Union that allowed women to vote and hold public office was Wyoming Territory, which passed legislation to that effect in 1869. This revolutionary action so appalled Eastern lawmakers that they almost did not grant Wyoming statehood when the territory applied for it in 1890. This legislation, however, may not have been radical thinking on the part of the Wyoming lawmakers. It was probably more of a public-relations gesture. Since there were hardly any women in Wyoming at the time and a territorial population of only about 9,000, lawmakers may have hoped that giving women the right to vote would attract more females to settle in the territory. In spite of this liberal gesture, the female population of Wyoming did not immediately increase. The Wyoming Territorial Government apparently had second thoughts about what they had done and voted to repeal the bill in 1871. The repeal failed by one vote.

By 1896, only three additional states had given women the right to vote. These were also Western states: Colorado, Idaho, and Utah. The staid and civilized East was shocked by such revolutionary thinking in the upstart West. It was not until 1920, and the passage of the Nineteenth Amendment to the Constitution of the United States, that women universally gained the legal right to vote.

❧ VICTORIAN SEX ❧

Sex is a biological process that is neither good nor bad. Only in more modern times has sex been viewed by most of western society as having a value and recreational aspect beyond the basic function of reproduction. Human attitudes towards sex, however, have always been heavily influenced by history, contemporary culture, and politics. Attitudes towards sex and prostitution in the Old West, therefore, were shaped by the opinions of the people who lived there during that particular time period.

The Victorian attitude of the superiority of men led to a male-oriented and culturally-supported myth that men needed, wanted, and enjoyed sex more than women. In Victorian society, this idea was indoctrinated into "nice" girls and many grew up with a fear of this supposed animalistic nature of men. Hence, many women either refrained from sexual activity or participated in it under less than optimal circumstances.

"Proper" Victorian women were supposed to be naturally virtuous and non-sexual. Even physician William Sanger wrote in his pioneering

Brothels offered a choice of girls, such as these women in fancy ball gowns photographed with their madam, Laura Evens, in Denver.
(Courtesy Colorado Historical Society, Mazzulla Collection, Box 22, FF 1294, scan #10026977)

study of prostitution in 1858 that "the full force of sexual desire is seldom known to a virtuous woman."[4] Women who did experience sexual urges or feelings were encouraged to suppress them. They were taught that any such stirrings were unladylike and shameful, and might even be physically harmful.

Indeed, it was thought that excessive sexual activity led to disorders of the reproductive organs, and women who enjoyed sexual excitement were considered to be on the pathway to madness. Nymphomania was considered to be a form of insanity that was best treated by incarceration in an asylum. Prostitutes, who by the nature of their work indulged in frequent sex, were viewed by the Victorians as having a distorted sense of sexuality and morality (and indeed this opinion is still common today). Proper Victorians would not believe the modern scientific evidence that many women have a higher sex drive and higher physical sexual capacity than men.

There were a few contemporary medical writers who conceded that women had sexual urges, but in Victorian society this was not a proper subject for discussion. The public's attitude was that research into sexuality was not an appropriate topic, and that open discussion or publication of anything to do with sex was not for public consumption.

There were a few who disagreed with the mainstream medical views. Elizabeth Blackwell, for example, a physician and pioneering moral reformer, acknowledged that women had a sex drive, but she also wrote that sex should not be engaged in frequently as it was a strain on the human body and depleted vital energies. Orgasm in men was thought to cause physical debility and reduced intellectual development. In women, it was theorized to interfere with conception and thought to lead to sterility. The Victorians thought that only lascivious women experienced sexual pleasure. Menopause was considered to be linked to mania, depression, perversion, delirium, and many other unrelated illnesses, including arthritis and syphilis.

Accompanying the idea that Victorian women were supposed to have no sex drives and no interest in sexual matters was the concept that no woman could gain the distorted sexual attitude of a prostitute of her own volition. The conventional thinking was that she must have been raped or seduced — and then probably while under the influence of drugs or alcohol.

Common Victorian names or adjectives applied to a prostitute, such as "fair, but frail," promoted the idea that these women were not in control of their own biological drives and hence of their own destinies. Far from being frail, however, most Victorian prostitutes were healthy, robust women with normal, if perhaps somewhat uninhibited, sexual ways and a strong desire to make easy money. It wasn't until the early Twentieth Century that "victimization" theories were discarded, as a gradual realization came that complex social factors, along with the stresses and changes brought about by urbanization, were contributing catalysts for commercialized prostitution.

⟨◆⟩ MARRIAGE AND SEX ⟨◆⟩

Sex within marriage was begrudgingly acknowledged and was looked on as a base physical drive of men that had to be occasionally satisfied by dutiful wives.

The concept of men having an extremely high sex drive that had to be satisfied due to continuously smoldering male passions was referred to by contemporary writers as the "volcano theory." Men were considered to be like dormant volcanoes and, unless they found regular release for their sexual pressures, they would explode and produce a veritable torrent of rape, adultery, violence, and even homosexuality. Though sex outside marriage occurred occasionally, it was condemned.

From many women's points of view, sex was a vehicle for procreation, to be hastily consummated with an attitude of martyrdom and by a long-suffering wife. Some physicians recommended sex no more than once a month, and then only under ideal conditions when neither partner was fatigued or under the influence of strong emotions. Women were advised to remain indifferent to their husband's sexual advances in order to restrain the male's natural passions. In spite of these authoritative pronouncements by experts, contemporary personal diaries have shown us that many Victorian wives enjoyed sex.

Because women grew up being told that they would not and could not enjoy sex, many did not. The minimization of female sexuality did not encourage sexual arousal or response. Men were led to believe that women's disgust for sex was so great that they went through the mechanics of the act as fast as possible. This, in turn, tended to increase many women's attitudes of indifference towards physical relations, which in turn made the husband work even harder to get sex over and done with quickly. Sage advice passed down from mothers to daughters about to be married was to lie in bed passively and think of some other subject until the event was over.

Sex education was ignored in the Victorian era, either from a desire to protect a child's innocence or from the parent's own embarrassment of the subject. For adolescents, and particularly for young women who were protected from the facts of life, the shock of the truth about sex within marriage could lead to horror, disgust, or shame. Information in contemporary marriage manuals, even those written by physicians, was couched in such vague and euphemistic terms that the publications, in fact, did not contain much useful guidance at all. Information on birth control was considered obscene and was banned.

Much of the Victorian attitude towards marriage and sex was based on three ideas: a belief that women could be categorized as either "good" or "bad", that there was a double standard of sexual behavior for men and women, and that brides had to be virgins.

Sexual repression for "nice" women and permissiveness for men clearly divided women into two distinct categories. "Respectable" ladies — wives, daughters, and sweethearts — were considered to be pure, virtuous, and sexually innocent women. These women were put on imaginary romantic pedestals, an idea left over from the practice of courtly love and worship from afar that was practiced in England and Europe during the Middle Ages. These women were expected to be ladylike, proper in dress and manner, good housekeepers, virtuous, and virgins when they married.

On the other hand, "bad" women were to be enjoyed. They were prostitutes and other sexually-available women. For Victorian gentlemen these women were not marriageable, but were in a category that allowed and encouraged strictly sexual relationships. From the male point of view this led to a practice that often meant that they had a home life, with or without sex, and a sex life outside the home. Because of this attitude, "decent" frontier women could not associate with or have any friendships among any of the inhabitants of the red light district. Respectable women were taught that the taint of the profession would rub off on them if they even talked to a prostitute.

These attitudes resulted in double beds and double morality. For women, there was the enforcement of chastity before marriage and monogamy after marriage. Men, on the other hand, were expected to gain sexual experience before marriage. This led to the quandary of how men were supposed to get this experience when nice Victorian girls were supposed to be virtuous before marriage and faithful after marriage.

The attitude of "boys will be boys" allowed young men to gain experience with "fast" women, but the reverse was not considered acceptable.
(Courtesy Denver Public Library, Western History Collection, F-20793)

For an unmarried man to gain sexual experience, one of the few acceptable options was to go to a prostitute. Adultery was considered to be a far worse option than simple sex between two unmarried people, because adultery threatened the stability of the family unit. If adultery occurred and the participants were exposed, the woman was usually blamed for having seduced the man, and the errant male was mildly censured with a knowing smile and the admonition that "boys will be boys."

One of the contributing factors to the tolerance of sex with prostitutes was the ever-present fear of pregnancy for the Victorian wife. For the wife who had been married for some years and who had already defied possible death to produce a large family, any further pregnancy could be an unbearable thought. Contraceptives were known and used, but the methods available at the time were notoriously unreliable. The only completely successful method of preventing conception was total abstinence. Abortions were performed, but they were extremely dangerous because of the lack of modern medical knowledge and aseptic techniques, and the lack of antibiotic drugs to prevent the infections that were almost certain to follow.

Contraception was generally looked on with disfavor as a male method of separating sex from procreation and by which men could satisfy their lusts without the responsibility of having children. Some opponents of contraception felt that sex without the intent of pregnancy was itself a form of prostitution — even sex between husband and wife. Thus, contraception became mentally linked with prostitution, because it was assumed that only prostitutes would do such a thing. The extension of this thinking was that abstinence was the correct way to limit family size.

So, in effect, Victorian prostitution was sometimes used as a form of contraception. Wives who did not want any more children either overlooked or, in some cases, encouraged visits by their husbands to prostitutes as an outlet for their supposedly uncontrollable sexual needs. Wives may not have liked their husbands' outside sexual liaisons; but, as opposed to the burden and dangers of pregnancy, they tolerated or at least overlooked them. Having been taught to believe that men would go wild without a release from sexual pressures, turning a blind eye to prostitution was seen as one method of preserving the chastity of unmarried girls and of protecting married ladies from adultery, rape, and other forms of sex not approved by Victorian society.

The virginity of a bride was very important to the Victorian bridegroom, since it was equated with purity and he had been taught that only a pure woman was a desirable marriage partner. Thus, for a woman, virginity was an essential asset for obtaining a good marriage partner. Girls who had strayed before marriage were ostracized as "fallen women." They were thought unlikely to make good marriage partners and their only recourse was to become a prostitute. Thus, viewed in its widest sense, sex became a buying tool. Men were forced to bargain with a woman to give up her chastity through an arrangement of marriage and the promise of permanent economic support.

The Victorian tradition of a prohibition of premarital sex for females of the middle and upper social classes was rooted in ancient culture, when women were regarded solely as the property of males. A man taking a wife wanted her to be perfect, like any other goods he bought. Previous sexual experience in a woman was regarded as an interference with those property rights.

This obsession with virginity and the purity of women often caused marital havoc. The attitudes towards "decent" women that were indoctrinated into the thinking of Victorian males caused many of them to suffer from sexual dysfunction, such as impotence and premature ejaculation, in their marriages. Such dysfunction stemmed from overwhelming feelings of guilt produced in married men because they felt that they were defiling the very women they had been taught were pure, non-sexual, and respected. As a result, after marriage, many married men turned to prostitutes for the majority of their sex, rather than to their wives. Even then, general feelings of guilt about the purity of women, instilled from childhood, often resulted in a lack of enjoyment of these quasi-illicit relationships.

The Victorian era was also a time when women frequently married men much older than themselves. Though this practice often had an economic basis, it was brought about, in part, by the hope that an older husband would have a lower sex drive than a younger marriage partner.

❧ ATTITUDES TOWARDS PROSTITUTES ❧

Attitudes towards women engaging in prostitution have always closely reflected the contemporary social, cultural, moral, and political climates prevailing in a particular society. For example, married men with families settling in Nebraska Territory lived in a different social environment than a large collection of single men in an all-male Sierra Nevada mining camp. Thus, the two groups acted differently towards prostitution. The men in the farming group were usually under the stabilizing influence of their wives and had the responsibilities of a family. The men in a newly-developed mining camp, on the other hand, had practically no stabilizing influences, had only their own sense of law-and-order to rely on, and usually had no women of their own for social companionship or sexual release. Their social void was soon filled by saloons, gambling halls, variety theaters and, of course, by prostitutes.

One point that is sometimes overlooked is that many working-class men in the developing West could not afford to marry and support a wife and family, thus contributing to the presence of a large population of single men. Census records show that middle and upper-class men, such as mine superintendents, engineers, lawyers, and merchants, were more likely to be married than lower-class working men, such as the miners who toiled underground. Emigrants who came from the East often saved for years to be able to bring their wife and family — if they had one — to join them out West.

When families arrived in the West, they brought with them cultural and social values from the East, which eventually produced a stabilizing effect on the frontier. They also brought with them many of the types of entertainment that they had enjoyed in the East, such as church groups, candy pulls, sewing parties, crocheting groups, dance parties, and gossip sessions. Social gatherings, called "bees," were organized to accomplish some particular work task, such as sewing bees, quilting bees, or barn-raising bees. Saturday night socials and dance parties were also very popular, and women living on widely-scattered farms or ranches thought nothing of riding forty miles in a buckboard to attend a dance. Activities such as these were typically organized by and for women and their families.

On the other hand, the social life of a single man in a remote mining camp typically revolved around the saloon. This venerable institution offered a relaxed, masculine social atmosphere, where a man could drink, gamble, and talk with his male friends, and meet a willing woman. Many of these men relied on saloons to replace the social environment of the home and on prostitutes for sex.

Prostitutes and saloons held a curious place in the society of the early frontier. At some point, prostitution became technically against the law in almost all communities, but it was generally tolerated for various social, financial, and political reasons. Gambling was also often declared illegal by local ordinance, and the saloons that housed the gamblers and gambling tables were the target of anti-liquor crusaders and saloon reformers. Prostitution and gambling, however, continued in most communities, but with a lower profile.

The Red Rooster Tavern in Twin Lakes, Colorado, was built in the late 1870s as a merchandise store, then changed names and evolved in 1884 into a saloon, gaming club, and dance hall with a brothel located upstairs.

(Author's collection)

There appears to have been more tolerance towards prostitutes and prostitution in the West than in the East. In the East — at least publicly — prostitutes and prostitution were vocally condemned as immoral. In the mining camps and cattle towns of the West, however, the prostitute's way of life was not generally considered to be contemptible. It was accepted by most of the male population as a way of making a living for certain women. Possibly this was due to prostitution being more flagrant in the booming and easy-going Western towns, or perhaps the early miners and cowboys were more tolerant of other people's activities, particularly when it was an activity in which many of them participated. The acceptance of prostitutes in the contemporary social structure can be judged by considering that prostitutes were sometimes called "single men's wives." As a way to appease Victorian sensibilities, prostitutes were often referred to as "single women," and their clients were "gentlemen callers." The women also were said to live in "boarding houses."

Then, as now, sex was a highly marketable commodity, with many willing sellers and many more eager buyers. As a result, prostitution became established across the West in hundreds of red light districts that ranged in size from one or two parlor houses or cribs in small towns or mining camps, to brothel areas that encompassed several blocks in the larger towns, and up to whole sections of a city — such as San Francisco's Barbary Coast. Because of Victorian sensibilities, prostitutes and brothels were usually relegated to a specific area of town, and respectable people were reluctant to even admit to the existence of a red light district, let alone to talk of what might take place there.

Prostitutes usually congregated and worked on one street in one specific section of town, hence the terms "The Line" or "The Row" were used to describe the row of parlor houses or cribs that housed the street girls. Even after wives and children appeared and the mining camps and cattle towns matured into more stable and civilized towns, the soiled doves of the red light district were still present. Respectable folks usually tolerated the saloons and prostitutes to some degree, because they felt that bawdy women served as a safety valve and a controlled outlet for the sexual urges of miners, cowboys, and other single men.

The Puritan ideal and romantic view of Victorian women led to a somewhat sentimental view of prostitutes and prostitution. Because Victorian morality and propriety didn't acknowledge the existence of sexuality and sexual drives for women, Victorian proprieties could not admit that some women voluntarily entered a profession that was perceived to be degrading. Several self-styled authorities wrote extensively on the subject, arguing the position that women never voluntarily sought a career in prostitution, simply because that was what the authors wanted to believe. To most Victorians it was inconceivable that some women might enjoy what most viewed as a life of squalid vice and sordid pleasures. Thus, to appease their sensibilities, the Victorians invented euphemisms to describe what prostitutes did for a living and rationalized various causes for their entering into prostitution.

Curiously, the attitude towards women was very black-and-white. Good women were considered to be completely pure in nature. However, once a woman strayed sexually or resorted to prostitution, even if only to feed herself and her family, she was thought to immediately become depraved. There was no middle ground — women were either totally good or totally bad. This reasoning was used to explain why a woman, who up until her "downfall" was considered to be pure, could remain a prostitute. She was considered to have become immediately and completely morally corrupt by her experience.

Because virginity was so important for a Victorian bride, if a woman were to gain sexual experience before marriage she was supposed to have fallen off her pedestal and lost her purity. The thinking was that once a woman had fallen from purity, her only option in life was to become a prostitute. Hence, she was called a "fallen woman" or the even more romanticized and flowery "fallen angel." When describing prostitutes, the Victorian literature is full of such euphemisms, calling them by delicate names such as "wronged woman," "abandoned woman," "soiled dove," "erring sister," and similar seemingly-innocuous phrases.[5]

One common thread among these theories was the popular notion that prostitutes were formerly chaste women who had been led astray and seduced by unscrupulous men who were craving to satisfy their own lust. Having been led astray and lost their virginity — euphemistically called their "virtue" — these women were supposed to have been callously flung aside to fend for themselves, while their seducers went on to new conquests. Thus, women who became prostitutes as a result of this experience were spoken of as having been "seduced and abandoned." One variation on this theme was that unscrupulous employers commonly forced unwanted attentions on women who worked for them and seduced them under the threats of dismissal from their jobs.

Another common Victorian romantic myth was that some women turned to prostitution to support an out-of-wedlock child that was conceived from such liaisons. Though some of these theories may seem reasonable at first glance, from a realistic standpoint they were incorrect, as will be discussed further in Chapter Two.

Chapter 2
SHE WAS FAIR, BUT FRAIL

"Here lies Charlotte,
She was a harlot,
For fifteen years she preserved her virginity,
A damn good record in this vicinity."
(from a cemetery headstone in Ouray, Colorado)

S ome contemporary Victorians saw prostitutes as existing in poverty and squalor, surrounded by violence, living on alcohol, and dying young from disease or suicide. Others saw them as having a life of carefree luxury, indulging in dissipation and easy living. The truth was somewhere in between.

Why Victorian women became prostitutes is a complex question, and one that has no simple answer or origin in well-defined social or psychological causes. There were, of course, many of the same reasons for women entering prostitution in the West in the late 1800s as there have always been. Namely: women who wanted easy money, women who enjoyed sex (though studies have shown that prostitutes generally do not enjoy sex with their clients), women lured or forced into prostitution by men for various reasons, and women who had a way of life requiring large amounts of money (for example, to support a drug habit or a pimp). However, beyond these reasons, prostitution was often forced on women who had no training or background to make a living wage. Prostitution was sometimes the last resort before starvation.

In the latter half of the Nineteenth Century, the outlook and opportunities for a young woman making her way into the world by herself were limited. For women without an education, prostitution often appeared to be a reasonable alternative to the menial drudgery

The Green Front Boarding House was a notorious brothel that consisted of two adjoining houses owned by Myrtle Butler and Pearl McGinnis, on the west end of Virginia City, Montana, in the thriving red light district on Wallace Street. The area was later absorbed into Virginia City's Chinatown.

(Author's collection)

that might be the only choice available to them. Becoming a prostitute was more appealing to many working-class Victorian women than going blind sewing clothes in a poorly-lit garret, working long hours as a domestic servant, slaving over a stove and doing laundry while surrounded by children stair-stepped in age, or begging on the streets. For others, prostitution was the only job that was available. Estimates made in the mid-1800s were that one woman in twenty had turned to prostitution at one point or another in her life in order to survive.

Before entering a career of prostitution, many women saw the prostitute's way of life as an adventure. Some were drawn to it by the lure of easy money, independence, and a glamorous life. Unfortunately, what many of them found was hard work, sickness, physical discomfort, and a life on the fringes of acceptable society. Prostitution did, however, offer a chance for many women who were down-and-out to achieve a measure of personal and financial independence. In a sense, then, prostitutes were the first businesswomen to appear in the Old West.

⇜ OCCUPATIONS FOR WOMEN ⇝

The accepted goal for young Victorian women was marriage and a family. Middle-class and upper-class parents raised their daughters with that result in mind. Employment, if any, for middle-class women was considered to be appropriate for only a short time before marriage. Poorer lower-class women, who typically had no education or useful skills, looked forward to a life of housework, child-bearing, and home-making.

In most cases, "education" for well-bred young women involved virtually no formal schooling, but rather consisted of learning to sketch or to paint, playing the piano, practicing needlework, reading romantic novels, and other similar diversions that were considered to be essential social skills for a young lady. In essence, the lack of formal education meant that genteel young women were not trained for any practical work and certainly not for any skilled occupation. In many cases, even the more practical aspects of daily life, such as housework or cooking, were not on their list of accomplishments, because it was assumed that servants would be available in an upper-class home to perform these mundane tasks.

Women from the poorer classes could typically not afford an education. They were usually so poor that they had to go straight into the work force and perform menial jobs to make enough money to survive. Even for the lower social classes these were not glamorous occupations that a young girl could look forward to with great anticipation. Cooking and cleaning were undoubtedly as exciting to young girls in the 1850s and 1860s as they are to young women 150 years later. The alternative was to marry young in order to have a husband for support. In retrospect, the attitudes of both rich and poor were impractical for a nation undergoing rapid urbanization and industrialization.

As a result, marriage was an essential factor in social and economic survival for a female who came of age in Victorian times. Before marriage, support came from their fathers and, after marriage, from their husbands. Thus, a woman depended on the male head of her household for economic survival.

Under most circumstances, if anything happened to a man who was the head of the household (such as death, severe illness, bankruptcy, or desertion), a lower or middle-class wife would have limited ways of bringing in money. Employers were reluctant to hire older or married women, and many upper or middle-class women in this position were reluctant to be hired because working would invite social embarrassment. At least for the lower social classes, employment opportunities were somewhat wider; because, in addition to being a wife and mother, a woman could become a factory worker, servant, housekeeper, or cook for a middle-class or upper-class family. Upper class women were expected to have enough private income to support themselves. The expectation was that "ladies" did not work, but working-class women did.

Even if a marriage was an unhappy one, divorce was considered to be socially — as well as financially — unacceptable. However, divorce was not totally unknown, and its incidence was higher in the West than in the East, because women on the frontier had a much better chance of remarrying quickly due to the shortage of females.

Desertion was another situation that the Victorian wife wished to discourage. Apart from the social horror of scandalizing friends and family, there were limited prospects for work or marriage for a single woman without training in useful skills and perhaps six or eight children to support. If for no other reasons than practical and economic ones, a wife generally stayed with her husband.

Should a woman not marry, and she had the appropriate qualifications, she might become a school teacher or private governess. Though not every young woman could gain such as post, or was qualified to hold one, teaching was one of the few respectable career opportunities open for women. One reason that teaching was primarily a female occupation was the extremely low wages. A man who had enough education to be a teacher could usually earn more money and better status from other occupations.

A good teacher in a big city might make $60 to $120 per month, with the majority of the positions on the low end of the pay scale. In rural areas, and particularly on the early frontier, a teacher might only make from fifteen to thirty dollars a month. To help offset the low salary, a rural teacher was often provided with room and board by the parents of the school children. The length of stay with a particular family was proportional to the number of children that the family had in school.

Schoolteachers on the plains of the Midwest were often only teenagers themselves, and the turnover was high. Many young women in the Midwest viewed teaching as a temporary career until a better job came along or she could find a husband. Many women journeyed west with the intention of temporarily being a maid, teacher, or servant, while looking for a husband among the large number of eligible bachelors on the frontier.

As towns matured and school financing became more stable, teachers' salaries rose. In 1880, teachers in Leadville, Colorado, were paid eighty dollars a month. Job security, however, was non-existent and closure of the schools for vacation or epidemics usually meant that the teachers went without pay until the schools reopened.

Many young women, on their own with no occupation and no means of support, turned to prostitution as a last resort for making enough money to survive. Rather than finding alternate forms of employment for these needy women, Victorian society tolerated prostitution as one way that single women could support themselves.

✧ INDUSTRIALIZATION AND URBANIZATION ✧

The impetus in the mid-Nineteenth Century for becoming a prostitute was influenced by changing urban conditions and the rise in prostitution in eastern cities. Though, at first, this may not appear to be directly related to the West, the gold rushes of 1849 to California and 1859 to Colorado were accompanied by a horde of prostitutes from the East who emigrated to the West.

In the middle of the Nineteenth Century, when the population of the United States was increasing dramatically, jobs became more difficult to find in rural areas. The period of early settlement of the West coincided with the emergence of urbanization and the beginning of the Industrial Revolution. Centralization of factories in the cities, and the resulting growth of industrialization, led to a shift in population from a predominantly rural agricultural population to an urban industrialized nation. New developments in machinery and automation gradually replaced traditional methods of manufacture that were performed by artisans and craftsmen using hand labor. Mechanized manufacturing heralded the start of mass production and uniformity of products. As a result, the growing industrial cities were seen as offering an opportunity for work in factories, particularly for young women. The availability of mass labor boosted the rapid spread of industrialization, but the growing pool of surplus workers and increasing competition for available jobs kept wages low.

As a large number of women were drawn to the cities and factories, the labor force grew beyond the needs of manufacturers. The majority of the rural young women who arrived in the cities were not trained in skills that could be used in the factories, and thus they were often unable to find work to support themselves. As a result, many of these women were forced to turn to prostitution as the only means available for them to survive.

The women who were able to find work in factories spent their days toiling alongside men and children from before sunup to after sundown. Factory labor was hard, wages were low, and there were none of the benefits that are expected today, such as vacations, sick leave, or holidays. Much of the work was difficult, tedious, and often physically hazardous. Women who worked in the textile mills, for example, typically worked sixty hours a week, were paid one dollar a day, and could expect to contract lung disease within a few years. These were not particularly cheerful job prospects.

✑ WHO WERE THE PROSTITUTES? ✑

Today, medical researchers study the most intimate aspects of human behavior, and it is socially acceptable to discuss the results with friends. The Victorian era, however, could not condone intensive research into prostitution or prostitutes' lives, because it was a subject and social problem that did not publicly exist. Only limited information, therefore, has survived.

One of the leading published studies was carried out by Dr. William Sanger, while he was a resident physician at Blackwell's Island Hospital, a penitentiary hospital in New York. In 1855, he undertook a survey of 2,000 prostitutes. The statistics he gathered were from women who worked in New York City, so they should not be taken as applying directly to the Western frontier. However, because the time frame is the same and because many of the women who were prostitutes in Eastern cities followed the exodus of men to the mining camps of California and the Rocky Mountains, it is reasonable to look at Sanger's findings and consider their applicability. Other significant information about prostitutes was gathered by George Kneeland in New York and Philadelphia in 1912.

The prostitutes Sanger surveyed ranged in age from fourteen to seventy-six, with the majority being between the ages of seventeen and twenty-four.[1] Categorization of the respondents showed that 959 had been prostitutes for a year or less, 1,587 had been prostitutes for five years or less, and one determined individual had been plying her trade for thirty-five years. The educational level of the study group reveals the typical lack of education for Victorian females. Of the 2,000 women Sanger surveyed, 714 could read and write well, 546 could read and write imperfectly, 219 could read only, and 521 were illiterate.

Miners and cowboys probably wouldn't have seen anyone as glamorous as these dummies in a window in modern Deadwood, South Dakota, but the principle was the same.

(Author's collection)

Approximately half of those surveyed were domestic servants before becoming a prostitute, a figure that was also representative of the occupations of working women in general at the time of the survey. The second largest grouping stated that they had previously lived with family or friends. This would indicate that, willingly or unwillingly, the majority of these women used prostitution to support themselves when they were on their own.

The third largest grouping was composed of women who had been in the clothing trades, such as milliners, shop-girls, and dress-makers. That these women entered prostitution, attracted by the potential earnings, is not surprising when considering their working conditions. Sewing was usually contracted on a piecework basis, which meant that a seamstress had to produce many items to earn a reasonable wage. She often worked her fingers to the bone with the additional prospect of going half-blind from detailed work and poor lighting. The names "servant," "milliner," "seamstress," and "actress" were also common Victorian euphemisms for a prostitute.

One of Sanger's important questions was: "What was the cause of your becoming a prostitute?" The most common response (about one-fourth of the answers) was destitution. This is not surprising because there were no government-supported social and welfare programs in the late 1800s . An individual without job, money, or family support faced very real prospects of starving to death. If a woman was unable to obtain money for basic necessities by any other means, prostitution provided an easy route to quick finances for someone teetering on the edge of survival. Thus, the basic drive to survive often overcame a woman's moral objections and taboos against prostitution. Because of the very low wages of manufacturing jobs, even the women who did have jobs sometimes turned to part-time prostitution to earn extra money to survive.

The second most common response to Sanger's question showed that about one-fourth of the women became prostitutes of their own inclination and free will. Considering the limited option available to single, young women with little education, this is not surprising because the career offered a reasonable economic incentive.

The third most common response of those surveyed was "seduced and abandoned." This group made up about sixteen percent of the total. This reason contrasts sharply with about sixty percent of the women who openly admitted that they entered prostitution of their own volition for reasons such as inclination, drink, an easy life, and being too idle to work. Thus, while "seduced and abandoned" was a sentimental Victorian rationalization for prostitution, the facts do not support the theory.

Data gathered by George Kneeland in Philadelphia showed that of 861 prostitutes in his survey, 645 were single, 193 were married, and 23 were widowed. In many instances the married women were carrying on their occupation with the knowledge and encouragement of their husbands. Whether they were women who had married pimps and were forced to continue prostitution, or whether some of them were part-time participants who turned to prostitution as a way to supplement a meager family income was not explained. Sanger's study showed similar figures: 1,216 single women, 490 married, and 294 widowed.

Data gathered by Kneeland showed that of 645 single prostitutes, only seventy-three women had illegitimate children. Of the 2,000 women that Sanger surveyed, 357 of the single women had children. Though abandonment by a man and support of an illegitimate child was supposed to be one of the compelling Victorian reasons for entering prostitution, Sanger's and Kneeland's data does not show this reason to have been a major cause. In many cases the child was a result of prostitution, rather than being the cause.

Information gathered by Kneeland in New York City indicated that the largest category of "first partner" for a prostitutes' first sexual encounter was that of "stranger." Of those surveyed, about twenty-eight percent initially had sex in exchange for money, which is the traditional basis for prostitution. Only eleven percent submitted to first-time sex against their will, thus again discounting the theory of coercion and rape as a major cause for prostitution. It would also appear that Victorian theories of the seduction of workers and servants by unscrupulous employers as a major cause for prostitution were unfounded.

WHAT DOES ALL THIS MEAN?

Several interesting conclusions can be drawn from the information in the preceding surveys. First, the majority of prostitutes entered the profession of their own free will. A large percentage of prostitutes started their careers because they wanted to and after impersonal sex with a stranger for money.

A second important observation is that most prostitutes came from low-paying service and manufacturing jobs. This implies that their change of career may have come about to seek an easier working life and earn more money. More significant was that many women related that they had become prostitutes because of a lack of money and were forced by their circumstances to enter prostitution in order to survive. As one young prostitute poignantly put it: "[she] had no work, no money, and no home."[2]

THE AGES OF PROSTITUTES

Contemporary authors indicate that the ages of prostitutes in the Old West were similar to the information gathered by Sanger and Kneeland.[3] Most of the women were between eighteen and twenty-nine years of age, with a typical age of about twenty-five. Some entered the profession as young as twelve or fourteen; others continued at age forty and over. Some were as old as sixty. In many of the mining and cattle towns, the average age of prostitutes was less than twenty, and the typical length of their career was about six years.

The ages of the youngest prostitutes may seem appallingly low by modern standards. This can be put in perspective, however, by considering that the age at which a female could legally consent to sexual relations was as low as age ten for some Western states in the late 1800s.[4] One reason for the low age limits for consent was the lack of available females on the emerging frontier. In a society that was perpetually short of women, young girls in the West matured rapidly into women's roles. They were courted at a very young age by much older men and were sometimes married when only a few years into their teens. The associated problem was that the low legal ages effectively allowed the recruitment of adolescent girls into brothels.

The young age of most prostitutes is understandable, because younger women would be able to attract customers who paid better. After a few years in the business, when a woman started to age, she often found it difficult to compete with the younger women entering the profession. With their beauty fading, and disease and drug use often taking their toll, most prostitutes slipped into an inevitable downhill slide. If a woman stayed in the profession long enough, her career pathway led from the fancy parlor houses, to the low-class parlor houses, to the cribs. Often she then ended up as a common streetwalker or "two-bit whore" in a cowyard. Few started at the top in the elegant parlor houses, but no matter where they started, as they aged, all of them slipped down the scale.

Built on the site of the Alhambra Theater, a combination saloon, dancehall, and variety theater in Silverton, Colorado, the structure on the left originally had four cribs, two cribs downstairs and two upstairs. Each crib was sold independently as sort of a crib condominium project.

(Author's collection)

Once a woman entered prostitution, it was difficult for her to escape her past. It was virtually impossible, for example, for a woman to start another career in the same town in which she had worked as a prostitute. The social stigma attached to her past profession was just too great. In reality, however, most prostitutes did not have the desire, ambition, money, training, or interest to move elsewhere to start a new life. A few prostitutes married and left the profession, but many of them died at a young age as a result of excessive consumption of cheap liquor, venereal disease, drugs, or poor working conditions. A disproportionately large number of them committed suicide.

In addition to venereal diseases, other common diseases of the time, such as tuberculosis, smallpox, cholera, typhoid, and diphtheria claimed the lives of many prostitutes. Another cause of death for women in general was pneumonia. This was a particular hazard at the high elevations and cold climate encountered at many mining camps.

The lucky women left the profession or died early. A typical example of the unfortunates was Dolly Adams, a prostitute in San Francisco who started her career at eleven and died at age twenty-six of venereal disease and opium addiction. One of the lucky ones was Emma Walters, a former saloon girl who married the noted frontier lawman, gambler, and eventual newspaperman William Bartholomew Masterson. Masterson (who later changed his name to William Barclay Masterson) was better known as "Bat" Masterson.

❧ DRUGS AND DEPRESSION ❧

Some women apparently entered prostitution with the thought that it would be exciting, fun, and easy living. They soon discovered that the work of a prostitute could be just as routine, dull, and boring as any other type of work. What many women found was hard work, sickness, and slum-level living conditions.

Many prostitutes used recreational drugs that helped the women to socialize with customers when working and, while waiting between customers, helped them to cope with boredom. Stimulant drugs helped the women to appear lively and attractive in spite of a long night of customers. Narcotic drugs helped ease the physical discomforts of frequent sex and allowed a temporary escape from reality.

The use of drugs was not without its grim side. Many prostitutes suffered from alcoholism or drug addiction, and it was an accepted part of their life. Data gathered by Sanger showed that approximately half of the 2,000 prostitutes he surveyed were alcoholics and another one-third drank moderately.[5] Approximately ten percent of the women he surveyed said that they had initially entered prostitution because of alcohol or a desire for alcohol. In the high-class parlor houses, the madams kept a close eye on their women and would generally not keep one who was a serious alcoholic or who showed signs of excessive drug use.

✧ THE SUPPOSED PERILS OF WHITE SLAVERY ✧

Elaborate reasons that were formulated to rationalize Victorian prostitution were basically a result of the denial of women's sexuality. The theories supported the Victorian ideal that pure women were forced into prostitution and illicit sex by circumstances beyond their control. The "victimization theory" reached its peak with the frenzy that surrounded White Slavery, which was the supposed forced prostitution of innocent white girls.

Stories of White Slavery were widely circulated, in great part to impress and horrify young women in the late Victorian era. Grim accounts were whispered of women kidnapped and held prisoner in harems and brothels and then forced to become prostitutes against their wills. The term "White Slavery" was used to describe this practice to distinguish it from traditional Negro or black slavery that was common in the South before the Civil War.

"White Slavery" was originally applied to trafficking in people, not all of whom were slaves. Later usage became synonymous with the procuring of women for prostitution. Stories were told in hushed tones behind closed doors of how pimps or procurers went into small towns to scout for gullible young country women. They would promise them jobs in the city as maids, seamstresses, actresses, and governesses, or even beguile them with promises of marriage. Lurid tales, repeated by mothers to frighten their daughters, told how unwary girls were drugged with opium or plied with liquor until they passed out, only to regain consciousness trapped in the strange surroundings of a brothel, often without their clothing or shoes. Melodramatic narratives recounted how young women were raped and beaten into submission. Self-proclaimed authorities on the subject knowingly wrote that up to 80,000 young women fell victim to white slavers each year.

As grim as these stories sound, verifiable incidents of white slavery actually happening appear to be in the minority, and, as with all such sensational stories, their incidence and significance was blown out of proportion. White Slavery was never the menace to the average American woman that it was supposed to have been. There would not be much benefit to kidnapping innocent young women into a profession that had so many willing entrants.

This qualification, however, applied only to white American prostitutes. White Slavery did exist for some other ethnic groups. In San Francisco, many of the inmates of Chinese brothels were unwillingly imported from China. Some girls, as young as eight to thirteen years old, were brought to the United States and literally imprisoned as slaves in cribs and brothels. On the Eastern seaboard, procurers occasionally lured innocent young women who arrived on immigrant ships. There were also instances of pimps marrying young girls and then forcing them into prostitution.

The paranoia of White Slavery was kept at fever-pitch by books such as *Fighting the Traffic in Young Girls*, published in 1910 by evangelist Rev. Ernest A. Bell, founder and superintendent of the Midnight Mission in Chicago. The book eventually sold more than 400,000 copies. It warned explicitly of the author's perception of the dangers to young women found at ice cream parlors, theatrical agencies, railway stations, and dances. He wrote fervently that such places could lead a young woman to become "immodest, indecent, lawless....and [a] distributor of vile diseases."

The term "White Slavery" is usually attributed to Clifford G. Roe, the assistant state's attorney in Illinois, who used the description during his campaign against involuntary prostitution in the early 1900s. Supposedly, he was involved in a case where a girl had thrown a note out of the window of a brothel which read, "Help me — I am held captive as a white slave." However, the term more likely originated from translation of the *French Traite des Blanches*, or "Traffic in Whites," to distinguish it from *Traite des Noirs*, or "Traffic in Blacks," the traditional black slaves.

The term *Traite des Blanches* was used in Paris, France, at a 1902 conference, which discussed the problems of international trade in women and children. The term was also used at a Vienna conference on slavery held in 1815, but was applied to trafficking in people, rather than specifically to those who literally were slaves. Eventually *Traite des Blanches* became loosely translated as "White Slave Traffic" and referred to the procuring of women for the purposes of prostitution.

The first American law aimed at White Slavery was passed by the Illinois legislature in 1908. Clifford Roe's campaign was largely responsible for later federal legislation called the "White Slave Traffic Act," or the "Mann Act." This act, introduced by Congressman James Mann of Illinois in 1910, provided heavy penalties for the interstate transportation of a woman for "immoral purposes." The Mann Act, and subsequent state laws against a group of activities that were considered immoral, caused the sharp decline or closing of most of the country's organized red light districts prior to World War I. Denver's famous Holladay Street red light district, also known as Market Street, closed in 1915. New Orleans' Storyville, the last quasi-legal, municipally-sanctioned red light district in the country, was closed by the U.S. Navy in 1917. Prostitution after 1915 kept a lower profile and was carried out in less-obvious brothels. Prostitutes also developed other methods of marketing themselves, such as use of the telephone by call-girls.

❧ WHO WERE THEY REALLY? ❧

Census-takers during the time when prostitution was not publicly recognized by "proper" Victorian people often had difficulty in classifying the occupations of some young single women. In many instances, a prostitute in the Old West was unwilling to provide a census-taker with her occupation, real name, or place of birth because her relatives in the East believed that she was a respectable governess, teacher, or

Fancy parlor houses line this part of "The Row" in Cripple Creek, Colorado, in 1893, with some of the more disreputable cribs in the background.
(Courtesy Denver Public Library, Western History Collection, P-769)

seamstress. Whatever the reason, prostitutes in the Nineteenth Century commonly tended to list themselves in categories other than their true occupation. While obviously some of these women were legitimate in their occupation, half-a-dozen "housekeepers" living together in one building were almost certainly prostitutes.

The largest census grouping for working women in the West appears to be that of "domestics." Occupations listed as seamstress, laundress, actress, or keeping house, may or may not have been those respondents true occupations. In addition, some women supplemented their income by occasional prostitution, thus while seamstress, actress, or laundress may have been their primary occupation, this may not have accounted for their entire income. Though difficult to determine accurately from contemporary data, the second largest group of working women in the early West probably consisted of prostitutes.

As an example of these nebulous numbers, census data for Virginia City, Nevada, for 1870 shows that out of 2,190 responses from women older than fifteen years of age, 109 listed their occupation as prostitute and 48 as harlot. These two categories, then, comprised a little over seven percent of the total. Among the other responses, however, were 156 who listed no occupation, seven who claimed to be actresses, and numerous milliners and dressmakers. While it would be inaccurate to assume that any or all of these women were also prostitutes, it is possible that some were, and that they used these common Victorian euphemisms to disguise their profession. Thus, the real percentages of prostitutes is probably higher than it would at first appear. One individual in this census curiously listed her profession as "hotel de refreshment."

The situation was not much different five years later. The 1875 census showed that Virginia City had 3,572 women over the age of eighteen. Of these, 298 listed their occupation as prostitute and nine admitted to being madams. In this particular survey, 208 women called themselves servants and forty-two called themselves laundresses or seamstresses. Both of these occupations were common euphemisms for prostitute, and were also occupations that were used as a legitimate cover for prostitution. So, though most of these women may have been legitimate servants and seamstresses, some undoubtedly also belonged in the category of "prostitute."[6]

The occupation for 180 women in this census was listed as "none," which was also a common practice among prostitutes. Thus, even when using census data, historians vary in their estimates of the actual number of prostitutes. For example, one expert placed the number for prostitutes

Names used by Western prostitutes

The names that Western prostitutes gave themselves ranged from common Christian names to exotic nicknames. Most prostitutes used assumed names, because they did not want to use their real names when dealing with customers. The use of working names also added to the impersonal aspect of the prostitute's transaction.

Common names that the girls assumed were Minnie, Alice, Kate or Katie, Hattie, Mattie, Kitty, Fanny, Jenny, Mary, and Annie. Other popular names included Rose or Queen in some combination, such as Irish Queen, Spanish Queen, Texas Rose, Prairie Rose, Tall Rose, Wild Rose, or even the apparently descriptive Velvet Ass Rose. In the years after the Civil War, many prostitutes in the South and the West adopted a professional name that included Lee. This was a clever ploy, since many of their customers were former confederate soldiers or Southern sympathizers.

Some of the names were quite descriptive, as can be seen by the more colorful ones below. Reading through this list, one can only imagine the characteristic that gave rise to the name.

Big Mouth Annie	Grizzly Bear	Rowdy Kate
Big Nose Kate	Hambone Jane	Sappho
Bilious Bessie	Hook-and-Ladder Kate	Scarface Liz
Black Pearl	Jo the Whipper	Short and Dirty
Buffalo Jo	Kidneyfoot Jenny	Slippery Sadie
Cattle Kate	Lady Godiva	Sloppy Gertie
Cockeyed Liz	Leo the Lion	Squirrel-tooth Alice
Cotton Tail	Lily the Fox	The Big Bonanza
Crazy Horse Lil	Liverlips Lil	The Carson Banger
Dirty Gertie	Mexican Jennie	The Chinless Wonder
Dirty Neck Nell	Nellie the Pig	The Spring Chicken
Dog-faced Kitty	Noseless Lou	The Victor Pig
Dutch Jake	One-eyed Sal	The Virgin
Ella the Wolf	Pegleg Annie	Three-tit Tillie
Fatty McDuff	Ragged Ass Annie	Tit-bit
Few Clothes Molly	Rattlesnake Kate	Two-bit Lil
French Blanche	Red Light Liz	Velvet Ass Rose
German Muscle Woman	Red Stockings	Wide-ass Nellie
Greasy Gertie	Rotary Rosie	Wicked Alice

Saloons were places for gambling, socializing, and were often a contact point for prostitution. Beer, spittoons, gambling tables, and some framed art decorate this saloon in Leadville, Colorado, in the 1880s.
(Courtesy Denver Public Library, Western History Collection, X-297)

in Virginia City from the 1880 census at 134; but another claims that this figure is exaggerated and that only seventy-seven can be identified.

There are similar findings all over the West. The 1885 census for Aspen, Colorado, listed a population of 3,800 people. Of these, forty-one were saloonkeepers and thirty-one were bartenders. Four admitted to being prostitutes, and five were "actresses."[7] However, there was also a disproportionately large number of laundresses, listed as 48, undoubtedly some of whom were disguising their real careers. Because the women of the red light district in Aspen were rarely mentioned in historical records, it is difficult to obtain an accurate estimate of the actual number of prostitutes who worked there, but it can be assumed that there were at least several dozen. Even when a prostitute's profession was obvious, it might still be couched in delicate Victorian terms. For instance, the 1870 census of Ellsworth, Kansas, reported that a certain Harriet Parmenter "does horizontal work."

❧ REFORM ORGANIZATIONS ❧

Prostitutes, being the opposite of sexual purity, became a scapegoat for Victorian fears about sex. Saving these women from themselves often became the work of self-appointed social reformers, who referred to prostitution as "The Social Evil." The Florence Crittenton Mission, for example, tried to reform alcoholic women, prostitutes, and unwed mothers.

Another attempt at reforming prostitutes was made by the Order of Saint Mary Magdalen, a religious order that accepted female criminals and placed them in cloistered isolation for a life of spiritual contemplation. This religious order was under the sponsorship of the Sisters of the Good Shepherd of St. Paul, Minnesota, which made the order unusual, because church law did not normally allow women with criminal backgrounds to take religious vows and enter a convent.

For all their good intentions and efforts, most reform organizations did not make a serious impact on prostitution or women criminals. The discovery that most prostitutes did not want to change their way of life led to a notable lack of success. The Magdalens, for example, accepted less than seventy women over the course of their existence.

❧ WHY WAS SHE A HOOKER? ❧

The origins of some of the slang for "prostitute" have been obscured by antiquity or are subject to various interpretations. As one example, the common name "hooker," as applied to a prostitute, has several reasonable explanations. Some authorities feel that the term came from the practice of streetwalkers hooking an arm through that of a prospective customer. Others say that it came from the crib girls who stood in their doorways and tried to "hook" customers off the street.

A totally different explanation credits the name to prostitutes who plied their trade among the Union soldiers of General Joseph Hooker's regiment in Washington, D.C., during the Civil War. The brothels became known as "Hooker's Row" and the women as "Hooker's Division." The name for the women was supposedly later shortened simply to "hooker." Contrary to legend, this explanation is an unlikely origin for the name, because the term "hooking" for prostitution was in use in the 1830s and the name "hooker" was in common use for at least ten years before the start of the Civil War.

A fourth possible explanation is that the term originally came from an area of New York that was named Corlears Hook — loosely called

"The Hook"—that was at the easternmost end of Manhattan, bounded by East Broadway, Walnut Street, and Water Street. As early as the 1820s The Hook contained a heavy concentration of saloons, brothels, and many poor, working-class women who worked as prostitutes.

❧ A VISIBLE DIFFERENCE ❧

"Naughty" women, such as prostitutes and dance-hall girls, were the opposites of the pure, romantic Victorian ideal. In some cases, the difference between "respectable" and "naughty" ladies was visible as well as moral. A popular fad for prostitutes from some brothels in Western communities was to use heavy make-up that included white wax as a base, along with flour or cornstarch for powder. Other "naughty women" used sour milk or buttermilk as a facial cream at night to bleach their skin. On top of this, they added a liberal application of rouge and lipstick. The combination gave the women chalk-white faces with scarlet lips and cheeks. This fashion statement of the ladies of easy virtue gave them the name "painted ladies" or "painted cats."[8]

Because of this, respectable women generally avoided the use of heavy facial make-up, so that they would not be mistaken for what they considered to be degenerate members of the world's oldest profession. Respectable women were supposed to rely on diet and cleanliness to give them natural beauty rather than rely on artificial means of enhancing their looks. Some "proper" people even thought that the use of cosmetics led to paralysis and premature death. A few respectable women, however, did use modest makeup. Genuine rouge was expensive, so many women who could not afford the real thing used beet juice to redden their cheeks. Another trick was to pinch or slap the cheeks to make the blood temporarily rush to them and produce a healthy-looking glow.

Interestingly, some years later in the 1920s, the tides of fashion changed. The "painted woman" look became popular among respectable women and cosmetic sales soared. What had been disreputable in the late 1800s became fashionable and quite acceptable sixty years later.

Chapter 3

FROM PARLOR HOUSES TO CRIBS

"Any girls not able to dance and entertain men are not wanted here,
as this is no place for old maids and old women."
(sign in a parlor house)

A brothel was one of the few places that single young men, such as miners and cowboys, could go to relax and enjoy some social interaction. For men who lived in tents, in rough log shacks, or camped out on the prairie, the bright lights, noise, and companionship that saloons, gambling halls, and brothels offered was a relief from herding cows or from the harsh world of mining. In addition to seeking sex, men visiting brothels sometimes came solely for female companionship. The noise, drinking, and warm friendly atmosphere was an antidote to the loneliness felt by many single men.

Part of the attraction of drinking and womanizing was the relief from the physical danger that surrounded the men's daily working conditions, which might involve fighting Indians, herding cattle, or working in an underground mine. Temporary escape and relief from accumulated tensions through sex and drink has long been associated with those in danger, such as men at war. The presence of perilous working or living conditions, combined with the absence of family and home, has always fueled the desire for commercial sex.

Many names have been used to describe a house of prostitution: brothel, bordello, parlor house, crib, house of ill repute, or the plain, but descriptive, term whorehouse.[1] Whatever the name, the activities that went on inside were basically the same, though the building's trappings may have been different.

The Deerhorn Boarding House in Winfield, Colorado, was typical of where the young miners lived, which made saloons a cheery social place for a rendezvous.
(Glenn Kinnaman Colorado and Western History Collection.)

There was, however, a definite hierarchy among prostitutes and the places they worked. At the top were the fancy girls in the high-class parlor houses. They looked down on the women in the common parlor houses, who, in turn, looked down on the whores of the saloons, cribs, and dancehalls. At the very bottom of the hierarchy were common streetwalkers, who roamed the sidewalks looking for clients wherever they could be found. A type of caste system applied to race as well. American and French prostitutes were generally considered to be the best lovers and at the top of the social ladder. At the bottom were Chinese, Negro, and Mexican prostitutes.

Racial bias also existed for men visiting brothels. Typically Indian, black, and Chinese customers were not welcome at brothels that employed white women, but had to seek out prostitutes of their own race. Typical of segregated brothels was one in Junction City, Kansas, that had six black women and a black madam. Some white brothels did have colored prostitutes, but they were typically for white customers who were looking for a different experience.

∽• THE PARLOR HOUSES •∽

A man of the Old West seeking a woman for pleasure had a range of options to choose from, depending on the amount of money he had, the amount of time available, and his social status. At the top of the list of available selections, in terms of both quality and cost, was the parlor house. The women of the parlor houses were at the top of the prostitute's world — socially, economically, and professionally.

Just as saloons were more than a place to have a drink, the parlor houses were more than premises to purchase sex; they were also gathering places for leisure and relaxation. The warmth and brightness of the parlor house and its well-dressed women in fancy frills were often the closest thing to home that many men on the frontier experienced. The

The parlor of the Old Homestead museum in Cripple Creek, Colorado, is a representation of what it might have been like in the "good old days"; however, it is unlikely that the ladies would have been serving tea.
(Author's collection; courtesy of the Wild Horse Casino, current owner of the Old Homestead museum).

cheerful aura radiated by the house and its occupants contrasted sharply with a single man's harsh existence in the mines or lumber camps, and brought some brightness to what was often an otherwise drab and dreary working existence.

The parlor house was an establishment that existed exclusively for prostitution. The household typically consisted of four or five women, though the number might range from only two or three up to a dozen or more. In charge of the house and the girls was a madam, who was a combination of house mother, employer, and business manager.

The name "parlor house" covered a wide range of premises, varying from run-down houses to elaborate mansions with beautiful furnishings and maids or waiters. The women found working in these establishments matched their settings. The high-class establishments offered attractive young women, who were well-dressed and entertained their gentlemen callers socially as well as sexually. The lower quality parlor houses had slovenly prostitutes, who lounged around in housecoats, kimonos, the flimsiest of underwear, or even nothing at all.

The price for a visit to a parlor house was proportionate to the elaborateness of the establishment and the looks of the girls. The cheap parlor houses might charge only a dollar, or perhaps less, depending on the color and nationality of the prostitute. The better houses, with attractive women and a better clientele, might charge two or three dollars. On the top of the scale, the high class houses might charge five dollar and up for a "quick date" — with the emphasis being on the "up" for a fancy place. The price in very expensive houses was more likely to be fifteen or twenty dollars a visit, depending on the establishment and the length of the customer's stay. An overnight visit might cost up to fifty dollars, again depending on the quality of the house.

The elaborate and expensive parlor houses often served as a social center for rich mine owners or cattle merchants. A man with plenty of money could stay for several hours in sumptuous surroundings and enjoy a pleasant social evening. It might begin with a good dinner accompanied by fine French wine. After dinner, the customer would enjoy music provided by a piano player, or, in the very fancy houses, by a small orchestra. The music might be accompanied by a song from one of the women, if she had a good voice. Songs might be popular ballads of the day, or might be bawdy ditties or lewd lyrics sung to well-known tunes. Then the customer would name his choice of the girls and retire with her to an upstairs room. If he had enough money, he might stay overnight.

The number of customers entertained by a woman at a parlor house varied. The typical number was around ten to fifteen a day; however, this number was subject to wide variation. In the cheap parlor houses or cribs this number might approach forty or fifty men a day. In the high-class, exclusive parlor houses, the number might be as few as one or two customers a night.

A woman in a high-class parlor house tried, with some degree of success, to camouflage the obviousness of her profession by providing more than just quick, impersonal sex. By limiting the number of her customers and acting out a facade of respectability by providing social entertainment and dinner while fully and fashionably dressed, she made her client feel like he was receiving her special favors within a quasi-personal and semi-respectable relationship. Of course, by providing quality instead of quantity, the girl was paid handsomely by each man. Presumably, though, neither she nor her client really believed the charade they were playing out.

The parlor house building was typically a two-story structure. The ground floor contained the parlor, where the girls assembled to meet a customer. High class houses might have two or more separate parlors, so that a prominent citizen, there for a discreet visit, might be able to meet with a chosen woman without running the risk of encountering friends or business associates doing the same thing. Depending on how elaborate the establishment was, the ground floor also contained a dining room, a game room, the kitchen, and the maid's quarters. It was not unknown for the expensive parlor houses to be lavishly decorated with fine furniture, rich tapestries, oil paintings, crystal chandeliers, and plush carpeting. The upstairs floor was primarily devoted to the girls' bedrooms, where the man and his chosen partner would retire after he concluded the business part of the transaction with the madam.

A typical bedroom would have a bed, dresser, commode, one or two chairs, and facilities for washing. Many of the women owned a large trunk, which they used to keep their personal belongings and as a substitute strong-box for cash and valuables. Prostitutes also commonly carried money in their stockings. Humorous contemporary newspaper reports write of women who had been paid off in coins trying to walk down the sidewalk using both hands to keep their stockings from falling down under the excess weight. One tongue-in-cheek story from a Dodge City newspaper reported that a gust of wind blew so hard that it removed several dollar bills from the stocking of a prostitute who was walking up the street.

Most fancy parlor houses had a butler or maid who answered the door and admitted the customers. During the day, when the girls were asleep after working all night, the maid did the cleaning and house-keeping, and, in the smaller houses, often doubled as the cook.

⊱ MADAMS ⊰

The madams who ran the business side of parlor houses were usually not active prostitutes, but were instead managers who conducted the financial transactions with the customers, hired and paid the staff, and were responsible for the smooth functioning of the entire house. Among the madam's other duties were hiring the girls, attracting the customers, making any necessary arrangements with local police or other authorities, encouraging the flow of liquor, and keeping whatever business records were necessary. Madams usually chose this career because they were able to raise the capital to open a brothel and had the expertise to manage it effectively. Some madams were ex-prostitutes who had passed their prime, but had accumulated enough money to open their own house or had found a partner to finance them. Other madams were women who had gone into business solely for the money and had never actually been in the trade themselves. The madam might be an independent business woman who owned or controlled one or several cribs or parlor houses, she might be in partnership with a man who owned the house or the land under it, or had invested in the establishment, or she might be employed by a saloon owner or other business investor to run the house. Madams were typically not as young as their working women, and were at least in their thirties.

A particular parlor house was not necessarily a long-term business interest for a madam. Many madams traveled from town to town, setting up parlor houses based on the current demand. When a mining camp or cattle town went into decline, which most did after a few years, the madam usually moved on to the next gold strike or new end of the cattle trail and started her business all over again. A typical example of this mobility was Eleanor Dumont, who for a while called herself Madame Simone Jules. She was a young, attractive French woman, who later developed a growth of fuzz on her upper lip that gave her the nickname Madam Moustache. She opened a saloon and parlor house in 1854 during the gold rush to Nevada City, California. To attract customers to her gaming tables, she offered free champagne to gamblers. When the gold strike dwindled in 1856, she closed the business and moved on to Virginia City, Nevada, where she opened a brothel. As the fate of mining camps rose and fell, she moved around the West, appearing in Deadwood, South Dakota, then Eureka, Nevada, and finally in Bodie, California, where she committed suicide in September of 1879.

Though a madam might be an ex-prostitute, she was typically not available for sex with the customers. At this stage of her life and business career, a madam tended to have an exclusive (either temporary or permanent) liaison with one man.

In addition to being an employer and manager for the girls, the madam was often their friend and confidante. Other madams were martinets, keeping their women in line by physical force, if necessary. Another duty of the madam was to fire a girl at her discretion. A madam might get rid of a woman if she was not attracting enough business, if she was an alcoholic, or perhaps just to "rotate the stock" to bring in new customers with the promise of new girls.

The madam occasionally ended up being the referee and mediator when fights broke out between the women. Men in general, lovers in particular, and insults real or imagined might be the impetus for face-clawing, eye-scratching, hair-pulling, shin-kicking fights between the girls. One day in September of 1880, the *News and Courier* of Boulder, Colorado, reported on a fight that "resulted in the complete destruction of one of the ladies, whose head came in contact with an empty beer bottle."

Violence might also come from outside the house. Because of her sexual relationship with many men, a girl from a parlor house was often the cause of rivalry between customers, each of whom regarded her as "his girl." Typical of this was the situation of Arden Shea, a miner who had fallen love with Mollie Dean, a girl at one of the parlor houses in the red light district on Brownell Street in Georgetown, Colorado. One day when Shea came over to visit, he found her with another man. As a result, he killed her and then himself.

Some girls had a steady customer or boyfriend, which naturally led to a peculiar relationship between the two, since the girl's work was selling herself to other men. These odd three-way relationships were also the source of fights and shootings. Jess Munn was a miner in Telluride, in the San Juan mining area of southwest Colorado, who had a girl in one of the cribs on Pacific Street. Art Gigline, the town marshal, was also drawn to the same girl. Munn told the marshal to stop seeing her, and, when he didn't, Munn shot and killed him.

To promote a facade of gentility and respectability, and in order for the madam to maintain control of the financial side of the transaction,

Abandoned cribs along Pacific Street in Telluride, Colorado.

(Author's collection)

the girls of the parlor houses typically did not handle cash. The financial arrangements for sexual services were made with the madam, and she collected the money. To simplify this transaction, one common medium of exchange was a token or brass check, which was a quarter or half-dollar-sized brass coin.

The use of brass checks instead of hard cash in the bedroom had advantages for both the customer and the madam. The madam did not want the girls making independent deals or holding back part of her fee, so the use of these tokens eliminated individual negotiations and standardized the transaction. It also allowed the customer to know the exact price in advance. He paid his money downstairs, then, when he went upstairs, he gave the token to the girl. She in turn would give it back to the madam in the morning or on payday in return for cash, thus completing the circle of accounting responsibility.

Reproductions of brass checks made as tourist souvenirs occasionally show up in collections of Western Americana. Some were made with a sense of humor. One bogus design reads "Good for One" and, as a background, had an engraving of that common hardware item, the wood-screw. Other forms of advertising included business cards that contained a listing of a brothel's residents and services, or cards with photographs of some of the boarders in abbreviated costumes that showed off their charms.

Windows were rarely opened in the bedroom of some parlor houses, and, as a result, the interior often had a distinctive smell. The air was usually full of a heady aroma that was a combination of liquor, stale tobacco smoke, perfume, and sweat. Though certainly not hygienic, keeping the windows closed had several practical aspects. For one thing, madams did not want robbers entering by the windows. They also did not want the girls' sweethearts or other non-paying clients coming or going via this route and getting a free sample of what everyone else had to pay for. There were often bars over the windows to further hinder entrance or exit.

Though most madams were alert to the downside of recreational drugs, drug-use was a common part of a prostitute's life. Narcotic drugs helped the girls bear the chronic and often painful pelvic discomforts and bloating that accompanied continued sexual activity over long periods of time. Drugs were also used to take the edge off depression and boredom, and they often made it easier for a prostitute to handle a busy night of customers. On the other hand, some pimps and unscrupulous madams helped to create drug addiction in their women in order to force the girls closer to them. Though some madams watched drug use with a tolerant eye, most were strict and would not keep a girl who was a serious drug addict or an alcoholic.

Madams were viewed differently by their contemporary society than were common prostitutes. Prostitutes were considered to have fallen from a state of purity due to seduction by a man or some other fault that was not their own. Madams, on the other hand, were seen as shrewd business-women who took financial advantage of the sexual commerce of the "unfortunate" prostitutes. Madams, therefore, were often viewed by respectable women with an animosity that they didn't have for prostitutes.

∽ A TYPICAL PARLOR HOUSE ROUTINE ∽

The operation of a fancy parlor house was straightforward. The customer, arriving at the door, would be met and ushered in by a maid, or possibly by the madam herself, and be shown into the parlor. If this were one of the expensive houses, he would be given a free drink or it might go on his account. In the cheaper houses, he would have to purchase it himself.

The sale of liquor was an integral part of parlor house profits, and, as part of the operation, the consumption of large amounts of wine and champagne was encouraged. Liquor was sold at a large markup — up to five or six times cost — and was an extremely profitable part of the house business. For example, a bottle of wine might cost the customer fifteen dollars and a quart bottle of champagne could cost up to thirty dollars (at a time when a common miner made three dollars a day and a cowboy made thirty dollars a month). Because of these large potential profits, parlor houses were occasionally backed by liquor merchants; or a merchant would put up the initial cost of operating the house, with the understanding that the madam would supply only his particular brand or brands of liquor.

If the madam had admitted the customer to the house, they might settle the financial side of the transaction immediately and have it out of the way. Some houses had a cash register in the hallway, so that, upon entering, the customer immediately paid and received a brass check as a receipt.

If it was a fancy parlor house, there would probably be music in the parlor. Some very expensive houses had a three or four piece orchestra,

A madam and her four working girls, with the "professor" at the piano ready to entertain customers.

(Courtesy Colorado Historical Society, Mazzulla Collection, Box 23, FF 1342, scan #10031331)

but likely as not music would be provided from a piano by the "professor," as the piano-player at a parlor house was often nicknamed. The piano player was not generally paid a regular salary by the house, or was paid only a token amount, so he worked primarily for tips and drinks from the patrons of the house. There might be a sign on the piano as a reminder, in order to encourage lavish tipping. Most musicians found this arrangement quite lucrative, knowing that a man out for a good time usually tipped generously. If he didn't, one of the girls might give the musician a prearranged generous (but bogus) tip, with the expectation that the customer, not wishing to appear cheap, would do the same.

If the house didn't have a live musician, twenty-five cents (or fifty cents in a really high-class house) might coax a tune out of a player piano. In later years, wax-cylinder phonographs were added for musical entertainment.

If music was available, the girls might be willing to dance with a customer. This was not purely for fun, but also had a practical motive. Having the customer dance close to an attractive woman, especially if she were scantily-dressed, was one way to make sure that his appetite for upstairs activities was quickly aroused.

Liquor, music, and dancing helped to prepare the customer for the real business of the parlor house. More than that, lively music and dancing were inducements for the customer to buy more liquor, which produced much of the profit for the house. In some of the less-reputable houses, the madam might insist that a customer "treat" all the other customers and the girls to a drink in an attempt to increase the liquor sales and profits.

During these preliminaries, the girls would assemble in the parlor for the customer's inspection. In the very expensive houses, they would be fully and elegantly dressed; in the cheaper houses, they might be dressed in only scanty underwear. The Old Homestead, which was a very exclusive and expensive parlor house in Cripple Creek, Colorado, had a small upstairs room with a window, which allowed the client to view the girls in the nude and make his selection without being seen by them. The same type of inspection arrangement was available at the Dumas Brothel in Butte, Montana.

While inspecting the women and finishing his drink, the customer might engage in small talk with them. A particularly affluent customer might be allowed to kiss or fondle several of the women to assist him in making his choice — sampling the goods, so to speak. After these preliminaries, he would select one of the girls and the couple would go upstairs.

Typical working hours for the women of a parlor house were from noon until the final customers left in the early hours of the morning. Then the girls slept until the start of the next workday at noon.

The benefits for a woman who was a parlor house prostitute were that no sales activity was required on her part, she had a safe place to work, and she did not have to dodge the police or social reformers. Also on the plus side, the girl had a secure place to live and eat during her non-working hours. Many parlor-house girls received one day off a week.

The girls were either paid a flat salary or shared their earnings with the madam. Depending on the arrangements in a particular brothel, the split might be uneven, with the larger share going to the house. Though this might seem unfair, the parlor house girls were well-paid. A popular girl in a good house could make a $150 to $250 a week. In 1880, prostitutes in Helena, Montana, had an average monthly income of $233. Though many of the women were well-paid, they were also fast spenders and most of the time were in debt to the madams.

Depending on the arrangements of a particular house, the girls either paid the madam a percentage of their earnings for room, board, and laundry, or paid for their keep at a flat rate that might be up to fifty dollars a week Depending on the status of the parlor house, food might or might not be a part of the arrangement. In the fancy houses, food and lodging were usually included as part of the business deal, though obviously the girls paid indirectly by returning a higher amount of their earnings to the madam. The lower-class parlor houses often provided only lodging.

There was another side of life in a parlor house that was not so glamorous. Like any other job, prostitution quickly became dull, boring, and routine. Unlike some other jobs, a prostitute had to act happy and carefree all the time when she was entertaining a client. She had to convince each man that, though he was obviously not the first, he was the best, and the only one who had really excited and satisfied her.

The women in the high-quality parlor houses might have seven or eight evening dresses, as well as more traditional clothes to wear during the day. As part of the ties that bound them to the parlor house, the girls were often encouraged to charge purchases of their clothes and makeup to the madam's account at a local dry goods store. In some instances, the storekeeper made a kickback to the madam and added fifteen percent or twenty percent to the bill on top of his regular prices. This practice helped keep the girls perpetually in debt to the madam and ensured that they would remain with a particular house.

Though the girls' work was obviously intended to satisfy multiple male customers, many of them had private sexual lives that were apart from their professional. They might have a steady boyfriend or "a kept man" that they supported. Some women were lesbians and formed close "friendships" with other girls with similar inclinations, though madams generally discouraged lesbianism, because such a relationship might lead to a lack of attention to male customers. Whatever their private sexual inclinations, high-class prostitutes were all adept at theatrical moaning and groaning and making the customer feel that he was extra special in bed.

Because they were expensive, both to run as a business and to the customer, the expensive parlor houses were mostly found in large cities, such as San Francisco or Denver, or in very rich communities, such as the mining towns of Virginia City, Tombstone, Leadville, Cripple Creek, and cattle towns, such as Dodge City.

There was another, lower class of parlor house that did not have fancy girls or amenities. This type could be found in almost any size of town. Here the furnishings were often tawdry and the paint might be peeling. The customer had to buy his own drink, which was probably beer or wine. The women did not cost as much, but were typically older, coarser, and homelier, and could not compete with the younger, prettier, expensive girls of the exclusive parlor houses in the big cities.

∽ THE OLD HOMESTEAD ∽

An example of the exclusive parlor houses was the Old Homestead in Cripple Creek, Colorado. It was owned during its peak years by young and enterprising Pearl DeVere, who was previously a madam in Denver.[2] She arrived in Cripple Creek in 1893, at the age of thirty-one. Her elegant, two-story, red brick building, which still stands in the 300 block of Myers Avenue, was built after two major fires ravaged Cripple Creek in 1896.

Ironically for the red light district, the first fire on April 25, 1896, occurred on the second floor of the Central Dance Hall. It was caused by a stove that tipped over during a fight between one of the girls, Jennie LaRue, and her boyfriend. A strong wind fanned the flames; and it quickly spread out of control over a thirty-acre portion of downtown, destroying most of the business district. However, the town was resilient. By the next day, many businesses, including several saloons, were back in operation in tents. and other hastily improvised quarters.

The Old Homestead Parlor House in Cripple Creek, Colorado, has been converted into a respectable museum for the curious.

(Author's collection)

Two fires in April of 1896 devastated the red light district of Cripple Creek, Colorado. Moments after this photograph was taken, the El Paso Livery Stable (at the right of center) literally exploded when the fire reached dynamite that was stored in the stable. The small buildings in the foreground are part of the Myers Avenue cribs.

(Glenn Kinnaman Colorado and Western History Collection.)

But the worst was yet to come. Four days later, on April 29, a second, more devastating, fire started in the Portland Hotel. Another brisk wind rapidly spread the flames, and soon the fire was burning out of control in the town's new buildings and the few remaining downtown structures that were left standing after the first fire. The fire raged all afternoon, fanned by the wind. Luckily, in the evening, the wind died down and the fire was brought under control; but not before 5,000 people were left homeless.

Fires were common in many early Western towns and were often unintentionally fueled by kerosene and dynamite stored inside buildings. Though the conflagrations were disastrous for the townspeople, they did serve to clean out hastily-built wooden fire hazards, shacks, slum buildings, and disease-ridden trash dumps; thus paving the way for better-built towns. Puritanical reformers gleefully announced that the disastrous fires that plagued early towns were just retribution for what they considered to be recreations of Sodom and Gomorrah.

As a result of the fires in Cripple Creek, a new city of brick rose from the ashes. Among the new brick buildings was the Old Homestead parlor house. The sedately-shuttered exterior contrasted with the

A similar fire ravaged nearby Victor, Colorado, on August 21, 1899.
(Glenn Kinnaman Colorado and Western History Collection.)

uninhibited activities in the rooms upstairs. It was a very exclusive parlor house that catered primarily to the wealthy local mine owners who could spend in a night what it would take a common miner six months to earn. The competition, which was not as elegant as the Homestead, was Ella Holden's "The Library" and Pearl Sevan's "Old Faithful."

One of the primary attractions of the Homestead was its exclusiveness. A prospective customer had to make a formal application, then go through a waiting period while his standing in the community (and his bank balance) was verified. The Homestead was very expensive. The charge was fifty dollars for a short visit and the price for staying all night was $250.

For the applicant the wait was worth it. The Homestead had the most beautiful girls in the mining district, offered the best wines, and catered to the most exclusive clientele. Elaborate banquets and evenings of dancing were arranged at the Homestead by wealthy mine owners who wished to entertain their friends and business associates.

The shades of the Homestead were always kept discreetly drawn, and the door was answered by a maid dressed in a white cap and starched apron. Inside were crystal chandeliers, a baby grand piano, wallpaper imported from Europe (along with a paper hanger to install it), and two bathrooms with running water. The Cripple Creek city directory for the year 1900 listed a staff that included a cook, a housekeeper, two chambermaids, two butlers, and a musician. At the rear of the main building was a separate structure that housed several black prostitutes.

As with many who were involved in vice, owner Pearl DeVere died young. On June 5, 1897, she either intentionally committed suicide or accidentally took an overdose of morphine — the particular cause depending on the perspective of contemporary sources. She was buried on a hill in nearby Mount Pisgah Cemetery. Her original tombstone was made of wood and was later donated to the Cripple Creek Museum. It was replaced by a headstone of white marble with a carved heart, which can still be seen today. To indicate her popularity, her funeral procession was accompanied by a twenty-piece Elks band and four mounted policemen. The last known madam of the Homestead was Hazel Vernon, who ran it from 1900 to 1910.

BLUE, RED, AND GREEN BOOKS

Parlor houses were so well tolerated in major cities towards the end of the Nineteenth Century, that guidebooks were available that listed the addresses of different houses, along with the names of the girls and the entertainment offered in each establishment. These directories were not a new idea. Guidebooks to brothels had been in vogue for over a hundred years in Europe for the use and pleasure of the aristocracy.[3]

The most famous of the guidebooks in the United States was one to Storyville, the red light district in New Orleans. It was published in several editions from 1898 to 1915. This guidebook was generally called "The Blue Book," because the earliest edition had a blue cover and binding. Later editions were still generically referred to as "The Blue Book," even though the covers were blue, green, or red. The first edition, which appeared in 1898, was forty pages long, and cost twenty-five cents. It was titled *A Directory and Guide to the Sporting District*. The guide consisted primarily of a listing of the district's prostitutes and brothels, with some pages near the back that were advertisements for various cigars, brands of liquor, and parlor houses.

The guidebook to the parlor houses of Denver was sixteen pages long and was called "The Red Book," because of its red covers. Its title was *Denver Red Book: A Reliable Directory of the Pleasure Resorts of Denver*. It was published collectively by Denver's parlor houses to coincide with the Knights Templar convention held in August, 1892.

∽ THE CRIBS ∽

If a woman could not compete in a parlor house, the next step down the career ladder was to a crib. Much of prostitution in the West and Northwest was performed in cribs, which were small one or two room shacks with the front door opening directly onto the street, where an individual prostitute worked, but normally did not live. The girl's name was often painted on a sign over the door. Cribs were usually clustered in an area of town that was generically called "The Red Light District."

Parlor houses and cribs catered to different social classes and financial capabilities of clients. Parlor houses often served as a social center where a customer with money could take his time in selecting a girl, and where he might enjoy food, wine, and music in addition to sex. The hallmark of the cribs was speed of service. Cribs provided a place for fast, mechanical sex with a maximum turnover of customers. There were no attempts at social interaction or entertainment. The crib prostitute wanted to move on to the next customer as fast as possible.

The "rooms" of a crib were sometimes separated by hanging a curtain down the middle of a single room. The working room, which

This building in Buena Vista, Colorado, was a brothel known as the Palace Manor, when it was owned by madam "Cockeyed Liz" Spurgeon.

(Author's collection)

might be either the front room or the rear room of a two-room crib, was typically about ten or twelve feet square and was sparsely furnished. The main feature was a brass or iron bed. In addition there might be one or two chairs, a spittoon, and a washstand with a tin basin containing an antiseptic, such as carbolic acid solution.[4] There was a wood or coal-oil stove in one of the rooms to provide heat and also to provide warm water for washing and douching. Apart from the bed, furniture was not required in the bedroom, since prostitutes typically did not live in cribs, but only used them during working hours. In some of the poorer areas of a big city or in smaller towns, the crib might also be the prostitute's home.

The front room of a two-room crib was often used by the girl to display herself. Women would sit in the windows with the shades up or lounge in the doorway soliciting business from passing men with a smile and a friendly: "Come on in!" On San Francisco's Morton Street, renamed Maiden Lane by someone with a sense of humor, prostitutes waiting between customers were known to lean out of their crib windows with no clothes on the upper half of their torso. For ten cents — or two for fifteen cents — prospective customers could fondle their breasts.

A series of individual cribs were sometimes built together to form one large building, which was nicknamed a "cowyard" or "bullpen." Such buildings were usually three or four stories high with individual cubicles that opened off a central corridor that ran the length of each floor. These structures were located in large cities, such as Seattle, Portland, and San Francisco. Sometimes 300 or 400 girls worked in these buildings.

More common in the West was a row of small, single-story cribs that lined a street. During the early development of mining and logging communities, many prostitutes started out in tents and later moved into small wooden buildings. This string of shacks was usually not on the main street of a town, but was close to the downtown area.

Cribs were not necessarily always built in a row. Reno, Nevada, for example, had a series of cribs arranged in a horseshoe-shaped concrete building. Cribs were also not always one-story structures. In the larger cities they were often two-story buildings.

In large cities, crib rents were on the order of fifteen to twenty dollars a week, usually paid in advance, and often collected in cash. In small Western towns, cribs typically rented from ten to thirty dollars a month. If nobody lived in the rooms, the same crib might be rented by different women during different working shifts. Part-time prostitutes might rent a crib by the night for three or four dollars.

The frequency with which a prostitute's bed linen was changed was in direct proportion to the price charged for sex. In expensive parlor houses, the bed-sheets were typically changed after each client. Medium-priced houses changed them daily. In the cheap cribs, the grubby sheets might not be changed until enough customers complained, and by then, they probably had to be thrown away.

One identifying feature of many cribs was a strip of red or yellow oilcloth laid across the bottom end of the bed where the customer's feet would be placed when he was lying down. The reason for the oil cloth was crib sex was fast. In the interests of speed, the customer was not allowed to take off any of his clothes, except perhaps his hat, which was supposedly done out of respect for being in the presence of a "lady." The man was generally not even allowed to take off his boots, hence the oilcloth was placed at the bottom of the bed to protect the linen and to keep it from being torn by his heavy work boots, even though the cleanliness of the sheets might be dubious at best. Kissing was typically not allowed as, perversely, it was considered too intimate a practice for two people who did not know each other.

The price for crib sex varied, depending on the part of the country, the size of the town, and the nationality of the prostitute. Prices varied from twenty-five cents to two dollars, depending on the age and attractiveness of the woman. Typical crib prices were one dollar for a white American girl, seventy-five cents for a French girl, fifty cents for a Chinese or black woman, and twenty-five cents for a Mexican. Some women were as cheap as ten cents. One industrious crib worker in the gold fields named Big Matilda advertised that she was available for fifty cents, or three for a dollar. Her advertising cards also stated that she was "300 pounds of black passion."

The cheaper prostitutes were sometimes scornfully referred to as "two-bit" whores. Though there was not an actual coin of that denomination, a "bit" was equivalent to twelve-and-a-half cents.[5] Thus two bits was twenty-five cents, six bits was seventy-five cents, and so on.

When miners, loggers, and cowboys were flush with money, prostitutes in the cribs faced hard work. During a typical busy payday, a crib girl might expect from twenty to fifty customers, with an average of about twenty-five. On a good weekend, some were reported to entertain up to a hundred men in a single night. This figure would seem to be optimistic. Even allowing only five minutes for a client — which was typical — this would be close to eight hours of continuous sex.

Between paydays, business was usually slower, and during the off times of the day, the girls often had nothing to do but sit and wait in the window or doorway of their cribs. Early accounts of life in Cripple Creek, Colorado, and other large towns of the West describe "slumming parties" of well-dressed townspeople entertaining themselves by strolling through the red light district to view prostitutes waiting for customers in the windows of their cribs.[6]

Some of the displays put on by crib women were quite flagrant. In El Paso, Texas, for example, an ordinance was eventually passed to curb vulgar displays. Women were required to sit back from the windows and doors, to keep their skirts pulled down, and not to sit with their legs crossed in a vulgar manner. Some of the girls of El Paso must have been quite brash, as the ordinance also told them not to pull men into their cribs. Similar ordinances were passed in Cripple Creek and Denver, but none of them seemed to have any lasting effect on the trade.

Though prostitutes always worked with a certain amount of potential danger (for example if a customer became violent or insisted on some unusual activity), most of the women were able to take care of themselves. Mary Cook was a 285-pound madam who ran the Ivy

Green in Portland, Oregon. She smoked cigars and acted as her own greeter and bouncer, and she was perfectly capable of throwing a rowdy customer bodily out of the door.

Many of the high-class parlor houses did not have a bouncer. Most of their customers were more genteel and, apart from an occasional drunken spree, were well-behaved. However, just in case a client became rowdy, bedroom doors were typically left unlocked while the women were entertaining. If there were any need for help, it took only one scream from a woman in trouble and the other girls, one or two maids, a piano player, a butler, and the madam could be there instantly for assistance.

Crib women, who were used to dealing with unruly customers, either had a pimp nearby for protection or were able to take care of themselves. The Cripple Creek, Colorado, newspaper reported the case of a man who was confined to jail after he attempted to create a disturbance in the crib district. He had razor cuts on his body, teeth marks on his nose, and one of his fingers was severely chewed.

⁕ BUNCO ARTISTS AND CON GAMES ⁕

Human ingenuity being what it is, and the desire to make a dollar from prostitution either honestly — relatively speaking — or in other ways, was so great that some crib girls and their pimps had more than the usual way to take a customer's money. Stealing from clients was common in cribs and cowyards, both of which usually catered to a lower class of clientele than did the parlor houses. Expensive parlor houses wanted to keep a good reputation and did not tolerate stealing. Besides, they did not have to resort to trickery to separate the client from his money because he usually parted with plenty of it willingly. Most madams in parlor houses were scrupulously honest. Cora Davis of Tombstone, for example, would take a drunk customer's belongings, give him a receipt, and return everything to him when he sobered up.

One of the obvious ways of making extra money in the cribs was to steal it directly from the customer. Unlike the "honest" cribs, which dealt only in sex and required the client to keep his clothes on, in places of thievery the customer was encouraged to undress, or at least to take off his coat and trousers, which was the place his money would most likely located. The girl would hang his clothes on a hook or drape them over a chair by the window or by the door. While the girl and the customer were busy on the bed, an accomplice would reach through the door or open window and take money from the client's pocket, under the assumption that the man's attention was otherwise occupied.

If the woman and her accomplice were good at their business, she would put the client's clothes on the floor at the foot of the bed, out of the direct view of the customer while he was lying on top of the bed. The girl's accomplice would be hiding in the back room. During crucial moments when the customer was preoccupied, the accomplice would slip quickly and quietly into the room and then back out again after rifling through the customer's pockets.

Another straightforward method of stealing was to encourage a customer to have several drinks, so that by the time he and the girl got down to business, he was so drunk that he did not notice what was happening. This technique also had the benefit for the girl that, if the customer were drunk enough, she might not have to have sex with him, because male sexual functioning is usually impaired by alcohol. Large amounts of liquor could be used, or a drug such as laudanum would be slipped into a drink.[7] This would not necessarily make the customer pass out but would make his mental processes so fuzzy that he did not know what was happening.

Small, lonely two-room cribs often didn't have much more furniture than a bed.

(Author's collection)

If the customer was not sufficiently intoxicated, the woman could slip some other drug into his drink to make him pass out. Prostitutes commonly used the drug chloral hydrate, also known as knock-out drops (K.O. drops) or a Mickey Finn. This practice was the origin of the expression: "To slip someone a Mickey." Chloral hydrate was readily soluble in alcohol or water, acted within ten or fifteen minutes, and produced a sleep resembling natural sleep that lasted five hours or more. When the unfortunate customer woke up, he found himself on the sidewalk or somewhere in an alley, minus all his money.

Another person called a "hooker" (besides this being a name for a prostitute) was the hook artist. This was an accomplice who waited outside the crib until the vital moments were reached, then reached in through an open window or through the slightly-open door with a long thin pole with a hook and line on it. He would snag the hook in the customer's clothes and lift them outside. After he went through the pockets and took whatever he wanted, he carefully replaced the clothes inside the crib using his hook and pole again.

A more subtle method was used in so-called "creep-joints" or "panel houses." In these establishments, the rooms either had a second door that was cleverly blended into the wall or had a sliding panel somewhere in the lower half of the wall, below the customer's view from the bed. Another key part of the deception was that the woman locked the door from the inside. After preliminaries, the girl and her customer would retire to the bed. While the two were embracing, an accomplice would creep in through the hidden entrance (hence the name "creep joint"), rifle through the man's clothes, and creep out again. The men who did this work were called "creepers" or "panelworkers." This method had the advantage that if the customer noticed that his money was missing before he left the room, the woman could claim complete innocence. After all, she could truthfully point out that she had been on the bed with him all the time, and the door was locked from the inside. She would act just as mystified as the customer.

If the crib rogues did not like the direct approaches, one variation that required advance preparation was the use of a crib with a modified closet that had a disguised entrance in one of the inside walls. After the customer had undressed, the girl hung his clothes in the closet and closed the door. While the two were on the bed, the accomplice simply opened the hidden panel inside the closet and went through the man's pockets at his leisure.

There were also many con artists, who carried out various swindles. A straightforward deceit for getting money that did not require the girl to actually participate in sex was the old badger game, hence the women practicing it were called "badgers." A woman would make a deal with a man for sex and take him to a room where they would undress. Just when they had reached a compromising position, the door would burst open, and the girl's accomplice, posing as her husband or brother, would come roaring in.

The "husband" would threaten the customer with a gun or a knife. To add some fake realism to the situation, the girl might pretend to cry and put on a convincing performance of the "wife" caught in the act. Overwhelmed by all of this, the customer was glad to pay off the accomplice with money or anything else of value that he might have on him, then grab his pants, and leave as fast as possible. Another variation of this theme was to perform outright blackmail, especially if the client were rich or was a prominent citizen.

A more high-class con game was carried out in the fashionable hotels in the large cities. A beautiful, well-dressed woman would strike up a conversation with a rich-looking man and somehow work in a story that she was staying at the hotel, that her husband was away, and that she desperately needed money for some pretext or other. The story might unfold that she was frightfully embarrassed and had never done this sort of thing before; but, if the man would "lend" her some money, say $100, perhaps he would like to come up to her room, and she would repay him in the world's oldest way.

If he agreed, she would act extremely embarrassed by the whole situation and say that she would prefer to go ahead to her room by herself to make preparations, but that she would leave her key with him, so that he might follow in a little while. The money would change hands, and she would give him a room key. The ardent man, after waiting a discreet interval, would race up to the designated room, only to find out that the key she had given him did not fit the lock. It was quite likely that it did not fit the lock of any room in the hotel. Meanwhile, the woman was probably at another hotel nearby, selling another key to another unsuspecting man. If the woman were good, she could sell a dozen keys during a single night's work.

One interesting con-game, that lends support to the philosophy that there is a sucker born every minute, was carried out in early San Francisco by a lady known simply as Big Bertha. She claimed to be a rich woman looking for a good man to help her take care of her investments, but her condition was that a prospective suitor had to give her a matching amount of money, and she would invest all of it. Several gullible men willingly handed over money to her, and, when they realized that it was all a con, were too mortified to press charges.

Other methods of extracting money from customers were more straightforward. The patrons of some brothels, particularly in tough areas such as Hop Alley in Denver or the Barbary Coast in San Francisco, could almost expect to be drugged, beaten up, or robbed. If they were in San Francisco, some might even wake up to find themselves a forced crew members of a ship bound for the Orient. Others never did wake up, and their bodies were found in a dark alley or floating face down in San Francisco Bay.

One confidence game that preyed on the men's loneliness and desire for women was an advertisement that would appear in a remote town or mining camp that said a young woman wanted to travel to the camp but didn't have sufficient money to do so. A miner answering the advertisement would start an exchange of correspondence and eventually would receive a picture of an attractive young woman, who said that she wanted to get married. The eager, but gullible, recipient of this letter immediately sent her the fare for the railroad or stagecoach. Some weeks later, when no attractive young woman had arrived on the stage, the man realized that he was poorer, but wiser.

Chapter 4

CONTRACEPTIVES
AND DISEASES

"A night with Venus; a lifetime with mercury."
(wry Victorian play on words commenting on venereal disease)

*T*he Victorian woman, prostitute and housewife alike, faced a fairly significant chance of becoming pregnant when she indulged in sex, even when using one of the limited forms of birth control that were available at the time. Though the outcome for any one individual is subject to a high degree of variability, statistically, a woman engaging in sex without birth control, on a fairly-regular, randomly-spaced basis, will become pregnant once every two to three years. Modern studies have shown that a healthy woman trying to become pregnant has about an eighty percent chance of becoming so by the end of the first year. Thus, all other considerations excepted, a Victorian woman starting her sexual career at age eighteen and making no attempts to prevent conception, could become pregnant from ten to fifteen times before menopause. For her, the only reliable method of preventing pregnancy was total abstinence. For a prostitute, this presented an obvious problem.

❦ CONTRACEPTION ❦

Like other aspects of Victorian sexuality, contraceptives were begrudgingly known to exist, but their existence was not openly discussed in polite society. The available methods were primitive when measured in terms of modern medical technology, were often disagreeable, and were unreliable at best. In addition, contraceptives were expensive, and were therefore most often used by women who had access to them and had sufficient money to purchase them.

American medical books published in the mid-1800s listed three methods of contraception that were thought at the time to be relatively reliable: *coitus interruptus*, the vaginal sponge, and the condom. *Coitus interruptus*, also known as the withdrawal method, required the man to withdraw before orgasm and ejaculation. This method was one of the oldest forms of contraception and was most popular with married couples. The method was psychologically undesirable and physiologically unreliable. It required the man to withdraw at the crucial moment and forego gratification when his natural impulses told him exactly the opposite. Also, the preliminary secretions of some men contained enough sperm to allow conception to take place, even if ejaculation did not.

Another popular Victorian method of contraception was the vaginal sponge, a small square piece of sponge about an inch across with an attached thread or ribbon for later removal.[1] The sponge was inserted before intercourse to block and absorb sperm. In an attempt to further its effectiveness, the sponge was sometimes soaked in lemon juice or a quinine solution before use.[2] Quinine was later found to have only

The building on the left is Gilliam Hall; its two stories housed a bar and dancehall in Elkhorn, Montana, in the 1870s and early 1880s. Next door (on the right) is Fraternity Hall, which was used as a meeting house and had a lecture room upstairs.

(Author's collection)

modest spermicidal qualities, and thus was generally ineffective. Lemon juice, however, was partially successful, because it contained citric acid, which could immobilize sperm.

The third popular method of contraception was the condom, known colloquially as the sheath, *badruche*, or French letter. Though not totally reliable, this method proved fairly effective. Perhaps more important to the user than its contraceptive properties was the fact that the condom created an effective barrier for venereal disease. The problems preventing the condom from being totally effective as a contraceptive were the same ones present in its use today, namely the possibility of pinholes in the material, rupture during its use, or having it slip off after use and before withdrawal. Also on the negative side, condoms were looked upon with disfavor by some people, because they came to have strong associations with prostitution and the prevention of venereal diseases. Because of these connections, condoms were not popularly used within marriage as a method of birth control.

A few advertisements for contraceptives appeared in newspapers in cities such as Denver in the late 1860s, showing that early information and distribution were not ignored or lacking. The women of the rural West, however, were usually isolated from one another and were far removed from the minimal sources of information that were available. As a result, wives who did not want to increase their family size bought salves, potions, pills, and patent medicines that were supposed to prevent pregnancy. Some of these methods were effective, but many were not.

A good deal of the Western woman's information about contraception came by word of mouth from female friends; and, unfortunately, much of it was incorrect. Since the biology of female ovulation was not understood until the 1920s, there was inadequate knowledge of "safe" periods, and contemporary attempts to define non-fertile times were based more on wishful thinking than on science. Some medical manuals categorically stated that conception was least likely to occur at times in the female cycle that were later found to be the most likely.

Much of the information that was passed around among women fell more into the category of old wives' tales than fact. One example was the belief that as long as a new mother nursed her baby, she could not become pregnant. As a result, some women prolonged breast-feeding in the hopes of preventing pregnancy. Though there was some validity to this method (because breast-feeding usually temporarily suppressed ovulation), it was unreliable with the result that the frontier wife often had one baby at the breast and another on the way. This method was effective enough, however, that some prostitutes volunteered as wet nurses for mothers who couldn't nurse their babies, in an attempt to take advantage of the limited contraceptive effects.

Before the development of the technique for vulcanizing rubber by Charles Goodyear in 1839, condoms were made from sheep's intestines and were relatively expensive. Several types of cervical caps or diaphragms were also produced in the 1830s. One design for an early type of cervical cap was brought to America by German and Hungarian immigrants, who used melted bee's wax formed into a disc-shaped device to block the entrance to the uterus. The modern rubber diaphragm was not developed until 1883 by the Dutch physician Wilhelm Mensinga.

Early contraceptive devices were made of India Rubber, also known as "gum elastic," a sticky material derived from the unvulcanized resin exuded by the rubber tree that grows in tropical countries. Following the discovery of vulcanization of India Rubber by the use of sulfur and heat, contraceptive devices were generally available in what is now called "rubber," which is the cured form of the sticky resin. Most of these new contraceptive devices, however, cost more than working-class men and women could afford .

The continued development of rubber technology in the 1840s also led to improved designs of rubber syringes and, as a result, douching with various chemicals became one of the most widely used (though generally ineffective) female contraceptive practices. Popular preparations were solutions of lemon juice, alum, vinegar, quinine, zinc sulfate, iodine, and carbolic acid. As with other birth control methods of the time, some of these chemicals were effective, and some were not. In addition to its use as a contraceptive, douching was also used by prostitutes as a supposed safeguard against the many venereal diseases to which they were continuously exposed. As one might expect, many working-class women in small log cabins or houses without privacy, bathrooms, or running water did not care for these methods.

~⊙~ BIRTH CONTROL AS OBSCENITY ~⊙~

For several decades after the Civil War, contemporary Victorian morality with its emphasis on purity led to a condemnation of contraceptive information and devices, which were deemed to be obscene. Though birth control information was freely available in the first half of the Nineteenth Century, in the latter part of the century, the distribution of information on contraceptives or of actual devices for contraception became punishable by law. This attitude evolved because birth control came to be viewed as allowing a male to satisfy his lust without the responsibility of child-rearing. Some radical feminists even felt that contraceptives turned respectable wives into a type of prostitute because their use made women continually available for their husbands' pleasure.

The major Victorian roadblock to widespread knowledge of contraception during the late 1800s was a comprehensive anti-obscenity bill, called the "Comstock Act," which was passed by Congress in 1873. The bill was named for Anthony Comstock, a self-appointed censor of American morals.

Comstock started his career in 1872, when he "raided" two stores in New York and declared the books and pictures that he found there to be obscene. Following this "success," he contrived an appointment as special agent to the U.S. Post Office, and organized and was appointed secretary of the New York Society for the Suppression of Vice. Comstock persuaded Congress to pass legislation that prohibited the mailing of obscene material or advertisements for obscenity, a general category that was defined to include information about birth control. With this legal backing, Comstock destroyed 98,563 articles that he felt were an "immoral use of rubber." For the next forty years he tracked down articles that he considered to be lewd, obscene, or filth, the definitions of which he expanded to cover material other than birth control. During Comstock's career, he destroyed 73,600 pounds of books and 877,412 pictures that he considered to be obscene.

Similar laws, some of which even made the verbal discussion of contraceptive information illegal, were soon passed in several states, starting with New York. The Tariff Act of 1890 prohibited interstate shipment or foreign importation of birth-control devices or information.

Since written information on contraception was considered to be obscene, most medical writers avoided the subject. Even physicians were subject to prosecution for distributing birth control information. One of the best-known pioneers of birth control and women's rights, Margaret Sanger, was prosecuted for distributing birth control information. Sanger, a mother of three, started her career as a public health nurse in New York's ghettos. Her experiences led her to believe that family limitation would help to alleviate poverty in the slums. As a result of her work, Sanger served a short jail term in 1916, before court decisions in 1918 paved the way for nurses and physicians to give birth control information to women who desired it.

❧ ABORTION ❧

Should a woman's fears be realized and she indeed faced an unwanted pregnancy, she was forced to accept her condition. Abortion was a topic that was never mentioned in polite Victorian society. The procedure was illegal and was also considered immoral. Pregnancy was considered to be the natural and almost inevitable result of sex, whether it was desired or not. For those who had illicit sex outside of marriage, pregnancy was regarded as a punishment, or at least a situation to be viewed by others with a prudish Victorian smile of satisfaction.

Mechanical methods of abortion, which were couched in Victorian euphemisms such as "illegal operation" or "criminal operation," were available but were not usually considered a viable option. Prior to modern medical technology and antiseptic techniques, it was a very dangerous procedure with the attendant risks of excessive bleeding and subsequent fatal infection. The chances of severe illness or death from even a properly performed abortion were very high.

Certain drugs might be used in an attempt to bring on a miscarriage, but they were not without risk. Ergot and quinine were among those used. Ergot, which contains an alkaloid first discovered in a fungus that develops on moldy rye, was used by doctors to control excessive bleeding following childbirth. The ingestion of large doses could be used to induce miscarriage, but the user also risked toxic side-effects that included vomiting, convulsions, blindness, severe abdominal cramps, and the development of gangrene in the fingers or toes from prolonged constriction of the blood vessels of the extremities.

Quinine was not as reliable or effective for abortion as ergot, but a massive dose could be used to stimulate premature contractions. Again, the dose required to be effective was so large that it exposed the expectant mother to other hazards, such as kidney damage, anemia, or respiratory collapse. Large doses also had the unfortunate side-effect of loosening the teeth. Vigorous exercise, hot baths, deliberate falls down stairs, sustained horseback riding, douching with irritating or toxic chemicals, repeated large-volume enemas, or large doses of purgatives, such as epsom salts (magnesium sulfate), aloes, and castor oil, were other techniques that were used to try to induce a miscarriage. Patent medicines that made promises to "remove obstructions," or similar phrases, were generally useless.

Even if a woman accepted her condition and wanted to be pregnant, further perils lay ahead. She would have to endure the pain and

One of the girl's bedrooms at the Old Homestead Parlor House. At the foot of the bed is a slop-jar next to a ceramic bed-warming bottle, the latter affectionately known by users as the "porcelain pig."

(Author's collection; courtesy of the Wild Horse Casino, current owner of the Old Homestead museum).

possible complications of childbirth. Unless she were in perfect health and stayed that way throughout pregnancy, she literally risked her life to have the child. In Victorian days, before antiseptics, antibiotics, and an understanding of modern medicine, the chances of infection or a woman dying during childbirth were high. As a result, an unwanted pregnancy was usually a condition to be dreaded. Cesarean sections were particularly risky.

Following birth, child-bed fevers were a constant threat to mothers. The germs that caused disease were often spread unwittingly between patients by the doctor himself as a result of a lack of proper antiseptic techniques. The existence of microbes was known, but their presence was not linked to infection. Suggestions that infectious agents could cause disease had been made as early as the late 1700s, but it was not until years later that the causes of infections began to receive attention.[3] Some antiseptic agents, such as bromine, carbolic acid, and bichloride of mercury, were known and were employed to disinfect operating rooms and instruments, but their use was minimal. A few surgeons tried to promote the idea of boiling surgical instruments to sterilize them, but this practice was not widespread.

For those who survived the rigors of childbirth, the prospect of having perhaps twelve or fourteen children, stair-stepped in age, was not necessarily a particularly bright or welcome future. From this aspect alone the Victorian wife could hardly be blamed for dreading sex and its consequences.

In addition to the hazards of pregnancy and abortion, a prostitute was subject to two additional medical conditions that the ordinary married woman was not. One was exposure to the many different venereal diseases that were rampant at the time. In a perverted sense venereal diseases actually helped some of these women in their careers. Repeated and prolonged exposure to various venereal diseases made many prostitutes sterile, thus freeing them from the burdens of pregnancy.

There may, however, be another contributing factor to the Victorian observation that prostitutes did not seem to become pregnant as frequently as other women. A 1967 medical study of prostitutes indicated that a large percentage of women who are frequently exposed to sperm may develop an allergic reaction that lowers their fertility.[4] In addition, the women studied had twice as many spontaneous abortions than they had before becoming a prostitute. These two recent discoveries may be part of the reason that prostitutes in the Old West were not overwhelmed by children, as might otherwise be expected.

The other medical problem that most prostitutes suffered from was a variety of discomforts due to chronic pelvic congestion brought on by continued sexual activity. Because of this, many prostitutes were irritable, emotionally disturbed, and could not sleep well. It was considered to be a hazard of the job and part of the heavy drug use among Victorian prostitutes was an attempt to make their physical discomforts bearable.

✥ THOSE DREADFUL DISEASES ✥

Prostitutes, because of their profession, were continually exposed to venereal diseases and ran a high risk of catching them. Having multiple sexual partners also made them responsible for continuing the spread of disease. Estimates are that as high as sixty percent to seventy-five percent of Western prostitutes contracted some form of venereal disease at some time in their careers.[5] Male customers were the obvious recipients; however, it was not unusual for respectable Victorian married women to contract venereal disease from their husbands, who had picked up something while visiting a prostitute and brought it back home.

The word "venereal" is derived from the name Venus and is an ironic reference to the Roman goddess of love. The organisms that cause venereal diseases are ordinarily found only inside living humans and cannot survive outside the body for long; thus these diseases are primarily transmitted via direct sexual contact. Various venereal diseases, including gonorrhea, syphilis, and other lesser-known forms of diseases, spread across the frontier almost as fast as the settlers; and, by the late 1800s, venereal disease was widespread in the West.

Venereal disease was carried by white fur trappers and traders, though evidence has been found that syphilis existed among American Indians several hundred years before the time of Columbus.[6] The

Waiting for a customer. Fancy furnishings adorn the parlor at the Old Homestead Museum in Cripple Creek, Colorado.

(Author's collection; courtesy of the Wild Horse Casino, current owner of the Old Homestead museum).

trappers and other whites who migrated across country rapidly transmitted venereal diseases to Indian women, who, in turn, quickly passed them to their husbands or to other men in their tribe.

In the late 1800s, soldiers on the frontier during the Indian Wars also spread venereal disease wherever they went; much to the disgust of the men in local towns. The spread of syphilis and gonorrhea was epidemic following the Civil War, as ex-soldiers migrated across the country.[7] Estimates made in the 1880s were that approximately eight percent of all soldiers were infected. At some frontier posts the figure was estimated to be as high as sixty percent.

Condoms were used to try to prevent the spread of disease, and almost all prostitutes douched and used antiseptic salves and washes. Most prostitutes thought that hygiene was desirable, but not essential. Some actually avoided any hygienic practice as being troublesome.

When prostitutes used douches of strong antiseptic solutions, such as bichloride of mercury, mercuric cyanide, potassium permanganate, or carbolic acid frequently, the harsh chemical solutions contributed to the general physical discomfort suffered by most of them. With many customers during a busy working evening, douching might not always be a sufficient safeguard. Sometimes the mechanics of performing the procedure between customers was considered to be a nuisance that was easy to skip, especially if the woman had been drinking or using drugs. Among the crib women, whose mode of operation was patterned for speed and as many customers as possible, this practice was usually omitted on busy days.

A prostitute usually inspected and washed her customer with soap and water or an antiseptic solution before sex. She was not just being fastidious; she was protecting her future health by inspecting for signs of disease. If a customer claimed to have been "burned," the common term for contracting a venereal disease, she could say with dubious legitimacy that it could not have been her because she had washed him.

For customers worried about catching venereal disease, many parlor houses offered a refund if the customer caught anything. In most cases this was not cash, but was credit for a free visit at the same house. This was a mixed blessing. If the customer had really caught some disease, presumably the last place he wanted a repeat performance was at the house of prostitution where he had caught it.

In spite of precautions, most prostitutes inevitably caught some form of venereal disease. Among the more serious was syphilis, and deaths from advanced untreated syphilis were not unusual.[8] The

These wooden-frame cribs in Crystola, Colorado, reportedly operated until the late 1940s.

(Author's collection)

incidence of syphilis among prostitutes in the Old West has been esti-mated at close to fifty percent. Syphilis was caused by a bacterium called *Treponema pallidum.* In Europe, syphilis was originally called "The Great Pox," because of the characteristic rash that accompanied early infection. In 1530 a physician named Fracastoro published a poem about a shep-herd named Syphilis, who contracted the disease. It has been known by that name ever since. Colorful nicknames for the disease in the Old West were "old dog," "gambler's rot," and "the French disease." Early treatment of syphilis was very important, because the later stages of the disease caused irreversible damage to tissues, including bones, joints, eyes, brain, the rest of the nervous system, and the heart. It appeared more often in men than in women, and, if untreated, it was frequently fatal.

Any course of treatment for syphilis was expensive for the time, costing about $100. The primary cure for both syphilis and gonorrhea was mercury treatment, in which a small amount of mercury was taken by mouth or injected directly up the urethra with a piston syringe. Red mercuric oxide was also used as an ointment that was spread on syphilitic sores, and calomel (mercurous chloride) was taken by mouth. Mercury is irritating to human body tissues and, as a heavy metal, is highly toxic. Undesired side effects of the mercury "cure" included copious salivation, bleeding from the gums, uncontrolled diarrhea, and various neurologi-cal problems, along with disintegration of gums and bones. After fre-quent or prolonged treatments, patients inevitably lost their teeth and developed sores in their mouths. The high incidence of syphilis, and the resulting mercury treatments, led to the wry saying of the time: "A night with Venus; a lifetime with mercury." Even the side-effects of the treatment were more desirable, perhaps, than going to one of the less-sympathetic doctors, whose "cure" was to cauterize the resulting genital sores with a red-hot iron.

The mercury cure was used until 1910, when Salvarsan was developed by the Nobel prize-winning German physician Paul Ehrlich. Salvarsan, also known as "606" because it was the six hundred and sixth preparation to be tried, was an arsenic preparation (arsphenamine) injected intravenously into the body. It became the standard treatment for syphilis until the widespread use of the antibiotic penicillin in 1945.[9] Salvarsan was not without its drawbacks. The treatment was expensive, painful, and sometimes had severe side effects. It was difficult to administer and, in some severe cases, required a course of twenty to forty injections over the period of a year. It was, however, an effective and lasting cure.

Until the arrival of Salvarsan, and later penicillin, syphilis was basically incurable, though sometimes the mercury treatment killed the bacteria that the heavy metal contacted. Because lesions from the primary stage of syphilis tended to clear up spontaneously, the mercury treatment was credited with affecting a cure. More typically the disease went into a latent stage, which could last for several decades, until it reoccurred, and the infected person suffered a painful death. On Vancouver Island in British Columbia, the bark of the Devil's Club *(Echinopanax horridum)* was boiled in water into a tonic and then drunk as a cure for syphilis. History does not tell us if it was effective.

Another widespread venereal disease was gonorrhea, nicknamed "the clap" or "the gleet," which was caused by the organism *Neisseria gonorrhoeae.* Like syphilis, gonorrhea was not easily cured until the discovery of penicillin. Even today gonorrhea is second only to the common cold in terms of the incidence of communicable diseases. The disease caused various physical problems, which if untreated, could lead to death. In women, gonorrhea produced severe inflammation of the Fallopian tubes, and thus repeated attacks of gonorrhea caused most prostitutes to eventually become sterile.

Part of the problem with controlling the spread of gonorrhea was that while about eighty percent of infected men showed symptoms of the disease, about eighty percent of women showed no signs of infection. Thus prostitutes could continue to unknowingly spread the disease to many customers. In addition, the incubation period for the disease was between two and eight days, thus again increasing the probability of rapidly spreading the disease to many customers. Estimates made by contemporary physicians (based, however, on experience and opinions rather than scientific surveys) were that between fifty and eighty percent of all men between the ages of eighteen and thirty contracted gonorrhea.

For men who contracted gonorrhea, the ubiquitous mercury cure by direct injection, by mouth, or as an ointment was the usual treatment. Repeated injections of lead acetate (also known as "Goulard's powder") directly into the penis were usually effective, but many men were too embarrassed to go through such a course of treatment. In most cases, infected men waited and hoped that the symptoms would simply go away by themselves.

One alternative for those who had the disease was to send away for one of several patent medicines that advertised a sure cure for venereal disease, such as Bumstead's Gleet Cure, Red Drop, or the aptly-named Unfortunate's Friend. The medicine was sent directly to the purchaser's doorstep, typically in a plain brown wrapper. Many liquor stores stocked a similar cure named Pine Knot Bitters.

These small buildings behind a former hotel in Twin Lakes, Colorado, may have been built to house traveling freighters or may have been used for other purposes.
(Author's collection)

PART II

The Places

Chapter 5

SALOONS AND GAMBLING HALLS

"If you spit on the floor at home,
spit on the floor here;
we want you to feel at home."
(sign in an early saloon)

*T*he primary purpose of parlor houses, brothels, and cribs was to sell sex; but other frontier vice factories found that having prostitutes available increased their business. Therefore, as well as in brothels and cribs, women frequently plied their trade in saloons, dance-halls, and gambling halls. Men looking for loose women knew that establishments that sold liquor and entertainment were also home to willing partners.

∾ THE SALOON ∾

One of the enduring symbols of the Old West is the frontier saloon. This institution has always loomed larger than life in movies, television, and Western novels. Because one of the primary forms of entertainment and diversion in the Old West was drinking, saloons rapidly evolved into an important social force for men in early Western towns. As early towns matured, the basic saloon and drinking house was quickly augmented by gambling tables to provide diversion for the patrons between drinks. Gambling was a popular saloon activity and was one that increased the profits for the house.

The lowering of inhibitions and relaxation through the ingestion of alcohol has always been popular with men. Heavy drinking was not

Saloons served a social centers for men all over the West as can be seen in this convivial scene from 1900 in Turret, Colorado.
(Courtesy Denver Public Library, Western History Collection, X-13904)

universal on the frontier, but it was certainly commonplace and was not censured. Reports of individuals downing four or five or more drinks of whiskey a day were not uncommon. In the town of Bodie, California, the snows of winter frequently piled deep on the buildings and the temperatures regularly dropped well below zero. The frigid weather virtually shut down mining in the winter, and, as one old miner complained, there was "nothing to do but hang around the saloons."

One anecdote, in particular, emphasizes the perceived importance of the saloon by the residents of a developing town. When the first combination store and saloon near Placerville, Colorado, was constructed, it was built a mile from the existing cabins of the small community. The horrified settlers decided that they couldn't be that far away from a drinking establishment, so they abandoned the existing town site and re-built their cabins around the new saloon.

In addition to the solace of liquor, the male and female companionship that could be found in a saloon provided a warmth and emotional release for men, many of whom had spent a day in hard physical work and danger herding cattle, digging and mucking in the mines, or driving spikes on the railroad. Besides, drinking, gambling, and womanizing in a saloon were considered to be the healthy pursuits and methods of relaxation for the active, young (as well as the not so young) male population. Not unusual was the town of Arland, Wyoming, which was built to supply local cowboys with whiskey and women. The entire town consisted of a dance-hall, a brothel, a store, and the local post office. Apparently there was nothing else that the local cowboys needed or wanted.

Most saloon prostitutes were not particularly pretty or shapely. If they had been, they would have been able to work in the more-lucrative high-class parlor houses, instead of hustling drinks and themselves in saloons. In the isolated communities of the West, however, almost any female was considered by the women-hungry men to be beautiful. The two primary qualifications for the saloon prostitute were that she had to be friendly and she had to be willing.

Except for prostitutes and occasional waitresses, saloons were essentially male strongholds. Women customers were barred either by custom, or in extreme cases by local law, from entering saloons. A few

Reflecting the substantial brick architecture of a mature mining town, the Fountain Saloon was located in Cripple Creek, Colorado. Note the separate wine room entrance at the far left.

(Glenn Kinnaman Colorado and Western History Collection.)

saloons had separate entrances and facilities, such as a wine room, for women customers; but these establishments were in the minority. Even in towns where females were not technically excluded from the saloons, the male patrons often found ways to discourage all women, except barmaids and prostitutes.

Though most Western men drank to some degree or another, saloons typically received more patronage by single men. Married men with families to support usually did not have much extra money for such luxuries, since everyday living in a frontier town was expensive. Apart from the cost, a wife at home often did not look kindly on her man spending large sums of their money on liquor and gambling. Married men who did not drink or patronize saloons could find alternative relaxation and social contact at the local lodge of a fraternal organization, such as the Elks, Masons, or Odd Fellows.

Single men, by contrast, had no immediate family to answer to. Often they lived in a boarding or rooming house, and "home" was a small room furnished only with a bed, a washstand, and a few personal belongings. For them, the saloon became a social club in which they met fellow bachelors and passed the time in gregarious pursuits. Because the social aspect was an important aspect of saloons, temperance movements did not make much progress in the West until close to the end of the Nineteenth Century, when the population shifted from predominantly single men to men with families.

The saloonkeeper was usually one of the first residents to arrive at a new mining strike or logging camp, and his saloon often served as the social hub of the infant town.

In a more practical sense, saloons and gambling houses were a good source of income for the owner.

In addition to filling the obvious roles of a drinking and gambling establishment and a contact point for prostitution, saloons often served other functions in a newly-founded town. They were used as meeting halls, churches for itinerant preachers, trading posts, employment agencies, temporary mortuaries, post offices, and hotels. Saloons and their bartenders were gossip centers for the latest news or the newest joke making the rounds. A newcomer to town could usually get a drink, a bath, a cigar, a meal, and a haircut at this all-purpose institution.

Though barbers and saloons would not appear at first to be compatible businesses, some saloons encouraged a barber to practice his trade in the back of the building. Customers who publicly denied drinking could thus go in for a haircut and also slip down a few quick drinks at the same time.

In a booming frontier town there always seemed to be room for another saloon; and, indeed, the measure of a town's success and wealth could usually be judged by the number of saloons. The faster saloons were established, the more successful a town was considered to be. Contemporary guide books often listed the number of saloons in a town as an indicator of the community's success, right next to information about churches, hotels, and banks. As a town reached maturity, however, and took on an air of respectability, this open attitude towards saloons usually changed. The same saloons that had served an important social function in the early days of a town's development were looked down upon by married women and reformers, who tried to sweep saloons, gambling halls, brothels, and similar places under the community rug.

Most early towns were proud of their saloons. By 1860, just a year after its formal founding, Denver had thirty saloons and dancehalls. Minot, South Dakota, had twelve saloons by the time it was only a few weeks old. In 1881, the rowdy silver-mining town of Kokomo, Colorado, had a hundred saloons along its main street. In 1879, Leadville, Colorado, which soon gained (and probably deserved) its reputation as the most wide-open boom town on the Rocky Mountain

"Saloon Row" in Colorado City, Colorado; the tall brick building was originally Jake Schmidt's saloon and gambling house.

(Author's collection)

mining frontier, proudly boasted 120 saloon, 19 beer halls, and 118 gambling halls.

By 1890, residents of Colorado City, Colorado, boasted that if a drinker wished — and many did — he could get twenty drinks in a row and never go into the same saloon twice. Many of these saloons had dance halls and gambling tables on the second floor, along with exits at the rear of the building that went to the brothels behind. The Colorado City saloon district, appropriately known as Saloon Row, stretched for four blocks along the south side of West Colorado Avenue. Behind this row of saloons and gambling dens, across the alley on West Cucharras Street (then called Washington Avenue), was the red light district. Local legend has it that there was a network of tunnels that connected the saloons to the brothels, which also allowed clandestine access to the saloons from the other side of the street. This area was so active that the second city hall and jail, built in 1892, was located on South 26th Street; because the old one, which was four blocks away on 29th Street, was considered too far for the frequent trips and arrests made by the police.

Typical of the early saloons in Denver was Hi Dingwall's combination saloon and dance-hall. The saloon had two bars, one located in the front of the dance-hall and the other at the back, so that the patrons could not avoid buying a drink by whichever door they entered. The cost of a dance was a dollar, with seventy-five cents going to the house and twenty-five cents to the girl. The music was fast-paced, and the actual playing-time was short. At the end of each vigorous trot around the dance-floor, the man was expected to buy a drink for himself and one for his partner. The cost of the drinks was fifty cents a shot.

By 1860, the little settlement that was Denver had grown rapidly. One survey showed that the town had thirty saloons, dancehalls, and gambling houses to serve a population of 5,000. One example was Mundy's Sample Room, which offered choice wines and liquors, the finest cigars, and "delectable female companionship."

The saloon district in Denver grew up along Larimer Street, which had once been the city's main street. By the 1880s, fifteen major gambling houses were located on Larimer Street between City Hall and 19th Street. Denver's red light district on adjacent Holladay Street was rated third in the nation for raucous activity, right behind San Francisco's Barbary Coast and New Orleans' Storyville. Notable establishments were the Arcade, the Chicken Coop, the Mammoth Pavilion, the Little Casino, and Murphy's Exchange, also known as The Slaughterhouse because of the many homicides in the place.

By 1881, Denver's population had grown to about 36,000. At the same time, some of the rowdy saloons of the early days had matured into elegant establishments. One such place was the Navarre, which offered fine dining with discreet gambling upstairs. The Navarre Building was originally constructed as a girls' boarding school named Brinker's Collegiate Institute, before becoming a gambling hall with an upstairs brothel in the former student's dormitory. For secluded meetings of a "personal" nature, there were private dining rooms with separate entrances, along with discreet waiters who entered the room only when called by a signal button.

Legends still persist concerning an underground tunnel in the late 1890s that supposedly connected the restaurant to the Brown Palace Hotel on the opposite side of Tremont Street. The tunnel was said to have been built to facilitate after-dinner meetings of a very personal nature and allowed hotel guests to make surreptitious visits to enjoy the pleasures of the Navarre and vice versa. Transportation through the tunnel was supposedly provided by a short railroad track with little trolley cars that were pulled by Chinese coolies. Whether or not the tunnel was actually used for guests to pass back and forth between the two buildings is still a matter of conjecture. A short section of track was visible in the basement of the Navarre until recently. The semi-secret tunnel lay unused for many years until destroyed in the 1950s by the installation of new telephone, power, and gas lines down Tremont Street.

THE MYTH AND THE REALITY

Television and motion pictures have given us rich visions of Western saloons, complete with ornate woodwork, elaborate furnishings, huge plate glass mirrors, crystal chandeliers, and rows of long-legged, pretty girls dancing the can-can. To someone expecting this type of extravagance, the real-life saloons found in most early frontier towns would be a disappointment. Some frontier saloons did later evolve into elaborate establishments with stage shows and lavish entertainment, but they were more commonly found in larger cities, such as Tombstone, Portland, Seattle, or San Francisco, where gold dust flowed like water and there were enough customers to support such excesses.

The larger saloons provided music from a small orchestra to attract and entertain patrons. The "orchestra" might range in size from only an accordion and banjo, to a more formal group, which might include a cornet, drums, fiddle, and piano. The logical extension of music was dancing, both by entertainers on a stage and by customers on a dance-floor. Often the only way a lonely bachelor could put his arms around a woman was to dance with one, and, in this way, surreptitiously live out some of his fantasies.

The glamorized saloon image is also one of pretty serving girls looking for a good time with the customers. In reality, this was typically true only in the larger population centers. In the small saloons, the women were just as likely to be overweight, coarse, older women who could not compete with the younger prostitutes and were now plying their trade in a row of cribs behind the saloon.

In some saloons the owner or bartender might be married to a prostitute. In such cases, it was not unusual for him to act as her pimp, not only tolerating her activities, but actually expecting her to solicit customers. These were often marriages of convenience or were a business arrangement to tie the woman to the man, rather than being the more conventional emotional attachment.

The women found in saloons were not all necessarily prostitutes, some were merely barmaids who served drinks. However prostitutes were certainly found there, and the chances were good that most of the women who were not regular prostitutes would negotiate for business if the price was right.

Though many of the contemporary accounts describe the saloon girls as "pretty, young, and vivacious," some of the images were probably colored by the lack of females and a longing for feminine companionship. Contemporary photographs show that the girls of the saloons, the dance-halls, and The Line looked just the same as women of any era. Some would be considered outstanding beauties, some were just as homely as the men they were entertaining.

∾ THE SALOON EVOLVES ∾

The early saloons in a newly-founded town or mining camp were often only canvas tents, hurriedly brought in and erected while thirsty customers waited impatiently to sample the brew. A canvas tent was the cheapest way to start a saloon and was the easiest way for a saloon-keeper in gold-mining areas to protect his investment. If a fledgling mining camp prospered and grew into a permanent town, the saloon could be easily moved from a tent into a more substantial wooden building. If the size of the gold strike did not live up to its early expectations, and the camp did not last, the saloon-keeper could pack the tent back into his wagon and move on to the next strike.

Economy, speed, and simplicity often marked early drinking establishments. In the proprietor's haste to start serving eager customers, the bar might be a makeshift affair consisting of a rough-sawn board thrown across two whiskey barrels or beer kegs. Early saloon buildings were often put together so rapidly that daylight could be seen through the cracks in the walls. Some fast-moving saloon-keepers served drinks off the tail-boards of their wagons, until they could erect more permanent structures. The men in these camps were often so impatient to drink that the tin cups or mugs used to serve the local brew were constantly in use with no time to wash them between customers.

The selection of drinks in early tent saloons was usually limited. Often the only choice was whiskey ladled into unwashed tin cups out of a nearby barrel. Beer was very popular with the men, but was slower to arrive in many early towns, because of the difficulty and expense of freighting it across the prairies. Beer was too bulky, fragile, and inexpensive to be shipped for great distances, until the arrival of a railroad provided cheap freight rates. To solve this problem, an enterprising businessman usually erected a brewery soon after permanent structures were erected, and made beer locally. San Francisco had a brewery by 1850 and Denver had one as early as 1859. Working in a brewery was a popular job because employees in many breweries were allowed to drink as much beer as they could manage.

As permanent towns were established, the early tent saloons of wood-frame and canvas évolved with the rest of the buildings, and the saloons became permanent structures made from logs or rough lumber. If a fledgling town lasted long enough and business was good enough, the saloon evolved into a more ornate frame building of finished boards. Throughout the West, two-story wooden buildings made of sawn lumber were characterized by false fronts to give them a substantial and imposing air. Tables and chairs, and eventually pictures, mirrors, and fancy glassware, were added. As a saloon matured, non-drinkers — and there were a few — who might have taken a temperance pledge, could order ginger-ale, ginger beer, lemonade, sarsaparilla,[1] or other non-alcoholic beverages. Early bars made of rough boards evolved into elaborate wooden counters with ornately-carved fittings.[2]

The exterior appearance of a saloon depended on the building materials that were available locally. At a mining camp where trees were readily available, an early saloon was typically a low-roofed, dark, log-walled

In its heyday the Grand View Saloon at Midway, Colorado, was one of the most popular saloons in the area and offered billiards, cards, and whiskey. Now only ghosts of the past haunt the dilapidated building.

(Author's collection)

Saloon construction varied widely depending on the building materials available. Lil's Saloon in the Mohave Desert in Calico, California, was made from adobe.

(Author's collection)

building. On the plains, where trees and wood were scarce, the saloon was often an earthen dug-out with sod walls and a sod roof. In the desert southwest towns, the walls might be adobe, stone, or mud and brick.

A typical early saloon in an established mining town in the mountains was a narrow, deep, log building with a long wooden bar that stretched from front to back along one of the longer walls. Windows were small and sparse. The inside consisted of a large, open, low-roofed room that ranged in size from fifteen feet wide by thirty feet deep to perhaps thirty feet wide and eighty feet deep. The floor was often hard-packed dirt, and the walls were unfinished logs or were covered with planks or bare plaster. The swinging batwing doors popularized by the movies were not in general use in most saloons. Standard doors were more common, though sometimes they were never closed, such as in some Kansas towns during the cattle-shipping season.

The dark, gloomy inside of a saloon was dimly lit by oil lamps, which hung from the ceiling and gave off black smoke and greasy fumes. The patron entering one of these establishments was greeted with a characteristic aroma that was a combination of unwashed customers, stale beer, coal oil fumes, and the smell of strong tobacco.

Saloons were often simple places with only a bar, a stove, and some tables for drinking or gambling.

(Author's collection)

Running along the front of the bar would be a brass foot-rail for the thirsty patron to hook his boot heel on. Placed at strategic intervals alongside the rail were brass cuspidors; however, photographs of the interiors of early saloons show that the aim of the tobacco-chewing patrons was notoriously inaccurate. To counteract this, the floor was often liberally sprinkled with sawdust to soak up drips, foam, and spills from beer glasses, as well as dropped food, poorly-aimed tobacco projectiles, and anything else that might end up on the floor. Even when dirt floors were replaced by plank construction, sawdust was still spread on the boards to soak up beer, tobacco juice, and other falling debris.

During the early development of a town, sawdust on the floor might also double as bedding. Because there was typically a shortage of housing as a new town boomed, saloon tables and floors were often rented out after closing hours to new arrivals or transients. The typical charge was twenty-five cents a night. This practice, coupled with the unsanitary habit of patrons spitting on the floor or at the stove to hear the sizzle, was one cause of the rapid spread of various lung diseases, such a tuberculosis, among many of the new arrivals in a camp.

Many early bars were made with rough wood boards and offered booze straight from the barrel, such as at this recreated saloon at Bents Fort, Colorado.
(Author's collection)

Typical barroom patrons gather at the White House Saloon in Cripple Creek, Colorado. Note the stains on the floor by the spittoon and the saloon mascot at the far right.

(Glenn Kinnaman Colorado and Western History Collection.)

As the entertainment center for early towns, a man could have a drink, relax among friends, play a friendly game of cards, and conduct business. Some saloons offered mail boxes, where customers could receive letters. There might be a bulletin board, where "help wanted" or "for sale" notices could be posted. Many a medical emergency, such as a bullet wound or a broken bone, was tended while the patient lay on a gaming table.

A saloon was often pressed into service as a church. Before permanent churches were established, the religious needs of early frontier communities were served by itinerant preachers, who rode from camp to camp by stagecoach or on horseback, stopping to preach — and taking up a collection — at each new settlement. In an infant town there was usually no church building, so preachers used the saloons. When a preacher came to town, drinking and gambling were temporarily suspended, and the nude paintings on the walls were discreetly covered up while services were held.

The saloon was usually the largest building in a new town, and it almost always had a ready-made potential audience for church services. Besides, many saloon-owners felt that it was their civic duty to allow the use of their buildings as makeshift churches, and they were pragmatic enough to know that, after listening to a fiery preacher for an hour or two, the audience usually had very dry throats that needed to be wetted. Saloon owners often donated liberally to roving preachers in the hopes that the sermons wouldn't contain too many negative references to saloons and drinking. After the preacher left, the gaming tables and nude paintings were uncovered, and the saloon again offered excitement, recreation, and relaxation for hard-working young bachelors.

In more mature towns, saloons were everything that the name conjures up. An atmosphere of noise and confusion usually reigned. The sounds of the "orchestra" and perhaps some harmony from a performer (or disharmony from the audience), blended with the click of dice and the whirring of roulette wheels. Shouts, cries, laughter, and curses from drunken revelers blended together and filled the air. Chestnut Street, in the boom town of Leadville, Colorado, boasted establishments such as the Keystone Saloon and the Theatre Comique. Here the atmosphere was so frenzied that customers on the main floor might find themselves being pelted by food and liquor bottles thrown by drunken patrons up in the balcony.

As well as the basic necessities — at least from the customer's viewpoint — of drinking and gambling, and the availability of women, an enterprising saloon owner might stage other masculine entertainment. Cock fights and dog fights might be arranged as special events, along with wrestling matches and boxing bouts between bare-knuckled pugilists.

⟨◦⟩ SALOON ART ⟨◦⟩

As well as having food and women available, saloon owners and bartenders soon found that customers liked to rest their eyes on something while drinking. Saloon walls were usually decorated with a variety of ornaments and pictures, most of them typically masculine. Stuffed animal heads, mounted birds and fish, pictures of contemporary sports figures, seafaring scenes, horse racing, and portraits of American presidents were all popular subjects for the walls of saloons. One of the most popular pictures found over bars was a huge lithograph of *Custer's Last Fight*, commissioned and distributed by the Anheuser-Busch Brewing Association of St. Louis, Missouri. By far the most widespread and popular type of art in this male haven, however, was the bar-room nude. Despite mental images to the contrary, these pictures were not lewd or obscene, but were in some ways quite decorous.

Popular images were larger-than-life paintings in elaborate gilt frames of standing or reclining nudes, gazing dreamily off into space. Most of these oversized pictures showed the Victorian ideal of the feminine figure, discreetly draped in the right places — albeit with the scantiest of veils — but nonetheless showing an alluring exposure of voluptuous bosom and beefy thigh. The word "beefy" is not used lightly, because the Victorian male's taste typically ran to plump feminine figures with large bosoms, tiny waists, and rather large hips. These paintings depicted women who were often heroically proportioned, almost to the point of overweight, the visual effect being somewhat like a bass violin. Contemporary men considered Victorian women to have ideal forms when they weighed 160 or 170 pounds in an age where women were typically only 5' 3" or 5' 4" tall.

Most of these pictures were placed behind the bar so that a customer could discreetly ogle the scenery while tipping back his glass. To lend an air of respectability, many of the nude paintings had a distinctly classical theme. Popular scenes were *Diana in the Bath, Venus Surprised* (just for variety there were also versions called *Venus in the Bath* and *Diana Surprised*), *The Bath of Psyche, Venus Dressing at the Bath, Venus Disrobing for the Bath*, and *Cleopatra at the Bath*. These displays of feminine pulchritude obviously showed a well-endowed, semi-clad young woman undressing to take a bath. Variations on the same theme

The Orient Saloon in Bisbee, Arizona, in 1900 with a faro game in progress.
(Courtesy National Archives)

showed similar voluptuous young things preparing themselves for a nap, or reclining nude or semi-nude, on a variety of couches, beds, and similar boudoir furniture.

This obsession with bathing would seem to be an unlikely subject for men who took so few baths themselves, but the painters knew what they were trying to evoke in the viewers. By portraying imminent nudity, yet innocence and a degree of modesty, they were able to produce more satisfying art for the Victorian viewer than if they had painted pictures that were outright pornographic.

One rather clever way of combining saloon art and profit was the use of small pin-ups as change. If the price of beer was a bit (twelve-and-a-half cents), a drinker paying with a quarter might receive a saloon token as change. The use of tokens was profitable for the saloon owner, because the patron either used them for more drinks, or did not redeem them at all, which was even more profitable. To encourage the patron not to redeem them, some saloons used tokens that had a portrait of a nude woman on them, which made the drinker only too happy to keep it.

Chapter 6

LIQUOR AND DRINKING

"I once spent a week in Virginia City's saloons one night."
(apocryphal comment by a visitor to the Comstock)

T he sale of alcohol and sex were closely related in the West, thus the male population commonly linked women and drinking. Alcohol was consumed in large quantities and helped provide relaxation and a temporary escape from the harsh realities of living on the frontier. In 1878, the editor of the *Dodge City Times* loosely estimated the consumption of whiskey in his town for that year to be about 300 barrels.

Drinking made life endurable for men who were often lonely, and who may have had only cold beans for breakfast, lunch, and dinner. If the men felt any guilt about drinking, which they rarely did, they could console themselves with authoritative comments from fellow drinkers that whiskey strengthened the heart and improved the lungs. Alcohol — taken purely for medicinal purposes, of course — was said to cure a wide variety of other ailments, such as bites from mad dogs, chills, malaise, palpitations, fevers, kidney ailments, and general debility. A self-fulfilling prophecy of some drinkers was that because alcohol was used as a preservative, by association, alcohol should also preserve a drinker's tissues and lengthen his life. Others felt that a drink before a meal prepared the stomach for food and that a drink afterwards helped the digestion.

❧ BOOZE AND ITS MANY VARIATIONS ❧

By the 1880s, whiskey was widely distributed across the West, and the term "drinking" usually referred to imbibing bourbon whiskey.

Occasionally, the name "whiskey" also referred to rye whiskey; however, rye was more commonly a drink of the Midwest. Scotch whiskey was not introduced to the Western frontier until after the turn of the century. Various mixed drinks were available in big cities, such as San Francisco, Denver, or El Paso, but they were generally frowned on in the mining camps and smaller towns of the West as "sissified drinks." Wine was commonly available, usually shipped from California.

The price of drinks was proportional to the relative remoteness of the saloon. In Dawson, Alaska, during the Klondike gold rush, so-called "whiskey" sold for fifty cents a shot and saloons in turn-of-the-century Dawson took in up to $15,000 on a good night. By comparison, a shot of whiskey in Cripple Creek, Colorado, at the same time typically cost about half that amount.

High profits from selling liquor was always a tradition on the frontier. At the mountain man's rendezvous, whiskey that cost a trader thirty cents a gallon in St. Louis was sold by the drink and brought as much as twenty-four dollars a gallon in profit. To further increase the trader's profit the whiskey was sometimes diluted with water.

Dave's Place, Creede, Colorado, in 1892 apparently imported and sold fine bourbon from Kentucky.

(Courtesy Special Collections, Tutt Library, Colorado College, Colorado Springs)

The old advertising man's motto of "take a negative feature of a product and turn it into a positive advertising claim" served even in the Old West. The Wells Fargo Saloon in Junction City, Kansas, boldly advertised that it had the worst liquor and the poorest cigars on the frontier. Looking at it from another angle, the owner may have been one of the forerunners of truth in advertising.

As towns sprang up throughout the West, breweries and distilleries quickly followed. If for any reason their output of liquor faltered, a panic might set in. A shortage of liquor was considered to be a serious situation, almost on an equal with a shortage of food. However, a shortage of liquor was not a major setback for some of the early bartenders and saloon owners. If there was a potential shortage, they simply made their own.

Though saloon liquor was usually alleged to be bourbon whiskey, its true heritage was often dubious, because the appearance and general taste of bourbon was easy to simulate for unsophisticated palates. The content of a whiskey bottle may have been anything. The liquor might be home-made, either because of a shortage of the real thing or, in many cases, due the ever-present desire of a business-man to turn a tidy profit.

Sometimes the fact that the liquor was homemade was proudly advertised. In most cases, however, a dubious mixture was started in a barrel in the cellar or back room, and then somehow found its way into fancy bottles at the bar upstairs. Usually the thirsty drinkers didn't really care either way.

Raw alcohol was often purchased in a fifty-gallon barrel and then diluted and spiced up with various chemicals. This adulteration could provide a yield in bar drinks of three or four times the original quantity of alcohol. The various brews that were concocted and bottled in the back room and aged overnight were invariably called "fine old bourbon whiskey." Even the real thing, if it were available, might be doctored, watered down, or otherwise corrupted between the storeroom and the customer's glass. This practice extended the number of servings and hence raised the profits for the saloon owner.

Some drinkers were so unsophisticated that one enterprising individual in Denver bottled a mixture of brown sugar, water, and yeast and sold it in Leadville and Denver as champagne for five dollars a quart. A few of the more gullible miners were reportedly able to become quite inebriated on it.

❧ HOW TO BREW YOUR OWN ❧

The recipes for some of the "overnight" whiskeys sound bizarre today. Though the formulas for some of the home-brews may sound humorous when reading their ingredients, they could cause serious harm to the unwary recipient. These potent brews frequently resulted in alcohol poisoning or other chemical side-effects, and drinkers occasionally even died as a result of ingesting some of the strange concoctions.

The basis for "overnight whiskey" was usually grain alcohol that was diluted and mixed with a variety of ingredients to color it and give it the taste of legitimate liquor. As a result, the drinks packed a powerful jolt, leading to the variety of colorful names that were attached to them. Liquor "experts" were supposedly able to determine the strength of the liquor by studying the bead, which was the bubbles that formed at the surface when the liquor was shaken; so soap was often added to the mixture to produce a good bead.

One recipient of many of the strange brews was the American Indian. Whiskey was one of the prime bartering tools in the fur trade, despite a prohibition by Congress and the presence of the U.S. Cavalry,

The Bird Cage Theater in Tombstone, Arizona, had a reputation for the wickedest drinking and gambling place between New Orleans and the Barbary Coast.

(Author's collection)

which tried to prevent the manufacture and importation of whiskey for the Indians. Cunning traders often bargained a bottle of home-made liquor for a prime buffalo robe. The Indians, unfortunately, did not know any better and had a low tolerance for alcohol. They had some preconceived notions about whiskey, and as long as it met these expectations, the drink was considered to be good. For example, they felt that liquor had to be strong enough to make them sick, and it wasn't any good unless it did so. Unscrupulous white traders soon realized that various additives could make the Indians just as sick without wasting good alcohol. Thus, it became a common practice to make Indian "whiskey" with a dash of soap or a few plugs of tobacco, both of which had the effect of inducing vomiting.

One recipe for Indian whiskey called for a gallon of raw alcohol, three gallons of water, a pound of tea or black tobacco to give the mixture color, some ginger, and a handful of red peppers to give it a kick. A variation of this all-purpose drink was to add a quart of black-strap molasses to the mixture and call the resulting concoction rum. As well as being sold to the Indians, this potent drink was brewed for the mountain men at their rendezvous.

Another recipe for Indian whiskey, one that was obviously made in wholesale quantities, started with a barrel full of creek or river water. To this was added two gallons of raw alcohol, two ounces of strychnine to give the drinker a jolt, half-a-pound of red pepper to give spice, five bars of soap to produce a good bead and make the Indians sick, and three plugs of tobacco to add color and increase the emetic qualities. Since Western creek water was often full of suspended silt and mud during the spring run-off, the resulting "whiskey" may have also had a very distinctive texture.

Shepherds in Idaho brewed a home-made liquor called "sheep-herder's delight." It consisted of raw alcohol, a plug of tobacco, some prune juice for color and taste, and a dash of strychnine to give it a good jolt. Presumably the mixture was diluted with water before being aged overnight.

Gunpowder was occasionally used for the same purpose as pepper and tobacco. Burnt sugar, molasses, tree bark, sagebrush, black bone meal, or dried peaches might be added to give color and flavor. Even more bizarre chemical ingredients, such as tartaric acid, sulfuric acid, ammonia, turpentine, or creosote, might find their way into the brew. One old recipe described how to produce fine "Irish whiskey" by adding creosote to cheap wine.

Two well-dressed bartenders ready to greet patrons at the bar of this saloon in Cripple Creek. Note the "misses" around the spittoons.
(Courtesy Denver Public Library, Western History Collection, X-660)

Sometimes distillery whiskey was simply watered down with water and colored with a little tobacco juice to make it go further. Dilution of the brew may help to explain why some bar-flies could spend hours downing drink after drink without falling flat on their faces.

Because of uncertainties in the heritage of some frontier whiskey, customers in the know often ordered "sink-taller whiskey." It was believed that a piece of tallow (beef or mutton fat) would float in whiskey that had been diluted or for other reasons had a low alcohol content, but would sink in liquor with a high alcohol content.

Another test, hopefully carried out in the outdoors, was to throw a little of the liquor onto a fire to see how high the flames flared. This is the origin of the Indian name of "firewater" for whiskey with a high alcohol content. Apparently the test had some validity. In June of 1881, a cigar was accidentally dropped into a barrel of whiskey at the Arcade Saloon on Allen Street in Tombstone, Arizona. The whiskey ignited and the resulting fire destroyed four city blocks of the downtown area and leveled over sixty businesses.

Though it may have seemed like a waste to many, whiskey was occasionally used for purposes other than for drinking. For example, it could be used as an antiseptic because of its high alcohol content. One popular formula for home-made shampoo called for a mixture of castor oil and whiskey, with lavender added to give it a pleasant scent.

If there was no alcohol available, the early fur trappers sometimes prepared a curious drink called "bitters," that was concocted from water mixed with ox-gall. It was described as being an "exhilarating drink," though it might cause vomiting. Another drink, which was described as being "an invigorating tonic," consisted of soaking the bark of aspen trees in sarsaparilla, then mixing the resulting liquid extract with an equal measure of whiskey.

✑ WOMEN, LIQUOR, AND DRUGS ✑

Drinking alcohol in a public saloon was an acceptable form of recreation for men, who often sought pleasure and release from their everyday cares. Consumption of alcohol by women, however, carried a social stigma, and women who appeared in public in a drunken state were considered immoral. Though drinking whiskey was generally considered a male pastime, women were not beyond a nip or two on occasion. Many women kept a small bottle of whiskey discreetly hidden among the kitchen supplies, and now and then took a swig or two for "female complaints." Though not as common as for men, alcoholism in women was not unknown. Records for the Nevada State Hospital in the early mining era indicate that a large number of women, both prostitutes and "respectable" women, were institutionalized for drug and alcohol abuse.

More often, women tended to seek their pleasure in private through drugs such as opium. Drug usage was not uncommon for many Victorian women, and recreational smoking of opium was a popular pastime across the West.[1] Though often thought of as drug of prostitutes and the lower criminal classes, opium was commonly used by middle-class women, some of whom were as young as thirteen or fourteen. Ironically, alcohol addiction was sometimes treated by a prescription for opium, and opium addiction was treated by the use of morphine, one of opium's powerful derivatives.

Though there were some concerns about opium addiction among the medical community, the drug's full effects were not clearly understood at the time and it was widely prescribed as a cure-all for pain of any kind, including so-called "female complaints." It has been estimated that sixty to seventy percent of women between the ages of twenty-five and fifty-five used opiates for relief of menstrual and menopausal symptoms. Other prescribed remedies of the time for these conditions included brandy and the use of ergot, a chemical precursor to LSD, that was also used in large doses to induce abortion.

Opium, laudanum (an alcohol solution of opium), and morphine (the most important opium derivative) were also used to treat legitimate ailments, such as consumption (tuberculosis), rheumatism, insomnia, and stomach disorders. Laudanum was a popular sedative. It was nicknamed "sleepy-stuff" or "quietness." Belladonna, also known as "deadly nightshade" or "banewort," was in common use as a pain reliever. It was popular with prostitutes, because it dilated the pupils, making the woman's eyes seem bigger and more attractive to her customers. Chloroform and ether, which had been available since the early 1830s, were originally used as recreational drugs, before their potential for use as anesthetics was realized.

This establishment in Victor, Colorado, proudly advertised its wares.

(Author's collection)

Narcotic drugs, such as opium, cocaine, morphine, and chloroform, were not controlled substances at the time and could be easily purchased over the counter at a local drugstore. As a result, cocaine and morphine addiction were common. There were no legal limits to prescribing opium in its various forms, and it was an ingredient of many patent medicines.[2] Patent medicines were available without prescription from drug stores, by mail order, or from traveling medicine show peddlers.

As well as opium, morphine, or cocaine, patent medicines also commonly contained a high percentage of alcohol. Kendall's Balsam contained sixty-one percent alcohol with five grains of opium per ounce. Old Sachem Bitters contained opium and alcohol; Wyeth's New Enteritis Pills and Mrs. Winslow's Soothing Syrup both contained morphine. Hostetter's Celebrated Stomach Bitters contained as much as forty-four percent alcohol.[3] Hostetter's was touted as being good for the treatment of dyspepsia, ague, dysentery, colic, and nervous prostration. Other examples were Baker's Stomach Bitters (forty-three percent alcohol) and Limerick's Liniment (which was also claimed to be good for diseases of horses), both of which consisted primarily of alcohol with a few token additives. Many patent medicines proclaimed themselves to be a "female remedy," thus temperance-minded women, who swore that a drop of liquor would never pass their lips, could naively dose themselves with a teaspoon or two a day of one of the many alcoholic concoctions that were available.

A popular icon for patent medicines was the image of an American Indian in full headdress on the label, which was supposed to make the customer think that its contents was an age-old natural remedy. A clue to the contents, however, should have been obvious, because "bitters" was sometimes used as a generic term for alcohol. Tonics, labeled as bitters, that were high in alcohol were Faith Whitcomb's Nerve Bitters (twenty percent), Burdoch Blood Bitters (twenty-five percent), Flint's Quaker Bitters (twenty-three percent), and Luther's Temperance Bitters (seventeen percent). This last name would seem to be somewhat hypocritical.

A particularly popular patent medicine was Lydia Pinkham's Vegetable Compound, which was advertised as the "only positive cure and legitimate remedy for the peculiar weaknesses and ailments of women." It was developed by Mrs. Lydia Pinkham of Lynn, Massachusetts, who claimed it contained only vegetable ingredients. It was said to be derived from various roots that were soaked in alcohol "as a preservative." This tonic, which was described at various times as being composed of twelve percent to twenty-one percent alcohol, with a large proportion of opium, was specifically recommended for pneumonia, tuberculosis, appendicitis, and especially for "the recurrent problems of women."

Narcotic drugs were also used to treat depression. From time to time, most prostitutes went through periods of severe depression and suicides were common. Christmas was always a dismal day in the cribs and parlor houses, and it was one of the few days of the year when there were almost no customers. Far from family and friends, the women felt deserted by the world and often spent the day in a haze of drugs or alcohol. Then as now, there were more suicides among prostitutes at Christmas than at any other period of the year.

The preferred method of committing suicide among prostitutes was an overdose of narcotic drugs, such as morphine or laudanum. Eleanor Dumont, for example, a professional gambler and brothel owner, became disillusioned by gambling and business losses. She committed suicide in Bodie, California, in September of 1879 by drinking an overdose of morphine. Others drank various chemicals, such as the potent antiseptic carbolic acid that was used for douching or washing the customers.

Distinct groups in the West seemed to have their own favorite methods of committing suicide. Miners might use dynamite to blow their heads off, and gamblers usually blew their brains out with a gun. Though prostitutes did shoot themselves, many of them, ever mindful of their final public appearance, used drugs or poison so that they would not be disfigured for their funeral. There were, however, exceptions. On October 11, 1897, Ruby Reed, a nineteen-year-old prostitute in Silverton, Colorado, shot herself in the head. Ella Wellington, a successful madam on Denver's Holladay Street, did the same on July 27, 1894. Others were not so successful. Timberline Rose of Creede, Colorado, shot herself six times, but survived this ordeal and evidently regained her health.

❧ SALOON REFORMERS ❧

Though saloons were often the center of social life in early communities, they were not without opposition. Liquor and the easy women that accompanied it, though popular with most men, were not always accepted by "decent" women. Anti-liquor crusaders soon banded together to try and save the men from themselves. Wives, daughters, and sweethearts, intent on creating social order, frequently tried to convert their men from drinking to some of the finer things in life — even though many of the men thought that drinking was one of the finer things in life. One such group was the Sons and Daughters of Temperance, which was organized in Virginia City, Nevada, in 1863 and met every Monday evening. Part of the attraction of the Temperance Movement for women was that it was linked to the early beginnings of the women's rights movement.

Gambling was another target for vice reformers. Many women considered gambling to be the work of the devil and believed that gambling should be outlawed on Sundays. To get around this, some saloon owners covered up or moved out the gambling tables on Sunday. It was back to business, however, the following Monday.

Liquor, in particular, was felt to be a calamity from which men must be saved, even if they did not wish to be. By way of bribery, one slogan of the temperance ladies was "Lips that touch liquor shall never touch mine." By association, the temperance movement considered alcohol and prostitution to be two interrelated evils. The reformers felt that the lack of family and community provided an atmosphere that led to a lack of restraint in a population dominated by young single males.

Reformers tried to shut down the many saloons and brothels in red light districts in towns such as Cripple Creek, seen here in 1890.
(Courtesy Denver Public Library, Western History Collection, P-1910)

Opposition to alcohol in the Old West was not new. Temperance workers were active in the East before the Civil War. At that time, their focus was primarily on reforming the individual by stopping him from drinking. Eventually realizing that this was a futile task, their strategy gradually changed after the war, and reform activities in the latter half of the Nineteenth Century turned to introducing laws to control the sale and distribution of alcohol. In the booming mining and logging towns of the West, it was a daunting task indeed. For example, in 1876, Virginia City, Nevada, had 10 liquor wholesalers, 5 breweries, and 137 retail outlets that sold alcohol.

As one strategy to try and shame men away from saloons, women organized anti-liquor crusades, in which volunteers stood watch outside saloon doors to record who went in and how long they stayed. To complement this activity, crusaders held temperance meetings. The general organization of such gatherings was that the ladies assembled and listened to anti-liquor speeches. Then, worked up to an almost religious frenzy by fiery speakers and anti-liquor songs, they marched to the nearest saloon carrying temperance banners and singing hymns. When they reached the saloon, they sang more hymns and knelt on the floor to pray.

The singing and praying didn't seem to have any noticeable effect on the drinking habits of loggers, soldiers, miners, railroad men, cowboys, and other hard-drinking males of the West. They just kept at it and treated the whole business as a game. As one form of retaliation, the men in some saloons set out lookouts. When they saw a band of temperance workers approaching, the men inside the saloon let fly with a barrage of all of the obscenities and profanities they could think of. This usually resulted in some red-faced ladies running back down the street with their hands over their ears. To the laughing saloon occupants, this served its purpose and kept the saloon a male stronghold. Presumably in the same tongue-in-cheek vein, one saloon owner in Buena Vista, Colorado, named his saloon the Road to Hell.

As another tactic, the men sometimes poured beer on the floor of the saloon or on the boardwalks outside the door in an attempt to prevent the ladies from kneeling and praying. If these tactics didn't have any effect, the men might invite the ladies to come inside and join them for a drink.

One of the few exceptions to such male antics was their treatment of the women of the Salvation Army. When these ladies came around, singing hymns and collecting for the poor, the men generally behaved with decorum and civility and were willing to contribute to the salvation of their fellow-men. However, it is probably safe to assume that the men were just as happy when their would-be saviors moved on to the next saloon, and they could resume their own pursuits of happiness.

Temperance and prohibition movements grew in the West in the 1870s and 1880s. The National Prohibition Party was founded in 1869. The militant Anti-Saloon League was formed in June of 1893. Some of their more militant supporters marched into saloons and smashed the fixtures and furnishings.

One of the leading groups that crusaded against saloons was the Woman's Christian Temperance Union (the WCTU), which was formally organized in 1874. The Union rapidly gained popularity and, by 1890, had about 160,000 members. Part of the mandate of the WCTU was the reform of inmates of jails and asylums, and the rescue of "fallen women," all of whom were considered to be direct or indirect victims of the saloon. Similar efforts were made by other organizations, such as the Florence Crittenton Mission, which, by 1879, had fifty-three branches throughout the country trying to reform alcoholic women, prostitutes, and unwed mothers.

Name your poison

Frontier liquor was often a peculiar drink and many colorful names were used to describe the potions that frequently had their origins in pure alcohol doctored in the back room or cellar of a saloon. It doesn't take much imagination to guess where some of these more interesting names came from.

Bug juice	Nosepaint	Stump puller
Cactus juice	Phlegm cutter	Taos lightning
Coffin varnish	Popskull	(also known as "Old Towse")
Corpse reviver	Redeye	Tarantula juice
Dust cutter	Rotgut	Tangle-leg
Dynamite	Sheep dip	Tiger spit
Firewater	Skull bender	Tonsil varnish
Gas remover	Skull varnish	Tornado juice
Gut warmer	Snake water	Trail varnish
Hell water	Stagger soup	Widowmaker
		Wolf whiskey

Anti-saloon fever reached its zenith with the turn-of-the-century ax-wielding crusades of Carry Nation, who was born Carry Amelia Moore in Kentucky in 1846. She came from a curious family. Her mother thought herself to be Queen Victoria, and Carry had an aunt who believed that she was a weather-vane. Carry herself experienced visions and strange dreams. Though she was fanatically anti-liquor, she also had other targets. She believed in sex education, opposed wife-beating, and championed equal rights for women. On the other side of the coin, she unleashed torrents of abuse against tobacco, immodest fashions, kissing, corsets, and fraternal societies.

Her first husband was a heavy drinker and a cigarette smoker. Her second husband, David Nation, received a savage beating at the hands of drunken saloon patrons at the Red Hot Bar in Richmond, Texas, in 1889. This incident was partly responsible for her anti-liquor fervor. Starting her "hatchetation" career at the age of fifty-four, she campaigned vigorously against "Demon Rum" across the plains of Kansas, trying to save men from the evils of liquor.

Almost six feet tall, weighing 175 pounds, and with a formidable appearance, Carry would stride into a saloon at the head of her crusading ladies and start in on the bottles, windows, mirrors, and pictures of bar-room nudes with her hatchet, destroying whatever she could reach. To spread the word to her faithful followers, she started a weekly anti-liquor magazine, appropriately called *The Smasher's Mail*. To the delight of her followers, she even appeared in a specially-written version of a popular Victorian morality play, *Ten Nights in a Bar-room*, in which she smashed up a saloon. She called her version of the play *Hatchetation*.

Legislation to establish National Prohibition — the so-called "Noble Experiment"—passed in 1919 with the Eighteenth Amendment to the United States Constitution. The law forced many saloons out of business. Some were torn down. Some were converted to other uses, such as restaurants or stores. Others turned to serving soft drinks or offering billiards. Prohibition ended in failure in 1933 and was repealed by the Twenty-First Amendment. It was too late, however, to save the traditional saloons. Their function was eventually replaced by cocktail lounges and restaurants that served liquor.

Chapter 7

DANCE HALLS AND VARIETY THEATERS

*"Any girl who is good enough for a high-class house
is too good for my joint."*
(a madam in an early San Francisco brothel)

As well as having prostitution in the more traditional establishments in the Old West, such as bordellos, cribs, and saloons, prostitution was rampant in other places where single men gathered for entertainment. Typical of these places were dance halls and variety theaters.

✧ DANCE-HALLS ✧

Dance-halls developed primarily to sell high-priced drinks and provide dancing, though gambling tables might be present. For the price of a few drinks and a set fee for each dance, a man could have a social (though often expensive) evening. Girls were freely available for a quick dance and then were supposed to persuade the man to buy drinks. As many as twenty women might be employed in a large dance-hall.

The women in dance-halls were not necessarily prostitutes. Their primary purpose was to hustle drinks, and most of them did not routinely offer sexual services. Some of the women who worked as dance partners were married women trying to earn a few extra dollars to make ends meet, while their husbands worked as miners or loggers. Some women were widows trying to support themselves. The women in these establishments were not looked upon as "lost souls" in a dishonorable profession.

Crapper Jack's saloon on Myers Avenue in Cripple Creek, Colorado, offered drinking and lively dancing.
(Courtesy Special Collections, Tutt Library, Colorado College, Colorado Springs)

Their job was to smile at the customers, to talk and dance with them, and perhaps to flirt a little, while also constantly trying to sell them drinks.

However, many of these women were prostitutes, who used the dance-hall as a place to meet potential customers. Profitable dance-hall and saloon sex was based on speed. If a man needed additional persuasion, dancing close to a woman would usually be enough to decide the issue. Fifteen minute intermissions between dances were not unusual and many of the women could be taken to a back room or behind the building to cribs, where they sold their favors to willing clients.

The price of a dance varied from twenty-five cents to a dollar, of which the girl typically gave twenty-five to seventy-five percent to the dance-hall owner. Between dances the customer was expected to buy himself and his partner several drinks at anywhere from fifty cents to a dollar a glass. Rather than liquor, the girl's shot-glass was often filled with cold tea, ginger ale, or colored water, instead of whiskey. This saved on expenses and she could continue to keep a sober head during the evening, while plying her trade. Some beer-drinking women were such accomplished drink-hustlers that they wore a type of diaper, so that they would not have to take time from the dance floor and miss any business.

Depending on her looks and vivacity, a dance-hall girl might expect to make from ten to twenty-five dollars during an evening.

The dance itself was usually short, often lasting from three to five minutes. The break was ostensibly to allow the musicians to "rest" but, in reality, was to allow ample time for the girls to hustle drinks. When the music played, the tempo was usually fast, so that the dancers moved vigorously and worked up a thirst. Most men were not particularly good dancers, and, in some dance-halls, the women wore heavy work boots to protect their toes from injury. Some of dance-hall girls made extra money from customers who had too much to drink by holding them close and picking their pockets while they danced.

In the 1850s and 1860s, a type of dance-hall called a "hurdy-gurdy house," or simply "hurdy-gurdy," was popular. The hurdy-gurdy, also known as a "wheel fiddle," was a type of hand-cranked, stringed instrument (essentially a mechanical violin) that was played by turning a crank that scraped a rosined wheel across the strings to produce the music. Hurdy-gurdy houses originated in the early 1800s, when itinerant peddlers in Germany were accompanied by attractive young girls, who danced and played the hurdy-gurdy. This technique quickly spread to other parts of Europe and eventually to the gold fields of California, where the girls were a great hit with the single miners. The name

Tents often served to house early dance halls, such as the Keystone Hall in Laramie, Wyoming, pictured here in 1868.
(Courtesy Denver Public Library, Western History Collection, Z-5810)

continued during the California gold-rush, when music for small dance-halls was often provided by a hurdy-gurdy. As a result, the women who worked in these establishments were referred to as "hurdy-gurdy girls," or simply "hurdies." On the early frontier, the hurdy-gurdy house was typically a tent with an dirt floor and lit by two or three smoky oil-lamps. Proprietors of dance-halls that had floors of packed dirt usually had to keep a sprinkling can full of water handy in order to keep the dust down.

The popularity of dance halls that were used strictly for dancing eventually declined. By the 1870s dance halls had mostly become quasi-brothels or at least recognized contact points for prostitutes. So the early dance-halls and hurdy-gurdys, and the women who worked there, ended up as another variation of selling sex.

Typical of the evolution of dance halls were those in Deadwood, at the center of the Black Hills gold rush in what later became Dakota Territory. When the first dance hall was started in 1876, it offered only the owner's wife and daughter as dancing partners. By June, there were two more dance halls, which were soon followed by a series of variety theaters. By 1877, seventy-five saloons, gambling dens, and brothels had appeared. A monthly "license fee" was imposed on each saloon to help bring money into the city treasury and to attempt some measure of control over the establishments.

One example of Deadwood's combination saloon, dance hall, and variety theaters was the Bella Union. The theater featured variety acts, and, when the show was over, seventeen private curtained viewing boxes were used by waitresses and chorus girls to entertain customers and sell themselves. The Bella Union was also used for gambling, dancing, and offered food at a lunch counter.

One of the legends from the Black Hills gold rush days, who appeared in saloons like the Bella Union was Calamity Jane. The stories that have arisen around characters like her have become so embellished over the years that it is hard to separate fact from legend. As best as known, Calamity Jane was born Martha Canary near Princeton, Missouri, in 1852 and moved west to Virginia City, Montana, in the 1860s. Among her exploits, real and imagined, were her claims to have at various times been an Army scout for General George Crook, a Pony Express rider, an Indian fighter, and the wife of Wild Bill Hickok. She was one of the Black Hills pioneers and tended bar in Deadwood during the 1870s. Her Army exploits were probably exaggerated, but she did work for a while as an Army teamster and could authentically swear like a mule driver.

Coarse, usually slovenly-dressed, and an alcoholic by the age of twenty-four, she was tall, wore men's clothes, smoked cigars, and caroused with the boys. She had a reputation as a brawling bar-room alcoholic and was not above occasional prostitution. Her popular name, Calamity Jane, supposedly came from the calamities of a venereal nature that occurred to her lovers. Rumor had it that in 1875 she spent time at a hog ranch near Fort Laramie. She has been reported, probably inaccurately, to have been an inmate of brothels from Virginia City, Nevada, and Bozeman, Montana, to Tucson, Arizona. Before her death in 1903 in Terry, South Dakota, she was reportedly seen in bar-rooms in South Dakota, Idaho, Montana, and Wyoming. In 1891, she married a Texan named Clinton "Charley" Burke, who drove a carriage in the Black Hills. Her tombstone in Deadwood has the name "Mrs. M.E. Burke" carved below the inscription of "Calamity Jane."

Dance-halls, as an institution, were very popular with men, though the "orchestra" providing the dance music might be only a piano, sometimes augmented by a banjo or a fiddle. The orchestras in small saloons were later replaced by an early version of the jukebox, which used a coin-operated Edison phonograph that played wax cylinders. In this manner, saloon owners cleverly saved money by not having to pay for live musicians and made additional money by having the customer pay for his music.

⌒ VARIETY THEATERS ⌒

Saloon owners and managers, even-mindful of the fact that more customers meant more dollars flowing into their pockets, constantly looked for better ways to draw paying customers away from rival saloons. One way was to provide different forms of entertainment, though adding stage shows, musicians, and other diversions never replaced the basic elements of drinking and prostitution. In the larger towns, the distinction between saloon, gambling hall, variety theater, and brothel became blurred, because all of these functions often blended together in one building.

Establishments such as the Bird Cage Theater in Tombstone, Arizona, operated around the clock to provide all these diversions and more. A woman who worked at the Bird Cage had to be prepared to serve in multiple jobs. She was expected to be one of the troupe of dancing girls who performed on the stage, and, if she had musical talents, perhaps she would sing a song or two. Between stage acts she worked as a barmaid, hustling drinks. She was also expected to be available

The Bird Cage in Tombstone, Arizona, had second-floor curtained boxes around the perimeter of the theater.

(Author's collection)

between acts to entertain customers in the heavily-curtained private cubicles that lined the upper sides of the main theater hall. Cowboys sometimes referred to women who entertained in the private booths as "box rustlers."

San Antonio, Texas, had a similar combination gambling house, saloon, and theater, called the Vaudeville. "Actresses" in skimpy outfits hustled drinks and themselves between turns on the stage. If a girl had a talent for singing, and frequently even if she did not, she might sing a song or perform a short dance. The women also conducted prostitution upstairs in a row of private rooms that was known as "Paradise Alley." As mentioned before, not all the women who worked at this type of theater were available for prostitution. Some were legitimate performers, and some were strictly barmaids. However, the goal of the management was to have as many pretty girls around as possible — a draw to bring in as many male customers as possible to spend as much money as possible on drinking.

❦ STAGE ENTERTAINMENT ❦

When stage entertainment was provided, audiences often made themselves part of the show by shouting, heckling, cheering, and booing.

Interplay between the actors and the audience became part of the entertainment. One of the more serious interactions occurred at a presentation of *Uncle Tom's Cabin* at the Bird Cage Theater in Tombstone in 1882. As the actress playing the heroine, Eliza, was being pursued across the ice by a real, but trained, bloodhound, a drunken miner suddenly rose up and shot the dog, to the great consternation of those watching the play. To show their displeasure, the miner was beaten up and thrown in jail. The next day, when sober again, the remorseful miner offered retribution.

Another humorous, but potentially deadly, incident involved a magician at the same theater who claimed to catch bullets in his teeth. An assistant fired a blank cartridge at him, then he would spit out a lead bullet he had previously concealed in his mouth. One of the zealous drunks took him at his word and fired a real bullet at him. Luckily, another customer deflected his aim, and the magician survived — but left the stage with unseemly haste.

Since single males in saloons and variety theaters were somewhat single-minded in their pursuit of women and drink (though not necessarily in that order), much of the stage entertainment was on the order of women performing in tights or dancing the can-can in short skirts.[1] Various theaters offered entertainment on a more cultural level, such as performances of Shakespeare, Gilbert and Sullivan, magic acts, jugglers, circus acts, classical music, and political lectures, but the basic visual delights of short-skirted, bare-shouldered girls dancing and bawdy burlesque acts were the mainstay of saloon and variety theaters.

Many of the women who performed in burlesque acts had more-than-ample hips and busts bulging from tightly-corseted costumes. One female manager proudly proclaimed that she wouldn't hire a woman performer who weighed less than 150 pounds. At the turn of the Twentieth Century, William "Billy" Watson managed a troupe called Billy Watson's Beef Trust. Some of his performers weighed more than 200 pounds.

There were enough all-purpose "actresses," some of whom who traveled a show circuit and appeared in bawdy skits, sold drinks between turns on the stage, and who were available for private entertainment in the curtained boxes of the theaters, that the name "actress" became a common euphemism for prostitute. Because of this association with prostitution, respectable people did not associate with actresses, and even actresses who were legitimate stage performers often found themselves ostracized by society.

Hovey's Dance Hall, Clifton, Arizona, in 1884 with patrons, a bar-tender, and dance partners lined up for the camera.

(Courtesy National Archives)

Stage acts experimented with different methods of exhibiting female flesh, but all of them were variations on the same basic themes. One variation was the strip-tease, though in order to maintain Victorian proprieties the women wore flesh-colored tights under the clothes they took off and never actually reached the point of nudity.

Along the same lines was the so-called educational story. This popular form of stage entertainment presented live versions of famous paintings, classical sculptures, or other works of art, portrayed by nude women, who posed silently without moving. Though the appearance was nakedness, they actually wore skin-colored tights.

These presentations were known as *tableaux vivants*, which is French for "living pictures" or "living scenes." They were also known as "living statues," or "living female paintings." This type of entertainment was originally popularized in the East in theaters and museums, where it was presented strictly as representations of classical statues and paintings. As time went by, however, some exhibitors realized that there were far more profits to be made in portraying any "art" that offered patrons the opportunity to view partially-clad, attractive young women. In large cities, private performances without the tights were available for those with enough money.

A typical example of a stage tableau portrayed scantily-clad girls, who were supposed to be Christian maidens being thrown to the lions — or at least to a moth-eaten stuffed lion. This was accompanied by theatrically-posed wailing and gnashing of teeth, and acrobatic positions that showed off the girls' figures. In addition to tights, costumes for the women often incorporated strategically-placed transparent wispy lace or gauze to enhance the erotic appeal. Another popular tableau was a live rendition of *Venus Rising from the Sea.*

For a young Victorian-era male, whose ideas about the female figure were always clouded by voluminous petticoats and skirts that reached the ground, these enticing views of the female form were enough to provide great stimulation. With today's sexually-explicit movies, fashions, swimsuits, and lingerie advertisements, it is easy to forget that a 150 years ago blatant nudity and frank portrayals of sexuality were unheard of.

Stage entertainment that involved girls dancing the can-can was popular among miners and cowboys, because the rowdy dance offered the lifting and waving of short skirts, high-kicking legs, frilly undergarments, stockings and garters, and occasional glimpses of an actual bare thigh. Though the can-can was declared "immodest and indecent" by one San Francisco newspaper in 1879, it remained a popular part of the repertoire of many variety theaters. Another popular form of entertainment was a female performer dressed in tights and doing acrobatics on a trapeze.

A routine titled the *Spider Dance* was popularized by a performer exotically named Lola Montez. She was born Marie Dolores (hence the name "Lola") Eliza Gilbert in 1818 in Ireland of an Irish mother and a father from the British Army. Before coming to America in 1851, she sang and danced somewhat unsuccessfully in Europe, and scandalized the European nobility with her two-year-long affair with King Ludwig I of Bavaria. Her special act involved "finding" a spider in or on her clothes. In the process of trying to rid herself of the "spider," which was constructed of cork, rubber, and whalebone, she went through a routine of wild gyrations. They included lifting her skirts and revealing her short petticoats underneath, removing some of her clothes, and the lingering exposure of her not unattractive legs. Her San Francisco career was meteoric in its rise and fall, and she quickly moved on to tour the mining camps of California. She eventually moved to Grass Valley, California, in 1853, where her re-created home is today a museum and visitor center. She died in New York City in 1861.

The specialty of Dolores McCord, who used the stage name of Adah Isaacs Menken, was her performance in *Mazeppa*, a drama loosely based on Lord Byron's poem of the same name. The word "loosely" is not used lightly here, because the original Ivan Mazeppa was a bald, bearded Cossack. However, the miners of Virginia City, Nevada, and San Francisco, California, did not seem to be surprised by the artistic license of Mazeppa's appearance as a voluptuous young woman. At the grand finale of the play, Menken was tied supposedly "nude" (though actually she wore form-fitting, skin-colored, tights partially covered by a short, filmy white tunic) to the back of a horse, which carried her off-stage. As might be expected, this was a very popular act with the miners. McCord's popular image must have made an impression with the men. One mine on the Comstock, suggestively called the Menken Shaft and Tunnel Company, artistically decorated their stock certificates with a picture of a naked woman on a galloping horse.

A more unusual version of *Mazeppa* appeared in San Francisco in the 1880s. The heroine for this version was the rather large con-woman named Big Bertha. After the end of her confidence career, she changed her line of work and performed on the stage. In the wake of her previous notoriety, she billed herself as the "Queen of Confidence Women." After several singing engagements, she appeared in a condensed version of *Mazeppa*. In this adaptation of the play, she appeared strapped to the back of a small donkey. Unfortunately, Big Bertha was all that her name implied, and one night the overburdened animal collapsed into the footlights, nearly ending theatrical careers for both him and his mistress. After this, she gave up acting and returned to singing.

Some of the entertainment was truly awful. The Waddling Duck was an overweight entertainer billed as a singer who could sing in two keys at once, but in actuality, could only screech in none. The Dancing Heifer and the Galloping Cow were two fat women who danced like elephants. A performance by singer Antoinette Adams in Virginia City, Nevada, was so bad that the miners made her sing until she was hoarse, and then took up such a large collection that she didn't have to sing on the stage again.

Chapter 8

REGULATING VICE

"If at first you don't succeed,
try, try again"
(advice in needlepoint hung on the wall of a parlor house)

*A*s well as trying to regulate saloons and alcohol, social reformers tried to control and eliminate prostitution. Though regulating prostitution in the Old West was a subject that was often discussed, like the weather, there was not much positive action taken. Regulation of prostitution was not a new idea. Ancient Greece and Rome tried to control the social and political effects of prostitution on family life and government. Schemes to control prostitution were tried later in Europe. Cities, such as Paris, confined prostitution to licensed brothels, and the prostitutes were made to undergo regular medical examinations. This official control of prostitution was called *reglementation*, from a French word meaning "a strict regulation by system."

Nineteenth century proposals to control prostitution in the West were aimed at trying to control the spread of venereal disease. The intent was to promote better health for prostitutes and consequently to prevent men from carrying diseases home to their wives.

❧ REGLEMENTATION AND SEGREGATION ❧

Bills to regulate prostitution were introduced in several state legislatures, but they were usually defeated. New Orleans, for example, sought for a long time to regulate prostitution in the city, but attempts were struck down in the courts as unconstitutional.

One successful exception occurred during the Civil War. The spread of venereal disease became so bad among the troops in Nashville, Tennessee, that on August 20, 1863, the local military commander legalized prostitution. The women were required to register their name and residence. They were tested for disease every two weeks at a cost of five dollars. Soldiers or women with any signs of sickness were immediately isolated in hospitals. The treatments of venereal disease were still primitive at the time, and this practice of quarantine did not eradicate the disease, but did control it. After the measures were instituted, the rate of venereal disease dropped from approximately forty percent to close to four percent.

The only large city in the United States that officially adopted a form of legal regulation was St. Louis, Missouri. On July 5, 1870, the Social Evil Ordinance was adopted, requiring the registration of all prostitutes within the city. Brothels were organized into six districts, each with a physician who made weekly inspections of the registered girls. Women found to have venereal disease were sent to the Social Evil Hospital, which was financially supported by the fees collected from prostitutes and madams.

Typical of the vice districts that the reformers tried to shut down were these "saloons and disreputable places" of Hazen, Nevada, seen here in 1905.

(Courtesy National Archives)

One of the ironies of the weekly inspection of prostitutes was that gonorrhea had an incubation period of two to eight days. In between inspections, therefore, an active prostitute could infect a large number of customers. Syphilis, by contrast, had an incubation period of about three weeks, making it easier for physicians to catch symptoms during their regular inspections. Another difficulty in controlling gonorrhea through inspections was that approximately eighty percent of infected women did not show any obvious symptoms. This problem was borne out in the St. Louis experiment, which was not successful in controlling venereal disease. Dr. W.G. Eliot, the president of George Washington University in St. Louis, reported in 1879 that the percentage of women treated rose from under four percent in 1871 to a little over six percent by 1874.

Though the lawmakers who crafted this legislation were well-intentioned, it was viewed by many as tacit approval of prostitution and the unlawful licensing of vice — both of which were contrary to the social and moral principles of the times. Others citizens argued that reducing the chances of infection would lead to an increase in lewd behavior by the male population. After much controversy, the law was repealed by the Missouri state legislature in 1874.

The few other attempts made to regulate prostitution via legislative methods were not able to overcome objections and become law. With the lack of success of the St. Louis law and other experiments at regulation, towns and cities turned mostly to segregation, which was the practice of protecting the community against immoral influences by confining prostitutes to a specified area and designating it as a red light district[1]. The creation of these districts was against the law, but segregation was a popular solution to the prostitution problem. The scheme allowed city fathers to keep track of and control organized vice. The Barbary Coast in San Francisco and Holladay Street in Denver were examples of two tolerated districts.

The most famous regulated district in the United States was Storyville, a legally-established red light district that existed in New Orleans from January 1, 1898, until November of 1917, when it was officially closed down by the United States Department of the Navy. At its peak, Storyville had 230 parlor houses and cribs, and over 2,000 prostitutes. The ordinance to create a restricted red light district was primarily the work of alderman Sidney Story, a respected citizen and businessman. The local press had a field day with the subject and gleefully named the district "Storyville" after him, much to his chagrin. The wording of the ordinance was carefully crafted so that prostitution

Drink and women were always targets for reformers. Champagne and other alcohol flowed freely at Laura Evens parlor house.
(Courtesy Colorado Historical Society, Mazzulla Collection, Box 22, FF 1294, scan #10027277)

was not actually legalized within the district, but was illegal outside it. The effect was to create an area where prostitution and other vice was allowed to flourish by default. The district was so well-known that it even had its own guidebook.

Though Storyville was created "legally," most towns created segregation by default. For instance, Boise, Idaho, created a restricted prostitution district called "The Alley" through a combination of confinement, fines, and law enforcement. Denver did not have an officially-segregated district, but the police succeeded in effectively keeping the brothels in the red light district on Holladay Street (Market Street) approximately between 18th Street and 23rd Street. If the houses crept outside the limits, public opinion — and the police — forced them back again.

There were several advantages to a segregated district. First, a known prostitution area could be better policed and prostitution-related crime controlled. Second, the better residential areas of the town were not bothered by prostitutes, and the residents could turn a Victorian blind eye to their existence.

Since the legality of prostitution inside the district was usually left in limbo, towns assumed the right to regulate its existence to one degree or other. In Kansas cattle towns, the Devil's Half-Acre in Abilene, Hide Park in Newton, and Nauchville in Ellsworth were, practically speaking, segregated areas that consisted primarily of brothels and saloons.

Segregation often just happened, rather than being planned. In Aspen, Colorado, the brothels and cribs gradually became established at the edge of town on Durant Avenue. This was next to the saloon district on Cooper Avenue and evolved more out of convenience and easy access to the taverns than by specific political enforcement.

When official efforts to produce strict regulation of prostitution were not successful, other forms of control were sometimes used. In some cities, the police required registration of madams and a list of her "boarders," for "identification purposes." Several cities required prostitutes to appear in person to fill out a registration form of personal information. Madams in the larger houses often had photographs taken of the women. The result of the tactics was to produce a list of madams and prostitutes that could be used for monthly collections of money, disguised as license fees, registration fees, fines, and business permits.

One idea tried in several cities was an attempt to control saloons by charging very high fees for liquor licenses. The theory was that high license fees could be used to control prostitution. One example of this occurred in Fort Collins, Colorado. By 1883 the town had thirteen saloon and five brothels that also sold liquor. In an attempt to control what the city saw as an escalating stream of vice, the license fee for selling liquor was raised from $300 to $1,000. The stringent measure worked. The number of saloons shrank to six, and many of the prostitutes left town.

In spite of some token efforts, there were usually few serious attempts to stamp out prostitution and drinking. The reason was simple. Money flowing from the red light district was often a major part of a growing town's economic base and was at the heart of potential graft and payoffs. The more practical businessmen of emerging towns also realized that prostitution and saloons attracted additional conventional business for them from miners, cowboys, loggers, and soldiers. Any elected official who succeeding in eradicating prostitution from his town would probably not have lasted long in office. If city fathers had really wished to completely eradicate prostitution, the simplest way would have been to revoke liquor licenses of saloons and brothels.

The jail in Colorado City, Colorado, was relocated to this building in 1892 in order to be closer to the saloon and red light district. Before it burned down at the end of the 1980s, the building housed a mattress factory.

(Author's collection)

Because of the Victorian double standard of behavior, laws against prostitution were strongly biased against prostitutes because they were women. Law enforcement officers frequently harassed, inspected, arrested, took to jail, dragged to court, and fined prostitutes. Such punishments did not fall on the men who were obviously equal partners in the transaction. This unequal arrangement satisfied contemporary morals but punished the ones who were least able to fight back.

∽ PIMPS ∽

As well as being on the receiving end of money for sexual services, most prostitutes had to pay a cut of their earnings to various individuals. Besides a madam, another common business partner was a pimp, or a kept man who lived off her earnings. These men were occasionally called "loafers," because that was what they did best. They were also called "sports" or "gentlemen of leisure." A pimp might serve as a business manager for a single prostitute or a series of prostitutes living and working alone. He would find clients, arrange for the meetings, and keep the girls out of trouble, either with customers or the law. For doing this, he usually took most of the money they earned.

Another name for a prostitute's "business manager" was *maquereau*, a French slang word meaning pimp or procurer. The name was often shortened to "Mac." A pimp or procurer who lured young girls into brothels was sometimes called a cadet, French slang for an "extravagant young man." This has been perpetuated in the name "cad" for a man whose behavior is not gentlemanly.

Alternately, the man in a prostitute's life might have nothing to do with making her business arrangements, but simply depended on her for his support. If a girl had a kept man, she supplied him with money for his clothes, food, liquor, cigars, gambling, and anything else he might want. In return he might supply her with drugs in order to create dependence on him.

✧ FINES AND LICENSES ✧

A prostitute had other payments to make. One was the semi-legal "contributions" that a prostitute usually had to make to be allowed to work. These payments might be monthly "taxes," "fines," or "license fees," as the payments were variously and euphemistically called. The money was used in many towns to finance the operation of the local police force or school district. Other, more direct, payments might have to be made to police or other officials as graft, protection, or blackmail money by madams, parlor houses, or the prostitutes themselves. Very often local sheriffs, and even judges, received a percentage of the fees and fines collected, as part of their salaries. This arrangement encouraged law enforcement officers to do a conscientious job of collecting fines.

One of the serious problems in an emerging town was how to finance civic services. The problem in mining towns, for example, was that miners were members of a highly mobile population, with departures and new arrivals daily. Similarly, the mines that the men owned or controlled constantly changed hands and fluctuated in value. Both factors made straightforward taxation of people or property difficult. Thus, one of the methods by which civic development was funded was through license fees. Respectable occupations, such as merchants, physicians, or lawyers, paid a nominal fee of anywhere from five to fifty dollars, depending on the town and profession. The brunt of tax payment then fell on members of the shady occupations, such as prostitutes, madams, gamblers, and saloon owners. These people and their establishments regularly paid license fees and fines. Saloons and dancehalls typically paid recurring license fees of anywhere from $50 to $450 per

This was where reformers thought that wayward women belonged — in jail — though this photograph is thought to have been posed as part of a campaign against vice.

(Courtesy Denver Public Library, Western History Collection, Z-64)

year. The amount of "fees" or "taxes" varied with what the traffic would bear and the geographic location. For example, dance-halls in Oregon paid $100 a month in license fees at the same time that dance-halls in Montana were paying $400 a year.

Paying for town services through taxation of vice was not a new idea. The practice appears to have started in the East and then migrated west. This type of financing was in place in California as early as 1850, when prostitutes and gamblers paid fees of from five to ten dollars, and brothels and saloons paid from ten to twenty dollars. All over the West towns routinely passed token ordinances against gambling and prostitution, but both vices were allowed to operate without interference, as long as they regularly paid their "fines." As a town matured, the tax base shifted to the more conventional type of taxation of real property.

As in many of the booming mining towns, the municipal government of Leadville, Colorado, paid for much of its expenses by a series of fines on prostitutes and license fees on gambling halls and brothels. Every month, madams paid fifteen dollars each as a "fine," and their "boarders" each paid five dollars. In 1879, the city collected $900 a month in license fees from saloons, brothels, and gambling halls. By the next year, as a result of the rapid population growth, the license fees increased to $1,700 a month. The money was used for payment of police salaries, so the officers were not too happy when the women were late with their payments.

In a similar manner, the city council of the mining camp of Aspen, Colorado, passed an ordinance that levied a tax of five dollars a month on each prostitute. The ordinance also included a tax of twenty-five dollars a month — cash only — on saloons, plus ten dollars a month on the first gambling table, and five dollars a month on each additional one.

If an economically-strapped prostitute, such as a street-walker or crib worker, was arrested and was not able to pay her "fine," it was not unusual for her to be allowed back on the streets to earn the money to pay it. A prostitute languishing in jail for not paying a fine was not an economic asset to anybody and actually became a financial burden to the community.

PART III

The Men

Chapter 9

WHERE MEN WERE MEN

"Men taken in and done for."
(sign in a brothel on Denver's Holladay Street)

ountain men, railroad men, soldiers, miners, and cowboys on the Western frontier were among those who had limited access to women. Each group composed mini-societies that fulfilled the criteria for encouraging prostitution. They were collections of young, virile men, isolated from normal social and sexual contact with wives and girlfriends; thus they turned to whoever was available. Prostitutes saw a male need, and a potential for earning dollars, so they filled the void.

✧ FUR TRAPPERS AND INDIANS ✧

The first white men to explore and pave the way for settlement of the American West were fur trappers and traders. From the early 1800s on, hundreds of men came west to trap beaver for the felt hats of fashion-conscious Eastern gentlemen and for export to European hat makers. Valuable beaver pelts became such a staple of trade that they were known as "hairy banknotes."

The mountain men chose to leave civilization and women to live a lonely existence in the high mountains. To help them make it through the long nights of winter, they often bought or bartered sex from Indian women. Sometimes the arrangement led to marriage, sometimes it did not. As well as sexual fulfillment and a convenient housekeeping arrangement for the trapper, setting up a liaison with a squaw had practical aspects. Living alone in Indian territory could be risky for a single white man. Having an Indian companion provided a trapper or fur trader with ties to the local tribes and led to some degree of security. An Indian woman could keep him informed of local activities via the tribal grapevine and warn him against any impending local unrest or potential danger. As well as the measure of personal safety that the arrangement provided for the fur trapper, it also often resulted in more favorable terms for trading with the Indians.

Sometimes the trapper purchased a woman outright. Many mountain men bought and sold Indian wives at the annual rendezvous,[1] the summer social and trading shindig where trappers gathered to barter or sell their winter's catch of pelts to the fur companies. This annual orgy of self-indulgence was used as an excuse to drink whiskey and have the good time that the men had been dreaming about all winter. As the big social event of the year, trappers could swap yarns and lies, try to out-brag each other with adventures, and catch up on local gossip. It was an opportunity to stage shooting matches, race horses, engage in contests of strength, and gamble away accumulated money and possessions. Most of the entertainment consisted of over-eating, over-drinking, fighting, womanizing with willing squaws, and general carousing. The drunkenness and revelry released merrymaking and mayhem that had been pent up for the previous year. The results were often that the whole previous season's wealth accumulated from trapping was squandered in one frenzied outburst. After an orgy of drinking, most of the men staggered back to their respective trapping areas nursing a week's worth of roaring hangover and with only enough supplies to start them off again in the fall.

Prices for a woman at the rendezvous were flexible, and the going rate was whatever the market would bear. A wife might be bought for two horses, or perhaps six pounds of beads, or even for as little as one blanket; though often an Indian father wanted to haggle and drive a good bargain for his daughter. If the girl were a chief's daughter, many furs would have to change hands before the deal was closed. Among items of value, firearms and Hudson's Bay blankets were highly prized by prospective fathers-in-law. Though bartering for Indian women did take place, early historians did not always interpret such transactions correctly. For example, though a bride's family might receive horses at a wedding, it was not always the purchase price of the wife. Among some tribes, it was the custom for the groom to give horses to the bride's family simply as an indication of the new husband's ability to be a good provider.

Most of the peaceful tribes did not mind relationships between white trappers and Indian women. Some tribes even welcomed it. A match with a mountain-man usually brought prestige to the bride and elevated her status among the tribal women. Through such a marriage, an Indian wife gained access to white man's possessions, such as jewelry, cloth, ribbon, and metal cooking utensils. In return she cooked for him, made and mended his clothing, was housekeeper for his tent or cabin, kept him warm at night, and bore his children. However, these marriages frequently earned the husband the impolite title of "squaw-man."

Varied customs and beliefs of different tribes provided rationalizations for Indian-white relationships. Some tribes believed that the children of mixed blood made good warriors. The Mandan Indians believed that a white man could transmit his powers via sexual intercourse, and that an Indian woman could in turn pass these powers on to her husband.

When trading posts were established in the West to provide trappers with a nearby ready outlet for their furs, intermarriage between traders and Indian women was popular.[2] If a woman were bought or bartered from her family, it might not be for the purposes of prostitution. Both the purchaser and the Indian tribe usually considered the two to be married. Even though an actual marriage ceremony might not have taken place, the couple settled among the Indians as husband and wife. Such relationships were considered to be quite respectable "marriages," and the man might even be adopted into the tribe. Bartering for a woman, however, was not always for a wife. In many instances, a man on the frontier wanted a temporary or permanent sexual partner but did not wish to marry her. A one-night stand could sometimes be arranged for as little as a plug of tobacco or a string of beads.

Some male-female arrangements that would be considered unusual by today's standards were not considered curious by their contemporaries. Among some Indian tribes it was customary for a man on a long hunt to go into partnership with a woman who would tend to the domestic chores and also be a sexual partner. At the end of the hunt she shared in the profits, and the arrangement between them ended.

Some liaisons were non-sexual and had quite harmless intentions. With the limited number of women available on the early frontier, prospectors in the Alaskan mining camps sometimes invited unattached women from nearby Indian villages to come to town for a dance. This was popularly known as a "squaw dance." It was also one method of courting, and the result for the miner might eventually be an Indian wife.

Not all Indian women, however, were considered to be desirable by white man's standards. In the Pacific Northwest, the Coastal Salish Indian girls normally did not wash. To compound this unhygienic state, they groomed their hair with pungent dogfish oil and, occasionally, with urine. Even the sweaty, unwashed local loggers, who were often not too hygienic themselves, tended to avoid them.

Victorian reticence to discuss any matters pertaining to sex was evident in accounts of white women captured by marauding Indians. Thus, contemporary accounts from westward travelers in the middle of the Nineteenth Century describe white women falling into Indian hands with the well-worn cliché of a "fate worse than death." Starvation, physical danger, and even death were hazards that were accepted by pioneer women, but the threat of capture by savage Indians was the worst possible horror of the trip west. A kidnapped white woman might be forced to be the sexual slave of a captor or several captors. She also might be successively raped by several warriors and then kept as the tribe prostitute. The contemporary expression that the Indians "passed her over the prairie" was the grim description of a fate that might await her. The reverse was also true and similar fears haunted Indian women. They were so commonly raped by white men that they are said to have developed a counter-strategy called "going for the sand." When white trappers showed up, Indian women went to the local creek and packed their vaginas with sand as a preventative measure.

It was not unknown for a white woman, who had been captured and had spent many years among the Indians, to adopt their ways and to accept the Indian village and way of life. Such a case was that of Cynthia Ann Parker, who was taken captive in 1836 at age nine by Comanche raiders. She grew up in captivity, eventually married a young Comanche Indian chief named Peta Nocona, and bore his children. She was the mother of Quanah Parker, one of the last great Comanche chiefs. When she was "rescued" twenty-four years later, along with her two-year-old daughter, she made several unsuccessful attempts to return to her Indian family. She finally starved herself to death in grief in 1864 after her daughter died. A similar story is that of Anna Morgan, captured by Indians in 1868. She bore a son, fathered by an Indian chief, several months after her rescue. Memories of her captivity and of what she considered the disgrace of the events that surrounded it, continually haunted her in later life, and she finally died in an asylum.

The status of an Indian woman among her own people covered a wide range, depending on the tribe. In some tribes, a woman was owned by her husband. Her function was primarily to work and bear children. Her husband's ownership was so complete that he could, and some occasionally did, offer her sexually to another man. For some tribes it was actually a gesture of hospitality to offer a woman to a guest for the night. Though some white men went along with this custom — sometimes enthusiastically — contemporary Victorian morality made most of the men at least outwardly disapprove of it, as a form of prostitution.

In some other tribes, the traditional role of husband and wife in Western society was reversed, and the woman owned all the property, including the dwelling, horses, and tools. The men didn't own much more than their clothes and personal weapons.

Among the Navajo of the Four Corners area (where Colorado, New Mexico, Arizona, and Utah come together) and the Papago Indians of Southern Arizona, unmarried women could establish their own homes and could set up liaisons with men, if they wished. This was generally considered a form of temporary marriage rather than prostitution.

As well as marriage customs, sexual customs and views on sex also varied among different tribes. Among some tribes, virginity before marriage was important; in others premarital sex was acceptable. Among some Indian tribes, girls were even encouraged to receive payment for premarital sex in order to accumulate dowries for their later marriage.

Among the Plains Indians, chastity was considered important; however, out of practicality, marriage was not always monogamous. There were many potentially-fatal hazards to being an Indian male; and, as a result, there was often a shortage of marriageable men. Many of the younger men were killed in the hunt or during periodic raids by nearby warring tribes. Because of the shortage of potential husbands, men were encouraged to have more than one wife. A man's number of wives eventually became a status symbol, indicating the number of women that an important warrior could support. The arrangement ensured that there was no excess of unattached females. It also had the practical aspect of spreading the household workload among several wives, since the men generally concerned themselves with hunting and attacking neighboring tribes.

As the frontier developed and changed, so did the relationship between whites and Indian women. With a surge of new settlers moving westwards, what originally started as friendly liaisons between trappers and Indian women evolved into commercial transactions. The Indians soon discovered that the influx of whites contained few females, and that the single men had many goods to barter. Goaded by increasing poverty and hunger after being driven from their tribal lands, the Indians saw this potential for barter and easy trade as the basis for commercialized prostitution.

As the frontier continued to expand, the early casual and generally friendly relationship between whites and Indians faded away and was replaced by mutual feelings of bitterness and hatred on both sides. As white women appeared on the frontier, contact with Indian women was looked down on, and commercial prostitution by white women took its place.

❧ HELL-ON-WHEELS RAILROAD TOWNS ❧

President Lincoln authorized the building of a transcontinental railroad in 1862. The final contract for construction went to the Union Pacific Railroad and the Central Pacific Railroad. The Union Pacific started building tracks westward from Omaha, Nebraska, on December 2, 1863, and the Central Pacific started eastward from Sacramento in January of 1863. The two railroads finally joined at Promontory Point, Utah, in 1869.

This sign that marks the site of Douglass City, Colorado, outlines some of the simple pleasures of the railroad construction workers who lived there, including "drinking, shooting, fighting, and knifing" in the town's eight saloons.

(Author's collection)

As the railroads penetrated the West, temporary construction camps followed to house and feed the workers. These camps were periodically torn down and re-built at a new location a few miles further down the track. Railroad construction camps spawned many short-lived boom-towns to provide diversion and entertainment (typically women, drink, and gambling) for the railroad workers. Most of the buildings were tent structures for maximum portability, because the entire town was expected to last for only a few weeks, or at the most, a few months. When a particular section of track was finished, and the construction camp moved on, the entire town packed up the tents and disassembled the shacks and followed the rails a few miles to start again at the new end-of-track. Because the temporary towns consisted mostly of tents and wagons, they were called "moving towns."

As the Union Pacific pushed its tracks to the west, it spawned mobile end-of-the-track towns that catered to the earthy recreational desires of the railroad construction workers. Every sixty miles or so a temporary town sprang to life, mushroomed, and then disappeared when the forefront of the railroad moved on. Vice of all sorts was available around the clock in these towns in an attempt to separate the tough railroad laborers from their hard-earned pay. Crime followed closely. Fights and killings occurred almost daily, and nearly all the men went about their business while armed.

Saloons and brothels were the mainstay of these towns, attracting gamblers, saloonkeepers, con-men, petty thieves, pimps, and prostitutes by the dozen. Whiskey flowed freely and venereal disease was rampant. Temporary railroad saloons might consist of a wooden platform for the floor, board walls three or four feet high around the sides, and then heavy canvas supported by a rough wooden framework for the roof and upper walls. Sometimes shacks were mounted on railroad flatcars for the ultimate in portability, which gave a town the popular name of "hell-on-wheels."

These violent railroad towns followed the Union Pacific tracks across the plains. Kearney and North Platte in Nebraska Territory, Julesburg in Colorado, and Cheyenne, Laramie, and Green River in Wyoming were some of the toughest, noisiest, and raunchiest towns in the West. They were not necessarily small camps. Julesburg in 1867, for example, had nearly 2,000 temporary inhabitants. In smaller fashion, the Kansas and Texas Railway (affectionately known to locals as "The Katy") spawned the towns of Denison in Texas, Muskogee in Oklahoma, and Coffeyville and Parsons in Kansas, all of which were

Only ghosts and a few old buildings remain high in the mountains at Douglass City, Colorado, which in its time was one of the wildest railroad construction towns in the area.

(Author's collection)

noted for brawling, gambling, boozing, wild women, and frequent homicides.

Interestingly, on the other side of the country, where the Central Pacific Railroad struggled over the Sierra Nevada mountains and the deserts of Nevada, hell-on-wheels towns were not a problem. Part of the reason was that the construction supervisor for the Central Pacific, James Strobridge, would not tolerate prostitutes, gamblers, whiskey, and the other diversions that followed the Union Pacific. It was also due to a lack of available white laborers. The Central Pacific used many Chinese workers, and the hard-working coolies did not have much use for bad whiskey and bad women. The greater part of their miniscule wages went to pay off the exorbitant passage fees that they had paid to travel to the United States. Many of them saved the rest of their money with intentions of eventually returning to their homeland and buying their own farms.

Back on the eastern side of the Continental Divide, as the Union Pacific's rails crawled west across the plains, so did the hell-roaring towns that the railroad tolerated.

❧ FRONTIER SOLDIERS ❧

Another male-dominated segment of society in the West was composed of soldiers. Following the Civil War, the regular army had completed its task in the East, and most field forces were deployed to the West to deal with Indian problems. After seeing action in the Civil War, life on the frontier was comparatively dull and boring for many of the men. Scouting and patrols relieved some of the boredom of daily life, but soldiering in the field was confined by weather to a period between April and October. Particularly on the plains and in the mountains, where winter weather was often severe, most of a soldiers' time was spent at the post. Even during the summer, there was very little real action or Indian fighting, though sometimes patrols scouted or served as escorts for wagon trains or stagecoaches.

Trapped in what was essentially a boring male world, it is small wonder that many soldiers dreamed of spending their time off with whiskey and women. Unfortunately for the soldiers, most Army posts were purposely isolated in the middle of nowhere, and no women were theoretically allowed except for officers' wives, those of some enlisted men, a few female servants for the officers, and the camp laundresses.

Ironically, only the laundresses had an official position at Army posts, having been authorized by Congress in 1802. The wives of the officers and enlisted men were described in army regulations as "camp followers," which was a generic term for all the civilians who had non-official functions at an Army post. The commanding officer of a fort could technically order any woman who was not working as a laundress off the post grounds.

Enlisted men often married laundresses. They were desirable wives, because they received free food, fuel, and post quarters, and were guaranteed payment of their laundry charges. Laundresses who were not married often did more than laundry, taking in washing by day and soldiers by night to augment their income through prostitution. It was common for unmarried laundresses to have illegitimate children living with them. Laundresses typically lived and worked on-post in a row of tents, shacks, dugouts, or sod buildings, nicknamed "Soapsuds Row" or "Suds Row." This was usually located behind the post stables and warehouses.

Some laundresses had marriages of convenience, living with a soldier until he was transferred or left the Army, and then arranging another "marriage." Some laundresses, who were legitimately married, continued to barter their favors to augment their official income, often with the knowledge and consent of their husbands. One post commander commented sarcastically that the primary duty of post surgeons was treating laundresses for gonorrhea and delivering their babies.

Though the Army's official position was against prostitution and other vice, post commanders in the field were pragmatic enough to realize that unfulfilled sexual needs would create tensions at the post. This situation could possibly lead to problems for wives and the other respectable female residents, unless provisions were made to allow for some sort of release. Therefore, some post commanders permitted women known to be prostitutes to live on-post under the blanket euphemism of "laundress," and it was not uncommon for post commanders and senior officers to turn a blind eye to their activities.

Not all government officials were as understanding as these commandants. One Indian agent at the Union Agency, in Muskogee, Oklahoma, wanted to stop the corruption of his charges and barred prostitutes, vagrants, liquor traders, and other undesirable characters from his reservation. His simplistic solution was to deport them to Kansas and Texas, and let someone else worry about them.

In a similar situation, Fort Union in New Mexico was located by itself on open grasslands in 1851, partly to escape the temptations of nearby towns that offered drinking, gambling, and women. The theory was sound but did not work out in practice. Almost immediately, Mexican prostitutes and whiskey vendors moved into caves and shacks in the hills near the fort and offered the soldiers what they wanted. The commandant at the time watched their activities but did not stop them. The next commandant was not so lenient. He burned down their shacks and ran them all off.

The job of laundress as an official Army position was phased out between 1878 and 1883. Though the phase-out was instituted in 1878, laundress wives of enlisted men were allowed to stay on until the end of their husband's five-year enlistment period, which allowed a few to remain until 1883.

Soldiers could sometimes find sexual partners among local women, who were allowed to enter and leave most posts freely during times of peace. They might also form a liaison with one of the women from a nearby friendly Indian tribe, who quietly slipped in and out of the post to earn a few dollars or trade for some extra food by dallying with the soldiers. Fort Laramie in Wyoming, for example, had a nearby village called "Squaw Town" that was made up of friendly Oglala Sioux who basically lived off the generosity of the residents of the fort. Some of the

Soldiers who drank, fought, and caroused to excess at Fort Union, New Mexico, often found themselves locked up in this solid-looking stone jail on the post .
(Author's collection)

women worked as servants for the wives of officers. Others were reduced to begging — living off government handouts and the largesse of the fort's inhabitants. The agency Indians were contemptuously named "Laramie Loafers" by other Indians. The unmarried enlisted men of the fort sometimes formed arrangements with young Indian women, either through marriage or by offering outright payment for sexual services.

A similar, but much grimmer situation, was forced on the Navajo Indians, who were relocated to the remote Bosque Redondo Reservation in eastern New Mexico after what was called the "Long Walk." The forced march was made from Fort Defiance in eastern Arizona to the reservation at Fort Sumner. Bosque Redondo was entirely unsuitable for farming. Crop failures, floods, plagues of grasshoppers, and a lack for game for meat left the Navajo unable to grow enough food to sustain themselves. Poverty was rampant, food was virtually non-existent, and many of the Navajo women had to turn to prostitution with the soldiers guarding them to eke out enough food to survive.

One advantage that the soldiers at Fort Laramie had that many other forts did not was that the fort was a stopping place and supply point for the frequent wagon trains that passed by on the Oregon Trail.

The soldiers took advantage of this situation and were alert to the possibilities of female company among women travelers. For more commercial contacts, the soldiers at Fort Laramie had nearby Three Mile Ranche, which was a combination stage stop, saloon, general store, and brothel, operated by Jules Ecoffey and Adolph Cuny.

Soldiers at an isolated post might have some success at the local post trader's store. The sutler's store, officially on-post to supply non-military goods such as coffee, bacon, and tobacco, often kept women, who supposedly worked as "domestic servants," but who were, in reality, prostitutes.

Small towns also sprang up near military posts to accommodate the men's desires. One example was the town of Loma Parda, which was located next to the Mora River about five miles from Fort Union, New Mexico. Dance-hall women offered all the diversions and amusements that the soldiers wanted twenty-four hours a day. A shuttle service ran regularly between the fort and the town, and a well-worn connecting footpath was available for those who could not afford the one dollar fare. Drinking, fighting, and whoring in Loma Parda became such a problem that the commandant at the fort finally put the whole town off-limits to soldiers.

For most post commanders, brothels and prostitutes were a constant nuisance. For example, though brothels were illegal under local territorial laws, there were two brothels in Sturgis, South Dakota, near Fort Meade, in the 1880s that were filled with colored prostitutes to cater to the colored troops stationed at the fort. Both places were the scene of periodic trouble. In 1884 a black soldier from the 25th Infantry was killed by a black prostitute, though the woman was later acquitted on the grounds of justifiable homicide. The next year, a black soldier beat a prostitute, killed the doctor who was treating her, and was lynched in an incident that sparked racially-motivated tension between the town and the soldiers.

One of the few off-duty pastimes for soldiers was drinking and, fueled by boredom, many soldiers became alcoholics. One place where soldiers could obtain their drink and women was the "hog ranch." Though their primary function changed with time, the delightful-sounding institutions did actually start out as farms for pigs to supply the military with pork. Depending on the post's location, meat such as beef, antelope, or buffalo was readily available to the soldiers by hunting, but pork was scarce. To alleviate this shortage, pigs were raised by independent pig farmers and supplied to the government on contract. Due to the arrangement, the pigs and slaughterhouses needed to be located reasonably close to the forts. Because of the potent smell, the pigpens were not allowed on the post itself and were required to be located far enough away for the smell to be tolerable. The official government distance five miles. Unless the commandant was strict, hog ranches were found anywhere from two to five miles away from the fort, though they were supposed to be downwind and downstream.

Since the hog ranches were convenient to the post and to the soldiers, they eventually became more than just a collection of pigpens and a slaughterhouse. They often included a saloon or other establishment where whiskey and beer were sold, and where there was a thriving business in prostitution and gambling. Sometimes small communities sprang up around this nucleus, which might include one or two stores, a few warehouses, and a blacksmith shop. Hog ranches flourished until 1890, when the position of post sutler was abolished.

The hog ranch at Fort Fetterman in Wyoming was just across the North Platte river from the fort. Soldiers wanting gambling, women, and drink had to sneak out of the fort and swim across the cold waters of the river. One would think that this experience would dampen their enthusiasm — to say nothing of their ardor. Fort Fetterman, built on a bluff just south of the North Platte River in Wyoming in 1867, was known as "Hell Hole" by many of the soldiers who tried to desert as soon as they arrived. One explanation for the name is that it came from the nearby hog ranch. The name "hellhole" was sometime applied to a brothel, because that is where people claimed that the inhabitants were headed.

Because of their low pay, enlisted soldiers could not afford "fancy" women, and the prostitutes at hog ranches tended to be of the less-attractive, hard-core variety. One author even humorously suggested that the name hog ranch was more appropriate for the human inhabitants and patrons than for the animal stock.

Cowboys, who were better paid than soldiers and could afford more expensive women, usually looked down on the women at hog ranches as "soldiers' women." The cowboys also resented the soldiers, because they felt that wherever the soldiers went they rapidly spread venereal disease among the local prostitutes. The cowboys may have been correct, because prostitution at hog ranches was partly responsible for a rapid spread of venereal disease among the western military. Estimates placed the number of soldiers who were infected with some form of venereal disease in the 1880s at about eight percent.

Because of the lack of women, non-traditional relationships were occasionally formed among soldiers on post. For example, there is the well-documented account of a company laundress in the 7th Cavalry named Mrs. Nash, who married three soldiers between 1868 and 1878. The first two stole her savings and deserted. Mrs. Nash, who also acted as a cook and midwife, was a rather tall, angular, swarthy Mexican, who kept a veil on the lower part of her face at all times. When Mrs. Nash died of appendicitis at Fort Meade, near Rapid City in South Dakota, "she" was found to be a "he." The rumor was that the man had been a refugee from Mexico and "married" Sergeant Nash in order to obtain political asylum. When the story came out, Mrs. Nash's last "husband," a private named Noonan, could not bear the taunts of his fellow soldiers, so he went into one of the stables and shot himself.

⟶ COWBOYS AND CATTLE TOWNS ⟵

One of the stereotypes of Western movies is the cattle town with its saloon and saloon girls. The major cattle drives only lasted for about fifteen years, from 1866 to 1881. During that short time, however, the legend of the cowboy became embedded in American folklore, and the cowboy's rip-roaring escapades stirred the imagination of people around the world.

Following the Civil War, the distressed cotton industry and depressed economic conditions in the South made the cattle business uncertain, and many sellers teetered on the edge of bankruptcy. However, an increased demand for beef in the growing industrial cities of the Northeast made some Texans reconsider the value of wild range cattle and try to figure out ways to bring the supply of cattle and the demand for beef together. Cattle worth perhaps only three or four dollars a head in Texas could be worth up to forty dollars a head at the slaughterhouses of Chicago or Kansas City. The big problem was the cattle were in Texas and the nearest railheads for shipment to the East were in Kansas and Missouri. The solution was to drive the cattle to meet the railroad.

The route north from Texas was long and dangerous, across miles of sun-baked prairie with hazards such as hostile Indians and dangerous river crossings with quicksand and deep water. While the cattle drives lasted, the life of a cowboy on the trail was a hard one for the young men. The drive north from Texas lasted for three or four months. During that time, all the cowboys saw were each other and cows — and those usually from the rear end.

Portrait of an unidentified young cowboy in typical gear, though he was probably wearing his best garb for the benefit of the camera.
(Glenn Kinnaman Colorado and Western History Collection.)

The chuckwagon and its questionable food was the only entertainment on the trail for working cowboys, often resulting to an orgy of indulgence when they finally reached the end of the trail.
(Glenn Kinnaman Colorado and Western History Collection.)

The usual working day for a cowboy was about eighteen hours long, seven days a week. The men were up before dawn and spent all day herding cattle and choking on their dust. During the drive there were ever-present dangers, such as being attacked by hostile Indians, trampled underfoot in stampedes, thrown from a horse, drowned in a hazardous river crossing, or attacked by cattle rustlers or guerrilla bands left over from the Civil War. Typical pay was thirty dollars a month plus food, thus earning the cowboy a total of less than $100 for the whole drive, normally paid in one lump sum at the end of the trip.

Trail bosses purposely kept their cowboys away from towns along the route because if the men started carousing, the cows would probably never reach the end of the drive. After several months of no liquor, no women, bad food, hard work, and no relaxation or entertainment, the cowboys were ready to spend their money on a wild time and wild women in the town where they ended the drive.

The saloons, gambling houses, and brothels of the cattle towns provided all the food, drink, and entertainment that the cowboys were looking for. Finally free from the dangers and dirty work of trailing cattle, and flush with money from several months of accumulated pay, the cowboys were ready to blow off some steam. They wanted whiskey, women, and a rowdy time. They wanted to get roaring drunk or, in cowboy slang, to "get roostered."

Each settlement founded in response to the cattle drives only lasted as a wide-open cattle town for three or four years. While they lasted, however, the Kansas towns such as Abilene, Wichita, Dodge City, Newton, and Ellsworth, burst from obscurity and were everything that a Wild West movie has led audiences to believe. Drinking, gambling, prostitution, fighting, and killing were accepted as part of the way of life when the cowboys were in town. Gamblers, saloonkeepers, and prostitutes gave a wave of welcome with one hand while grabbing for the cowboys' money with the other.

Many of the prostitutes in the cribs of the cattle towns were tough and coarse, because they had to be to survive. Often they were older women who traveled West looking for a new start, when they could no longer compete with younger and better-looking prostitutes in the East and in the fancy parlor houses. Luckily, at the end of a long cattle drive, most cowboys were not too particular.

Due to the potential danger from rowdy customers, some saloon prostitutes in cattle towns armed themselves. Small single or double-barreled derringers, named after their inventor, Henry Deringer (note the difference in spelling) were popular for self-protection with ladies of easy virtue. A woman could easily carry one of these loaded derringers in her hand purse or in the pocket of a dress.

A woman could also carry a derringer alongside her thigh (next to her money) in a holster or spring clip, or tucked into the wide band of one of the garters that held up her stockings. Concealed under voluminous skirts, a derringer might not be instantly available for a fast draw, but was certainly close at hand should danger threaten. Or a woman could slip one down the front of her bodice, a method of carrying a derringer that was popular with dancehall girls. A prostitute's derringer was often even a type of fashion accessory, plated with silver or gold and sporting mother-of-pearl handles. The common use of derringers by women, particularly prostitutes, led them to be nicknamed "boudoir cannons."

The more sedate residents of the cattle towns viewed the hell-raising cowboys with mixed emotions and usually with some distaste. On the one hand, cowboys and their payrolls brought a prosperity that the merchants did not want to discourage. On the other hand, the cowboys brought a lawlessness that was not always welcome, and they attracted many of the less desirable elements, such as gamblers, prostitutes and pimps, who were all competing for a share of the cowboys' pay. Cowboys, and their rowdy ways, were looked upon as a necessary evil to be endured and complained about, while greedily relieving them of their hard-earned money. The few lawmen in the towns were expected to keep a reasonable degree of law and order and ensure general safety for the citizenry by whatever means they could.[3]

◅ THE RISE AND FALL OF THE CATTLE TOWNS ▻

June of 1867 heralded the start of the rowdy cattle towns when a twenty-nine year-old cattle trader from Springfield, Illinois, named Joseph McCoy, put Abilene on the map as one of the wildest towns in the West. Abilene was the prototype of the booming cattle towns.[4]

The cattle season generally ran from May to September. During the off-season, the town consisted of about 500 people. By the middle of that year's season the population had increased to an estimated 4,000 to 7,000 people. Not all of these were cowboys. The rest of the town's population was augmented by trainloads of prostitutes, gamblers, con-men, and anybody else who wanted to help the cowboys spend their hard-earned dollars.

While they lasted, the boom times were great for the towns. Lawman Bat Masterson expressed the opinion that the principal and best-paying industry in Abilene was gambling. He noted that the potential for taxation was enormous. Individual gamblers paid between five and ten dollars and proprietors of gambling establishments paid twenty dollars in taxes a month. Occasionally additional "fines" of up to seventy-five dollars were imposed.

Like the other towns that followed, Abilene's life as a rip-roaring cattle town was short — lasting only a few years. As the railroad pushed further south and west to meet the cattle drives, the shipping terminus moved with it, and Abilene, then Ellsworth, were left behind to sink back into obscurity.

The streets that made up the permanent red light district in Abilene consisted of solid rows of saloons and gambling houses that were in full operation twenty-four hours a day when the cowboys were in town. During its heyday, the red light district in Abilene consisted of thirty wooden buildings with from ten to twenty rooms each. Between

Dancehall girls in their fancy dresses drinking beer and idling away time outside at a table between customers. (Courtesy Colorado Historical Society, Mazzulla Collection, Box 22, FF 1278, scan #10027280)

Kelley's Saloon, "The Bijou", Round Pond, Oklahoma Territory was typical of the saloons of the period.

(Courtesy National Archives)

200 and 300 prostitutes plied their trade, some working in shifts to accommodate the twenty-four-hour partying schedule. Rival saloon owners tried to outdo each other to bring in customers, including even hiring brass bands. Bar girls and highly made-up prostitutes in short dresses and gaudy jewelry beckoned through the windows and doors to the cowboys to come in and "have a good time."

Wealthy Texas cattlemen spent their time at high-class saloons, like The Alamo on Cedar Street, where gambling never stopped and the orchestra played twenty-four hours a day. Saloons in cattle towns often had names such as Alamo, Houston, or Lone Star to attract Texans by appealing to their patriotic spirit. For the same reason, many prostitutes in cattle towns used names evocative of the South, such as Dixie and Lee. The Alamo was a large place, about 40 feet across and 120 feet deep, with an ornate bar backed by a huge mirror, gambling tables, paintings of nude women, and glass-paned doors that never closed. There was a wooden boardwalk connecting the back of the saloon to a nearby brothel, so that customers going between the two wouldn't sink into the mud.

Regular cowboys, with less money to spend, went to the Applejack Saloon or the Bull's Head. The Bull's Head Saloon was one of the most infamous saloons and gambling halls in a town full of notorious establishments. The saloon was named after the genitals of a male longhorn, and the outside was decorated with a huge sign that proudly displayed the bull's prowess. Even the locals thought this was a little too crude and petitioned city officials to change the painting. Inside the saloon, whiskey sold for fifty cents a shot, and, for those who could afford it, a bottle of champagne went for twelve dollars.

Mattie Silks, who later became a prominent madam in Denver, arrived in Abilene in 1870 and started the first high-class parlor house, named the Gulf House. She opened a large, yellow two-story building, where customers were served only champagne, and which was reputed to house ten of the youngest and most attractive girls in town. Such beauty was not without its price. A simmering argument by Wild Bill Hickok and Phil Coe over Jessie Hazel, one of Mattie's girls, resulted in a gun fight, which ended with Hickok mortally wounding Coe. Coe was the co-owner of the Bull's Head Saloon with the notorious gunman and gambler Ben Thompson.

A continuing problem for the townspeople was how to walk the fine line of letting the cowboys spend their money and blow off steam, yet still control them without offending a source of revenue that could easily take its business elsewhere. During the summer months, when the cowboys were around, the town and its seamier inhabitants became completely lawless. Incidents such as the shooting of prostitute Louisville Lou by fellow prostitute Jenny Lyons over the attentions of her gambler boyfriend, Quade Hill, were not uncommon.

By the spring of 1870, the citizens of Abilene felt they had put up with enough of the cowboys' wild celebrations. To try and curb the thirty-two licensed saloons and to prohibit brothels within the city limits, laws were passed against gambling, fighting, and prostitution. Brothels were restricted to a section on the southeast edge of town, which became known as "McCoy's Addition," or more popularly known as the "Devil's Half-Acre," which was a concentrated area of gambling, drinking, and prostitution. If cowboys attempted to stray up to the "decent" part of town, they were liable to be arrested. However, the laws, along with an ordinance against carrying guns in town, proved to be "token" laws that were almost impossible to enforce.

By 1871, most of the permanent residents of Abilene were tired of the cowboys' rowdiness. They felt they had seen enough of cattle and cowboys, in spite of the boom in business they brought. Their viewpoint was not unreasonable. Cowboys were known for such antics as riding their horses into a saloon and demanding a beer for the animal. They also had a taste for shooting at the hanging oil lamps — and anything else that took their fancy. Bullet holes in the ceilings of the buildings that have survived attest to this practice.

Reformers in Abilene banned prostitutes from saloons and raised saloon license fees to $100, and then to $500, to try and change the rowdy and immoral image of the town. In 1872, the town was markedly antagonistic towards the cattle trade, and the citizens finally asked the Texans to take their herds and their business elsewhere. The results, coupled with a financial panic that was sweeping the country, were disastrous. By the spring of 1873, eighty percent of the businesses in town had closed. The town frantically reversed its position, but it was too late. Most of the business had already moved to Ellsworth, sixty miles southwest of Abilene.

Ellsworth was founded in 1867, and by 1872 it was shipping thousands of cattle. Ellsworth's red light district was called "Scragtown" or, alternately, "Nauchville." Ellsworth was the location for the apocryphal story of "Lady Godiva of the Plains." Supposedly one of the local prostitutes accepted a bet to walk stark naked down the main street in broad daylight. She did, and when she fulfilled her part of the bet, her outfit consisted of a pistol in each hand. Her reputation for marksmanship was such that none of the men present dared to look her way.

Rapid decline, similar to Abilene, took place in Newton, Kansas, which had a meteoric rise and fall as a cattle town. Newton was founded in March of 1871 with a population of two. By the time that the Atchison, Topeka & Santa Fe Railroad reached the town in July of 1871, the infant town already had a hotel and a saloon. By August there were ten dance halls. Rapid growth soon brought the number up to twenty-seven saloons and eight gambling halls. The thriving brothel district was called "Hide Park," and a variety of white, Mexican, and Negro prostitutes plied their trade there. The girls were headquartered in two dancehalls and three brothels.

In 1872, the railroad arrived in Wichita, putting it on the map as another end-of-the-line cattle town. In the winter, the number of resident prostitutes was usually between five and seven. In the summer of 1874, the year of its last big trail-drive, the number increased to between forty and fifty. Because the cattle business was seasonal, and the cowboys were only in town for three or four months out of the year, some prostitutes arrived in portable brothels called "catwagons," which traveled from town to town depending on the demands for business.

The rowdiest bawdy-house was owned by Margaret "Mag" Woods, who had a reputation for being as tough as nails. She later moved to Caldwell, another rough cattle town, and opened a combination saloon, dancehall, and brothel called the "Red Light," which was notorious for its violence. The girls of The Red Light were well-known for luring would-be patrons into the saloon, then knocking them over the head, and stealing their money. Two town marshals and Mag's husband, George, were killed in The Red Light. After George Woods was killed, the brothel became even worse. Before the new town marshal could close the saloon, Mag burned the place to the ground and left town.

The routine fine for prostitutes in Wichita was eight dollars a month, plus two dollars for court costs. The brothels where the girls worked paid fines of eighteen dollars a month, plus two dollars court costs. The fee for selling whiskey was twenty-five a month. In August of 1873, a typical month, money raised from fines on prostitutes was $390, and liquor licenses contributed another $625.

Dodge City, founded in 1872, was one of the last of the great cattle-shipping points and was sometimes called the "Queen of the Cowtowns." In 1872 it was a small settlement of about 500. In its peak year of 1882, Dodge City shipped 500,000 cattle. One of the fanciest saloons in Dodge City was the Long Branch. It featured the owner, Chalkley "Chalk" Beeson, on the violin with a four-piece orchestra that played in the main barroom during the peak summer business hours. No dancing, bar girls, or prostitution were allowed in the Long Branch. After temperance crusaders won their fight, and Kansas became a dry state in 1881, the Long Branch saloon became the Long Branch Temperance Hall.

Though Kansas officially became a dry state, liquor continued to be openly sold for several years. It was either dispensed by druggists "for medicinal purposes" or was openly sold by those willing to risk fines or imprisonment. In many communities, local lawmakers tolerated the sale of illegal liquor.

The higher class of saloons in Dodge City were located north of the railroad tracks, which ran down the center of Front Street. They included establishments such as the Alamo saloon, the Long Branch Saloon, the Saratoga saloon (later renamed the Lone Star), and the Alhambra saloon. Front Street was seventy-five yards wide to allow for the railroad right-of-way, which ran down the middle of the street.

The former Mattie's Boarding House, built in 1883, and the Welcome Saloon (right, added in 1909) make up the oldest surviving bordello building on notorious Blair Street in Silverton, Colorado.

(Author's collection)

Dodge City's red light district and the wilder places, such as the notorious Varieties Dance Hall (later renamed the Green Front Saloon), and the Lady Gay Saloon and Dance Hall, were south of the railroad tracks. In 1877 Dodge had seventeen saloons and dance halls, sixty prostitutes, and thirty professional gamblers. In 1879, during the cattle season, there were fourteen saloons, two dance halls, and forty-seven prostitutes.

In an attempt to clean up its image, Dodge City eventually banned prostitutes from dance-halls and did not allow new dance-halls to be built. This did not mean that prostitution was abolished. It was allowed to continue, but not as flagrantly as before.

The decline of the Kansas cattle towns was rapid. By the early 1880s, what had been cattle towns were primarily farming communities. The final death knell came in 1885, when a Kansas state law was passed to ban importation of Texas cattle or their shipment by rail across the state.

❧ THE LURE OF THE RED LIGHT ❧

One of the legacies that supposedly (but falsely) came from the Kansas cattle and railroad towns of the 1870s is the use of the expression "red light district" to describe the part of town where the parlor houses and cribs were located. In the early days of the Kansas-Pacific and Santa Fe Railroads the trains would often be assembled at night. As the story goes, the railroad brakemen made a habit of hanging their lighted red signal lamps outside the parlor house or crib where they were visiting. This way, when a train was ready to pull out, the dispatcher's call boy could easily locate the men. The term and the story has become part of Western lore. In spite of this common explanation, this was not the origin of the term. There was a much earlier use of red lights around brothels in the East and an earlier common use of the expression.

As a curious sidelight, for some unknown reason a few of the prostitutes in Virginia City, Nevada, in the 1860s hung blue lights outside their doors to indicate their business. By the mid-1870s, however, this practice had generally changed and conformed to the more common use of red lights.

Chapter 10

MINERS AND GOLD DIGGERS

"It's day all day in the daytime,
And there is no night in Creede."
(Cy Warman, editor of the *Creede Chronicle*)

*A*nother group of young, virile Western men that was isolated from women and needed all the traditional entertainment and recreational pursuits of active Victorian men were prospectors and miners. Fast growth and easy wealth, along with the large, faceless and nameless population of young men in early mining camps, were ideal conditions for drinking, gambling, and prostitution.

Mining played an extremely important part in the development of the American West. For every cowboy, logger, or railroad man, there were a hundred miners. Much of the story of prostitution in the Old West, therefore, revolves around miners and the mining towns that they created. Indeed, the initial impetus for whiskey and prostitutes on the frontier was the discovery of gold, because a rich strike was rapidly followed by a rush of single would-be prospectors hoping to make their fortunes. During the years between 1849 and 1900, gold rushes in the West enticed over four million people to travel to and settle the West from Colorado to California and Canada to Mexico.

The earliest white settlers of the West, the mountain men and fur trappers, were hardy, self-sufficient men who depended only on themselves for their livelihood. They hunted their own food, they (or their squaws) made their clothing, and they trapped, cleaned, and sold their own furs. They were independent, free spirits. The gold and silver prospectors and miners who followed them, by contrast, were men who depended on others for their existence. They were not self-sufficient and had no intention of being so. The early prospector was not interested in raising cattle or growing vegetables, building his own house, making his own clothes, or performing the other mundane tasks that were required as a part of everyday living. He wanted to spend as much of his time as possible prospecting and digging for gold in order to make a fortune as fast as he could. If a prospector were successful and made a rich strike, he had plenty of money. He would trade the gold he had dug out of the ground to someone who would perform these tasks for him, while he continued to search and dig for more precious metal.

As a result, a successful mining camp or district spawned a large support population of men other than prospectors and miners to perform services, such as grocers, butchers, storekeepers, and blacksmiths. In this way, a successful camp that started with only a few prospectors soon mushroomed into a bustling town that sold food, clothing, and other necessary supplies to prospectors and miners in the surrounding area. The miners' perception of necessary services included drink, gambling, and women. These voids were rapidly filled by saloons and brothels; and, of course, drinking, gambling, and prostitution were intertwined. A man who went to a saloon to drink might well be persuaded to gamble his money away or to enjoy other activities with a short-skirted dance-hall girl.

But gold and silver mining was also a boom or bust proposition. If the gold played out, the mining town that sprang up overnight might become deserted almost as quickly. The bartenders and loose women who populated these towns were there for the money; and, if the mines and the wealth played out, they disappeared and headed for the next strike as quickly as they had arrived.

The mining towns that did succeed and survive became synonymous with the Wild West. Deadwood in the Nebraska Territory, Bodie in California, Leadville and Creede in Colorado, Tombstone in Arizona, Bannack and Virginia City in Montana, and later Cripple Creek in Colorado, were just a few of the best known towns with famous red light districts. Many others were just as wicked. In 1879 Silverton, Colorado, had a booming red light district, centered on notorious Blair Street, with forty saloons and dance halls, twenty-seven establishments for gambling, and eighteen brothels. By 1883 the number of brothels had increased to forty. Even the long-vanished town of Irwin, which today lies unknown deep in the Elk Mountains of Colorado, had twenty-three saloons and nineteen brothels.

Silverton, Colorado, still tries to maintain its notorious image for the tourists. At one time nearly forty saloons, gambling houses, and dance halls lined two blocks of Blair Street in Silverton. Sixty girls worked in the brothels and cribs of the red light district.
(Author's collection)

When a mining town was started, women were a scarce commodity. In 1880, for example, there were 2,669 inhabitants of Ouray County, in southwestern Colorado, but only fifteen percent of them were women. Similarly, when Green Russell and John Gregory staked out claims in adjoining valleys in the spring of 1859 in the mountains about forty miles west of present-day of Denver, the area quickly grew to a population of several thousand people, but contemporary accounts tell us that of this number only a dozen were women. Five were the white wives of miners, and the other seven, as a contemporary writer slyly put it, were squaws living with white men "in the capacity of wives."

Similar to many other mining areas, minor gold deposits were found in southern Montana in the 1850s, but it was not until 1862 that a major strike was made along Grasshopper Creek. The resulting town of Bannack was typical of the short-lived gold mining camps of the West,

Deadwood, South Dakota, has retained some of its Old West heritage and flavor by converting to a modern gaming town.

(Author's collection)

and, as soon as the gold ran out, most of the miners moved to the next strike in Alder Gulch, about fifty miles to the east. Prior to the gold rush, the white population in the gulch consisted of 604 men and 65 women. Within three months an estimated 10,000 miners were digging in Alder Gulch. By June, 1862, there was a 320-acre town called Virginia City (Montana), mostly built with log cabins, but sporting several dance halls.[1] Business was so brisk that one couple staying at a hotel in Virginia City found only one sheet on their bed. When they asked why, they were told that the other sheet was being used as a tablecloth in the dining room. The sheet was reluctantly returned to them, but only under the condition that they rise early, so that the "tablecloth" could be put back into use. Women were apparently never far from men's thoughts in Virginia City. One debating society argued a proposition that was obviously a difficult dilemma for the miners: "The love of woman has more influence on the mind of man than the love of gold."

Like other rip-roaring mining towns, the abundance of robbers and road agents around Virginia City and nearby Nevada City made it dangerous for a miner to carry his gold dust with him. Most men went around town armed with a pistol, a shotgun, or a rifle. Miners stood guard on sluice boxes at night. Shootings and killings occurred almost daily, and crime became so bad that a vigilante group was organized to rid the town of the lawless element.

The rest of Montana was also not without its vices. Butte claims (perhaps a little grandly) to have at one time had the largest red light district in the West, encompassing a full two city blocks of sin.

❧ THE FORTY-NINERS ❧

Anywhere in the West where there was a large population of young, single males isolated from females was a prime target for prostitution to grow and flourish. One of the earliest areas in the West was the gold fields of the Sierra Nevada Mountains of California. Many enterprising individuals, both men and women, figured it was easier to extract gold from the miners' pockets than it was to dig it honestly out of the ground. Thus the discovery of gold was rapidly followed by saloons, gambling dens, and brothels.

The 1850 census showed that less than eight percent of the white population of California was female. In the mining camps, the figures were even more disproportionate, and men might outnumber women by a hundred to one. Many camps had no women at all. By 1852, women still made up only about fifteen percent of the state's population.

Men from all over the world filled the wild and raucous gold camps that dotted the Sierra Nevada Mountains. With new arrivals pouring in daily, towns sprang up almost overnight up and down the gold belt. Estimates place the number of miners at about 120,000 in the peak year of 1860. Many of the mining camps had colorful names, such as Poker Flat, Liars Flat, Red Dog, and Hangtown. The miners' obsession with drink can be judged from the name of two particular towns: Whiskey Diggings and Delirium Tremens.

In this essentially all-male world, men frequently tired of the sight and sound of each other. Women were such a rare sight in the gold fields that men would flock to a camp where a woman was reported, just to look at her and listen to her voice. There are accounts of men traveling forty miles to a neighboring camp just to stare at a woman. In these isolated communities, any woman, no matter how homely, was considered to be special and was treated with courtesy and respect. There is an account of one miner in the California gold fields who sold tickets for his wedding at five dollars each. Reportedly, he made enough money from the scheme to pay for the event and build a home afterwards.

The chance to see women of any kind was a great attraction. Traveling road-shows featuring female entertainers, such as legitimate singers or actresses, were extremely popular among the men, and an entertainer had to be absolutely appalling before the miners would complain.

At the occasional dances that were held in the camps, the shortage of women meant that some of the men had to pair up to dance. A handkerchief or bright bandana was often tied around the left arm of one of the dance partners to signify that he was dancing the woman's part. To further create the illusion, some men were known to wear women's petticoats or crinolines (hoop skirts) over their trousers when dancing the woman's part. Entertainment at some of the early gold-rush dance-halls was quite modest, and the music for the dancers might be provided by a hand-cranked hurdy-gurdy.

Along with hopeful prospectors flocking west to make their fortunes, others flocked west to make their fortunes from the gold-seekers. As well as the miners, the camps were filled with a large floating population of gamblers, saloon keepers, thieves, and con-men, all of whom saw an opportunity to relieve the miners of some of their gold. Close behind them came a tide of prostitutes, also drawn by the lure of easy money. Some 200,000 hard-working, muscular men filled the gold camps on the California mountain slopes, and these women saw their chance to indirectly get their share of the profits.

Apart from prostitution, two non-sexual services for which women were prized were cooking and doing laundry. Women who ran restaurants or boarding houses with home-cooked meals made almost as much money as some of the prostitutes. Washing clothes was another chore that few of the early miners wanted to do, and they were willing to pay handsomely for someone else to do it. In the early days of the gold rush, having a dozen shirts laundered might cost as much as twenty dollars. Some miners even sent their shirts to China or Hawaii (at that time called the Sandwich Islands) to be laundered, the garments spending six to nine months at sea.

✧ THE FABULOUS COMSTOCK ✧

The frantic days of the Forty-Niners lasted about ten years, and by the late 1850s, most of the rich placer gold had played out. As the California gold rush was fading a new strike was made on the eastern side of the Sierra Nevada Mountains, in what is now Nevada, when small amounts of placer gold were found on Mount Davidson. Limited placer mining continued fitfully, but the best was yet to come. Assays of a curious blue clay that was interfering with gold-sluicing showed an unexpected bonus. Embedded in the matrix of clay was a large amount of silver that was worth several times the original gold. Over a period of twenty-five years, before the silver ran out in the 1880s, the Comstock produced about $300,000,000 in gold and silver.

News of the Comstock silver discovery started a stampede to the east from the California gold fields and, by June of 1860, a shanty town by the name of Virginia City appeared near the strike. The town was named for one of the five original partners in the Comstock Lode, James "Old Virginny" Fennimore, also known as James Finney. The

"The Queen of the Comstock", Virginia City, Nevada, seen here from the cemetery, was the home of the Comstock Lode, one of the richest silver strikes ever made.
(Author's collection)

mine was so rich that it gave the name of "The Comstock" to the surrounding region, and Virginia City was referred to as "The Queen of the Comstock."

Where miners congregated, saloons and women were fast to follow. The first hotel in Virginia City was a fifteen by fifty-two-foot canvas tent. The sleeping area was fifteen feet by thirty feet and could accommodate thirty-six guests at a dollar a person per night. When gold was discovered a few miles to the south at Gold Hill in 1859, "Dutch Nick" Ambrosia erected a large tent that served as a combination saloon and boardinghouse. The rate for boarders was fourteen dollars a week.

By 1861, the population of Virginia City stood at a little over 3,000 people and, at its peak in 1875, contemporary estimates placed the population at around 20,000. As in other mining towns, the ratio of men to women was highly disproportionate. In 1860 there were 2,857 men, but only 159 women.[2] Figures from the 1875 Nevada State Census shows that of 6,112 adult men in Virginia City, 4,624 were living by themselves and 1,488 were living with women. Thus, only one man in four lived with a woman.

With great originality the major streets of Virginia City were named A, B, C, and D Streets. The majority of the saloons and gambling halls were on the east side of South C Street. To provide convenient access for patrons, most of the brothels were on D Street between Washington Street and Sutton Avenue, located right behind the popular saloons. There was an additional area of low-class brothels on C Street, between Silver Street and Flowery Street, that was called the "Barbary Coast" after the sleazy namesake brothel section of San Francisco.

Like other mining districts, the Comstock had its share of vice. By 1879 there were one hundred and thirty-one saloons and four breweries. Gambling, drinking and womanizing were common entertainment for the men.

The Comstock had token regulations against prostitution and saloons. Ordinances regulating both (though not eliminating prostitution) were enacted in 1863 but were seldom enforced. For example, one ordinance made it unlawful to operate a brothel west of D Street, south of Sutton Avenue, or north of Mill Street. In spite of the law, prostitution was still found outside these boundaries.

Virginia City had its ups and downs and unusual stories. In 1863, a fire that started by accident in Pat Lynch's saloon soon burned out of control and ravaged most of the business district. The fire lasted longer than it should have, because two of the fire engine companies, Engine

The cribs of Virginia City in its heyday were located along D Street, with convenient access from the saloons that backed up to them on C Street.
(Courtesy Colorado Historical Society, Mazzulla Collection, Box 22, FF 1280, scan #10038308)

Today the wooden buildings are gone and only the memories remain.
(Author's collection)

Company No. 1 and Young American Engine Company No. 2, started a gunfight over which was the better fire-fighting company, and thus who should fight the fire. One fireman was shot and killed during the skirmish. Other fires destroyed the Virginia City red light district in 1871 and 1875, but each time the district was quickly rebuilt.

An interesting example of the idealization of the frontier prostitute is told in the tale of Julia Bulette of Virginia City. According to stories that grew more colorful after her death, she was supposedly young, beautiful, wealthy, and adept at entertaining gentlemen with witty conversation in luxurious surroundings. Like the legend of the cowboys, the story of Julia Bulette grew more exotic over the years with the retelling. "Julia's Palace" on The Row in Virginia City was reported to be a sumptuous house renowned for the satin sheets on its beds, its beautiful girls, elegant French cuisine, and its cellar of fine imported wines and champagnes. Julia has been called the "Queen of the Comstock" and supposedly charged $1,000 a night for her favors.

Separating fact from legend, Julia Bulette was actually a somewhat plain but kindly woman, who was born in Liverpool, England, in 1832. She emigrated to Louisiana, where she married and then later left her husband. She is known to have been a prostitute in New Orleans before the Civil War. Thus, she was not as young as in the legend, but was thirty-one when she moved to the Virginia City in 1863. Julia was never a madam, and her "palace" was a two-room, clapboard, rented house with no kitchen or indoor plumbing, located among the cribs on D Street at Union Street. The parlor was in front and was furnished with chairs and a sofa. The bedroom at the back had a stove, bedstead, lamps, and a washbasin.

Though Julia didn't have the social status attributed to her by legend, she was apparently well-liked. She was popular with the men and was elected an honorary member of Engine Company No. 1 of Virginia City's fire department, one of the greatest social achievements in the male world. She had a fireman's badge and uniform and marched with the fire company in the local parades.

Unfortunately, Julia met an untimely end. In January, 1867, she was robbed and murdered by a man named John Millian, a Frenchman who worked in a bakery on D Street. Feelings ran high when the deed was discovered, and a massive hunt was quickly organized. Millian was quickly captured and publicly hanged in 1868.

Julia was not rich, as her story has alleged, and she died in poverty. Her debts were not covered by her meager estate. To pay final tribute to their friend and fellow-member her fire company, in full uniform and preceded by the Metropolitan Brass Band, marched in her funeral procession.

∾ BODIE ∾

Another mining district that blossomed and attracted the disillusioned Forty-Niners when they were returning home to the East was Bodie, California, located high in a flat meadow at 8,375 feet in elevation on the western side of the Sierra Nevada Mountains. The mining district at Bodie was established in 1859 but did not attract many prospectors until the discovery of a very rich strike on Bunker Hill in 1877. The mine's success was a magnet for miners, gamblers, and prostitutes, all attracted by the promise of gold. Between 1877 and 1882, the permanent population of Bodie swelled to about 7,000 people.

The red light district developed on the north side of town in 1864. Brothels and cribs were clustered on Bonanza Street, which was also known locally (with heavy sarcasm) as "Virgin Alley" or "Maiden Lane." Both sides of the street were lined with brothels and dancehalls, interspersed with cribs. For convenience, several of the saloons that lined the west side of Main Street had rear exits that led directly to the brothels and cribs.

Bodie had a short-lived reputation for being one of the roughest, toughest mining camps anywhere and supposedly averaged a killing a day. In 1881, one preacher picturesquely described the town as "a sea of sin, lashed by the tempests of lust and passion."

At one time, Bodie, California, had a reputation as one of the roughest, toughest mining camps in the West. Seen here today, it is arguably one of the best examples of a ghost town, preserving its authenticity through only limited maintenance.

(Author's collection)

Like many other mining towns, when the mines gave out, the population sank rapidly. By 1882, as the ore was mined out, most of the mines closed, and the population fell from a peak of 10,000 to around 500. A few brothels remained open on Bonanza Street, but most of the prostitutes left along with the miners to go to better prospects. By 1881, the local paper commented on how quiet the town had become; nobody had been killed for a week.

Bodie had such a wild and wicked reputation that it was the source of an amusing apocryphal anecdote about one of the residents. As the story goes, a young girl was told that she was moving to Bodie with her family. When she heard the news, she is reported to have a given a weary sigh and said: "Goodbye, God, I'm going to Bodie." One of the local newspapers supposedly took offense at this affront to the town's reputation and retaliated by changing the punctuation of the quote to read: "Good, by God, I'm going to Bodie!"

◈ LEADVILLE ◈

In 1860 the discovery of a small amount of placer gold in California Gulch in Colorado gave birth to a town named "Oro City." As in most mountain mining towns, the ratio of males to females was highly disproportionate. The 1860 census recorded 2,000 males and only thirty-six females. After the first limited discoveries played out, the mining district entered a period of decline that lasted through the early 1870s. Then the discovery of a rich lode of silver created a new mining boom, and, by 1879, many rich claims had been staked out. As silver started pouring out of the mines, thousands of miners rushed to the area, and a booming town called "Leadville" was on its way.

The population grew rapidly, mushrooming from about 5,000 residents in 1879 to close to 15,000 in 1880, making Leadville the second largest city in Colorado after Denver. Along with population growth came an inevitable increase in stabbings, shootings, and other crimes of violence. Leadville's reputation of mayhem and murder was well-deserved. At night, armed robbers lurked on almost every street corner, lying in wait to rob belated revelers making their way home. Stagecoach holdups were common, men were robbed in front of their houses, and guests in hotels were robbed in their own rooms. Men who carelessly flashed their money around were liable to mysteriously disappear, never to be seen again. Claim-jumping and lot-jumping was common. Men whose business required them to be out at night either

Chestnut Street and nearby notorious State Street around the corner in Leadville, Colorado, offered gambling, drinking, and prostitution to eager young miners.
(Courtesy Special Collections, Tutt Library, Colorado College, Colorado Springs)

traveled in groups for safety or walked in the middle of the street with a loaded pistol in their hand. A similar situation evolved in Soda Springs, Idaho in 1881, where one resident wrote of sleeping with a loaded pistol under his pillow and a shotgun by his side.

A shortage of marriageable women in Leadville attracted the other kind of women to cater to the miners. Parlor houses, along with a collection of variety theaters, dance halls, saloons, and cribs, soon sprang up on State Street and around the lower end of Harrison Avenue. The Red Light Dance Hall, the Bon Ton, and the New Theater featured short-skirted dance-hall and waitresses. Estimates placed the number of prostitutes in the State Street brothels at over 200, a figure that did not include streetwalkers or madams. The local newspapers frequently published stories about the red light district — complete with lurid details — and the town reveled in a national reputation for wickedness.

The saloons of State Street, later renamed Second Street, were the meeting place of many of the gamblers, thieves, and claim-jumpers that made up the early lawless element of the town. When they were not robbing someone else, the criminals fought among themselves. They challenged each other in the streets, in the alleys, in the saloons, in the variety theaters, and in the hotels. Fights often ended in a knifing or shooting, or (on several occasions) biting someone's nose off.

The fancier parlor houses were in the 100 block of West Park Street, later renamed Fifth Street, and on West Third Street. Popular establishments were run by Mollie May, Sallie Purple, and Frankie Paige. Three bizarrely-named parlor houses were The Slaughter House, The Chicken Coop, and The Bucket of Blood. To cater to the wealthy owners of the silver mines, many of the parlor houses were lavishly furnished and featured costly furniture, tapestries, rich velvet carpets, and oriental wall hangings. With silver flowing freely from the mines, excesses were not uncommon. The Texas House, a richly furnished gambling house, had oil paintings hanging on the walls to complement fine rugs and hanging draperies. The Church Casino featured a large Gothic window.

In 1879, a report in a Leadville newspaper boasted that the town had ten dry-goods stores, four banks, four churches and thirty-one restaurants. As one measure of the miners' likes and priorities, the report also boasted of 120 saloons, 19 beer halls, 118 gambling houses, and 35 brothels.

Typical of the saloons where a miner could go for relaxation was Wyman's Place, owned by Charles "Pap" Wyman. This establishment was a combination saloon, dance-hall, and variety theater, which also served as an occasional meeting hall for an itinerant preacher. The waitresses were pretty and were allowed to sit on a miner's lap to try and entice him to buy champagne. The girls were paid ten dollars a week and a commission on the drinks they sold. As well as being a popular and successful saloon owner, Wyman was a conscientious man and would not allow married men to gamble or spend all their money on whiskey. A large sign underneath the clock requested patrons to not swear.

Even though miners' tastes generally ran to women and whiskey, not all the entertainment around Leadville was lewd or lascivious. Tabor's Opera House and the Grand Central Theater provided quality entertainment to cater to more refined tastes. Wood's Opera House emphasized family entertainment. The Grand Central Theater had a matinee performance directed at women and children on Wednesday afternoons.

On the other end of the scale of refinement were bawdy variety theaters, such as the Coliseum, the New Theater, and the Theater Comique. Shows at the Theater Comique started at 9 p.m. and ended

This former brothel building, now a private residence in Colorado City, Colorado, was occupied by several madams at the beginning of the Twentieth Century. The building next door was the establishment of bordello-owner Laura Bell McDaniel.
(Author's collection)

about 2 a.m., and offered entertainment that was reported to be "in rather poor taste." The shows must have been popular, because receipts in 1879 were estimated to be $1,200 a day.

Miners from Leadville also liked to hop on the Denver & Rio Grande train and ride over to the town of Glenwood Springs for a change of pace and a night of fun. The Riverfront district — now Seventh Street — was the sporting district. It was directly across the street from the train depot and was lined with saloons and gambling halls. In the 1890s the district boasted twenty-three saloons and numerous bordellos. Typical of the "watering holes" was the Silver Club Saloon, started by owners John Richardson and Patrick O'Neil. Their building had some of the most luxurious furnishings in town. A saloon operated on the first floor with a high stakes gambling hall on the second. The second floor also contained a brothel in the back rooms.

❧ DENVER ❧

Though Denver was not a mining town, it grew up on the plains just east of the Rockies to supply the mining camps of the nearby mountains. In its heyday, Denver's red light district was rivaled only by the Barbary Coast in San Francisco and Storyville in New Orleans.

The infant city of Denver was founded in 1858 from an amalgamation of earlier townsites and had an estimated population of 1,000, of whom only five were women. As one of the few large cities that survived the boom and bust days of the early gold rush mining camps, Denver matured to become a center of commerce, finance, and culture in the Rocky Mountains. By 1882, an estimated 480 prostitutes worked in Denver.

Hardcore drinking started even before Denver was a town, during a celebration of Christmas Day, 1858, when mountain man Richard "Uncle Dick" Wootton arrived from Taos, New Mexico, in a wagon laden with ten barrels of Taos Lightning. "Old Towse," as it was affectionately known, was undiluted, home-made alcohol that was said to deliver a kick like a mule. Wootton originally sold whiskey from a tent that he called the Western Saloon. Business was so good that the tent was quickly replaced by a wooden building.

One of Denver's earliest official saloons and gambling dens was the Denver House, which opened on Blake Street in 1859, soon after the first gold-seekers arrived. It was a long, low, single-story building 130 feet deep and 35 feet wide. The construction was typical of many early frontier saloons. The outer walls were made of hewn cottonwood logs, the roof was covered with canvas, the windows had no panes, and the floor was tamped earth. The results of the tobacco-chewers' errant aim collected in puddles in depressions in the uneven dirt floor. Except for the long, unfinished pine-board bar, most of the free space in the interior was taken up by gambling tables that operated twenty-four hours a day.

Those who felt that they could sleep at the Denver House in spite of all the uproar could rent one of the six guest "bedrooms," which were partitioned off by canvas at the back of the building. A lack of developed facilities in many of the early towns meant that men and women often ended up sharing the same rooms at lodging establishments, and sometimes even the same primitive bed. Most hotels required single travelers of the same gender to share a double bed rather than let the space go unused. Partitions for the "rooms" were usually made of calico, paper, or canvas. Some "hotels" did not even have these flimsy dividers, and all the guests slept in the same room — men on one side and women on the other. Though miners had a reputation for always being on the lookout for opportunities with the opposite sex, they treated lady travelers in these establishments with great respect. Any unseemly advances towards a woman or improper behavior by a male lodger would often result in the man being beaten up by his fellow guests.

The Denver House was eventually sold to Robert Teats, who improved it, enlarged it, and changed the name to the Elephant Corral. The name was appropriate, because of a huge oval-shaped corral with eight-foot-high walls behind the main building, where guests could leave their wagons. Inside, gambling was a popular pastime. In one corner of the room was an orchestra, consisting of a fiddle, a cornet, a fife, and a piano, which belted out such favorites as "Yellow Rose of Texas" and "Sweet Betsy From Pike." The management of the Elephant Corral was generous enough to advertise that if a guest was killed on the premises, he would be buried at the expense of the house.

By the 1870s, Denver's red light district had become centered on what is today's Market Street, between 19th Street and 23rd Street. Market Street went through several name changes over the years. It was originally named McGaa Street, after William McGaa, one of the first residents of Denver, whose son, William Denver McGaa, was the first white child born in Denver. The name of the street was later changed to Holladay Street after Ben Holladay, an ambitious and ruthless business tycoon. Holladay Overland Mail & Express Company had a virtual monopoly on passenger and freight service between Atchison, Kansas, and Salt Lake City. When Holladay's Express Company was a mail contractor, Denver's mail piled up for over a week at Julesburg, a way station on the Colorado-Nebraska border, before being forwarded to Denver. To show their displeasure at this perceived insult to them, the residents of Denver changed the name of McGaa Street to Holladay Street in 1866.

The Row also gained such a reputation for wild and wicked ways that in 1872 the city physician Frederick Bancroft estimated that one man in three had contracted syphilis in the local brothels by the age of twenty-five. Upset by the continued notoriety given to the family name, Holladay's relatives petitioned for another name change for the street in 1887. Holladay Street duly became Market Street, because it was also the site of produce markets.

During the heyday of the Holladay Street red light district during the 1870s and 1880s, cribs and parlor houses lined both sides of the street for four solid blocks. A side street, named "The Blue Row," housed the cheapest prostitutes, who cost as little as ten cents.

Behind Holladay Street, and running parallel to it, was Hop Alley, Denver's Chinatown. It received its name because "hop" was a nickname for opium. Drug addicts of the time were named "hoppies" and opium dens were often called "hop joints." Denver had seventeen such places by 1880. Hop Alley was lined with opium dens, brothels with Chinese prostitutes, Chinese gambling parlors, Chinese laundries, stores for Chinese food, and other oriental products for Denver's Chinese population. Hop Alley was a tough section of town, and curious sightseers took a chance on robbery or mugging, or even worse, if they went there. For safety, visitors from other parts of town went there only in groups.

The "Queen of Holladay Street" was undoubtedly Mattie Silks, a shrewd businesswoman who moved to Denver from Georgetown, Colorado, in the mountains to the west, and opened a parlor house in 1877. One of Mattie's trademarks was her dresses which had a pocket on each side. One pocket held gold and silver coins (like many women of the time she kept her paper money under her dress in the top of her stocking). The other pocket was for a small, pearl-handled derringer that she was quite capable of using if needed.

Mattie Silks was born in Indiana in 1846 and ran away from home at the age of thirteen. Mattie started her parlor house career at the top, as a madam, at the age of nineteen. She claimed that she had never been prostitute, unlike many others in the trade. During the fast-paced era of the great cattle drives, she successively owned parlor houses in Kansas in Hays City, Abilene, and Dodge City. She owned a series of parlor houses in Denver, the last and most famous of which was the House of Mirrors at 1942 Market Street, which she bought from Jennie Rogers.

Jennie Rogers was another prominent Holladay Street madam. Her name became Leah J. Fries when she married a doctor in the East, before she ran off with a steamboat captain named Rogers. She moved to Denver in 1879 from St. Louis, where she was also a madam, and eventually opened a series of parlor houses on Holladay Street. Her biggest and best was the House of Mirrors, built in 1889. This large building was built from gray stone and had five faces carved in the upper stonework. The largest, at the peak of the roof, was a women in a low-cut dress that was believed to be Jennie herself. Another was a leering face of a man with one eye closed in a wink that was reputed to be the man who had financed the construction of the house. The lower stonework contained carvings with various phallic designs. Jennie also owned the connecting house next door, which she furnished as a Turkish harem. Two years after Jennie died in 1909, Mattie Silks bought the House of Mirrors and continued to run it as a parlor house.

The House of Mirrors had fifteen bedrooms, sumptuous furniture and heavy crystal chandeliers in the parlors, luxurious carpets on the floors, and a wine cellar in the basement. The name of the house came from its ornate ceiling-to-floor mirrors with elaborately carved frames that incorporated the figures of nude women. The building also housed a ballroom lit by electric lights, in which a five-piece black orchestra played. After Mattie took over, the cement steps at the front door was decorated with inlaid colored tiles with the inscription *M. SILKS.* In later years, Mattie's place was derisively called the "Old Ladies Home" or the "Old Ladies Roost" by the other madams. This was because Mattie did not follow the common practice of turning out prostitutes just because they were growing older.

Reformers periodically tried to regulate the brothels and cribs of Holladay Street, or at least tried to enforce ordinances to prevent the public flaunting of its wares. One law was that the girls had to keep their doors closed and the window shades down or the curtains drawn. They were also forbidden to sit in the windows of the cribs or lean idly in the doorways. The requirement that window shades be drawn was easily bypassed by "accidental" tears in the material that allowed conversation between a prostitute and a prospective customer. Rips in the material were also used to provide not-so-accidental peep shows of what the customer could expect inside. After the first outburst from the reformers died down, enforcement generally relaxed, and business soon was back to usual.

The clashes that developed out of the periodic ordinances passed to try and control the red light district developed into a series of running skirmishes between the reformers and the girls of The Line, some of which had rather humorous aspects. On one occasion an ordinance was passed that required each "public woman" to wear a yellow ribbon to indicate her profession. In response, some of the girls dressed in bright yellow outfits, from gloves and dresses to hats and shoes, and paraded around the downtown business district. Embarrassed lawmakers rapidly repealed the ordinance. The girls may have won some of the battles; but the reformers eventually won the war. In 1915, the City of Denver closed down Market Street's sporting houses, and the former red light district became part of Denver's downtown industrial district.

ᴄᴏ· TOMBSTONE ·ᴏᴄ

Silver, as opposed to gold, was responsible for the creation of the rip-roaring town of Tombstone in southern New Mexico Territory, in what would later be south-central Arizona. The town was founded after the Tombstone and Graveyard claims were staked by prospector Ed Schieffelin in 1877 in the San Pedro Valley. Schieffelin called his first claim the Tombstone, because cynics told him that if he prospected in the desert among hostile Indians all he would find would be his tombstone.

The real boom didn't start until after 1879, when Tombstone was laid out on 320 acres of a nearby level spot called "Goose Flats." The short boom lasted until 1883, when a gradual decline set in from which the town never recovered. In spite of this, over $37,000,000 worth of ore was dug from the mines. Reliable estimates placed the population of the city at its peak at around 6,000 people, though other estimates placed it at between 15,000 and 20,000.

The city quickly gained a reputation as a wide-open town with a thriving red light district. After reading contemporary accounts of daily life in Tombstone, however, some of its reputation may have been exaggerated. For example, there were not as many murders in Tombstone as might be thought by visiting Boot Hill cemetery. In reality, many of the corpses buried in Boot Hill were from other nearby towns that did not have their own undertaker.

In spite of the exaggeration, cowboys from the surrounding area came to town to blow off some steam. One indicator of the level of their antics was when Virgil Earp was appointed town marshal, he felt it necessary to set up some rules of behavior for the cowboys. Along with understandable ordinances against drunkenness, carrying guns in town, and the public discharge of firearms (except on holidays), was one that prohibited anyone from riding their horse into any saloon, gambling hall, or dance hall.

Movie screenplays and cowboy fiction have tended to emphasize Tombstone's dramatic side. Much of the town's reputation was deserved, and most of the Tombstone saloons and gambling halls that lined several blocks of the north side of Allen Street never closed. If respectable ladies walked on that side of the street they were liable to be mistaken for the other kind of woman and harassed by attentions and offers that they did not want. Eventually the red light district migrated to the southern part of the town, east of Sixth Street.

The number of liquor licenses issued in the city numbered 110 during Tombstone's peak boom days in 1881. Because liquor could legally be sold by drugstores and parlor houses, this was not an indicator of the number of saloons in the town. The taxes on saloons and the red light district provided over half of the financial support for the local school

The stage at the Bird Cage Theater in Tombstone, Arizona, was the scene of many riotous and racy burlesque shows.

(Author's collection)

district and the city government. Gambling houses paid a "license" fee of ten dollars a month. Brothels that sold liquor paid twenty a month in "taxes" but only had to pay seven dollars if they did not serve drinks.

Many of the mines and mills were located in nearby Charleston on the San Pedro River, about ten miles southwest of Tombstone; but miners and mill workers flooded to Tombstone in search of female entertainment. Tombstone's prostitutes drew men from other towns along the river, such as Contention City, Millville, and Fairbank. The town also attracted soldiers from Fort Huachuca and other nearby army posts. Women, drinking, and gambling were the pursuits for many off-duty soldiers, and when military payday arrived, so did additional prostitutes. Some came for temporary stays from as far away as Tucson.

The better-known saloons in Tombstone were the Crystal Palace, the Oriental, the Alhambra, and the Bird Cage, all of which were located on Allen Street between Fifth and Sixth Streets. When the Oriental opened with a dazzling display of twenty-eight-burner chandeliers, it was considered by local residents to be the most ornately furnished saloon outside of San Francisco. The Crystal Palace Saloon was built as the Golden Eagle Brewery in 1879, then changed to the Fredericksburg Lager Beer Depot before becoming a fancy saloon with crystal glasses

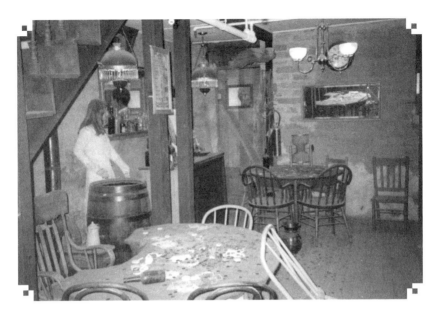

Reportedly a poker game in the bar and gambling den beneath the Bird Cage Theater in Tombstone, Arizona, continued for longer than eight years.
(Author's collection)

and large plate-glass mirrors. Virgil Earp had his office over the Crystal Palace when he was the town marshal.

Several theaters were erected to provide legitimate entertainment, such as plays, opera, and musical shows, supplemented by magicians, minstrel shows, and vaudeville acts. Better known theaters were the Danner & Owens Hall, the Sixth Street Opera House, and Schieffelin Hall, the largest and best-known theater in the Southwest. Theaters became so popular that the city imposed a daily license tax of five dollars to improve the civic revenue.

The Bird Cage Theater, which opened on December 23, 1881, was located on the corner of Allen Street and Sixth Street. It grandly called itself an "opera house," though it was actually a combination of a gambling casino, a dance hall, and a bar that employed three bartenders. Evidence of the wild times that gave it the reputation for the wickedest place between New Orleans and the Barbary Coast are the 140 bullet holes that can still be seen in the walls and ceiling.

The audience which visited the theater sat around tables on the main floor and drank beer and whiskey, while peering through a haze of tobacco smoke at the leg-exposing vaudeville show on stage. The stage was not large, only fifteen feet wide and about fifteen feet deep, but it was still large enough for the "actresses" to perform rousing dances. Before electric lighting arrived in town, performers were illuminated by flickering gas jets located along the front of the stage.

The shows at the Bird Cage were typical burlesque acts, primarily featuring girls, girls, and more girls. For the edification and entertainment of the prospectors and miners, typical stage shows featured young women in various acts that were intended to appeal to young men. This meant that most of the performances consisted of scantily-clad girls with a lot of make-up cavorting around the stage to loud music. This included acts with women dancing while dressed only in tights, others singing while dressed in short skirts and bright stockings, and some, of course, dancing the can-can. The Parisian can-can, with women performing high kicks and revealing black stockings and frilly underwear, was considered at the time to be a scandalous dance.

Shows typically started at 9 p.m. and ran until 1 a.m. or 2 a.m., with the acts becoming bawdier as the evening wore on. When the show was over, the main floor was cleared of tables, chairs, and benches; dancing and drinking continued until dawn.

Like many other variety theaters, the Bird Cage was well-known for its pretty waitresses. It was also well-known for its fourteen private boxes that were built into the walls along the sides, about fifteen feet above the main floor of the theater. Between stage shows, the members of the audience in the boxes could draw heavy curtains across the viewing area and continue their study of the actresses' and waitresses' talents at closer range. This type of theater with private boxes for prostitution was sometimes called a "box house." Directly beneath the stage on the main floor were private rooms for prostitution, a bar, and a gambling table that is reputed to have hosted the longest running poker game in western history. The apocryphal game ran for eight years, five months, and three days.

The Bird Cage Theater has been cited as the inspiration for the popular Victorian song, *She's only a Bird in a Gilded Cage*, composed in 1900 by Harry von Tilzer and Arthur Lamb. The story, however, is unsubstantiated. A "bird cage" was also the nickname for a wire gambling cage in the shape of an hourglass that was used for rolling dice.

Apparently assuming that the audience was tiring of always looking at exposed female flesh, and wanting to provide some variety, the Bird Cage tried entertainment of a different sort in 1881. Three men dressed in tights with women's undergarments over them came on stage and danced. Apparently they were ahead of their time, and the audience was not yet ready for transvestite burlesque acts, because after watching in silent disbelief for a few moments, the enraged patrons grabbed the manager from the stage and beat him up.

◦◦ AND A FEW OTHERS ◦◦

At the mouth of a narrow gulch on the eastern edge of the San Juan Mountains of southwestern Colorado was a notoriously wicked silver camp named Creede. The town was founded in 1889, following a rich silver strike by Nicholas Creede and George Smith. The town of Creede rapidly developed a reputation for violence and sordid pleasures. As with many of the other mining boom towns, gambling houses and saloons were among the first structures completed in the new town. They were open around the clock. During the summer of 1890, the population grew at the rate of 200 to 300 people a day. By early 1892, the infant town had thirty saloons to serve an estimated 10,000 inhabitants and was shipping $1,000,000 worth of ore each month. Attracted by the gleam of silver, many of the early residents were saloon keepers, gamblers, dancehall girls, pickpockets, and con artists.

The lower portion of Creede, where the gulch that containing the town and Willow Creek emptied onto the flat floor of the valley below, was called "Jim Town." With irony, some residents called it "Gin Town," because of the large quantity of spirits that were consumed in saloons there. Both names were eventually dropped in favor of using the name "Creede" for the entire town.

Creede was the last home of Bob Ford, the man who supposedly shot outlaw Jesse James in the back. Ford operated a combination saloon, gambling den, and bawdy house called the "Exchange Saloon." On June 8, 1892, he had a difference of opinion with deputy sheriff Ed O. Kelly, when Ford accused Kelly of stealing his diamond ring. The result was that Kelly blew Ford apart with two barrels from a shotgun, an event that local opinion held to be poetic justice. At Ford's funeral, most of the town's prostitutes and gamblers accompanied the coffin to Sunnyside Cemetery, which was located on appropriately-named Shotgun Hill, where they held a celebration and drank copious amounts of wine and champagne around the gravesite.

Telluride, fifty miles over the mountains to the west, boasted a red light district popularly called "Popcorn Alley," that was lined with cribs, saloons, and other houses of entertainment, such as the Pick and Gad,

Big Swede, the Monte Carlo, the Senate, and the Idle Hour. Among the two-room cribs of The Row on Pacific Avenue was an unusual double crib that was said to be used for training novice prostitutes.

Like other towns, Telluride suffered a major fire in 1890. It was set by a dissatisfied customer, who tried to burn down the Silver Bell, a combination dance-hall, saloon, gambling den, and bawdy house at the corner of Spruce Street and Pacific Avenue, named after the notorious street of the same name on San Francisco's Barbary Coast. Everyone escaped safely, except the "professor," a lady piano player who broke her leg when the firemen's net collapsed as she jumped into it.

❦ CRIPPLE CREEK ❦

The town of Cripple Creek, on the west side of Pikes Peak in central Colorado, had a later start than many of the other wild mining towns, because gold was not discovered there until October of 1890. As with many of the other boom towns, hopeful prospectors and miners soon poured into the district, and, within a year, 2,500 people lived there. By 1896, the population had grown to an estimated 10,000. By 1900, the Cripple Creek mining district had 475 operating mines, was served by three railroads, and had produced $18,000,000 worth of gold. Cripple Creek eventually became the second largest gold district in the world and produced a total of over $475,000,000.

In 1893, Cripple Creek had eleven parlor houses, twenty-six one-woman cribs, and four dance-halls. Like other boomtowns, the Cripple Creek red light district was a source of revenue for the city. Each month, madams were fined sixteen dollars, the parlor house girls paid six dollars, and the dance-hall girls and crib prostitutes paid four dollars.

By 1896, Cripple Creek had six churches and two banks, compared to seventy-three saloons. One of the finest and best-known saloons and gambling halls was owned by Johnnie Nolon, a soft-spoken Irishman and one of the camp's respected citizens. A miner down-and-out on his luck knew that there was always a free meal and a dry floor to sleep on at Nolon's. The Salvation Army band could often be found outside his front door, collecting for the unfortunates.

The red light district in Cripple Creek was centered around Myers Avenue, named after Julius Myers, one of the town's founders. The Myers Avenue tenderloin area had as racy a reputation as any red light district in the West and did its best to live up to its reputation. At the turn of the century, there were twenty parlor houses and between 250 and 300 prostitutes worked in Cripple Creek. In 1896 an estimated 350 women were working the trade, and there was so much demand for their services that the women often worked all night long. Before the establishment of the red light district on Myers Avenue, saloons such as the Buckhorn and the Anaconda had prostitutes available in their upstairs rooms. A girl working in the dance-halls received fifteen cents a dance. Beer was five cents a glass and came with a free saloon lunch, so long as the customer bought a sufficient amount to drink.

The main concentration of saloons, dance-halls, and cribs stretched for two blocks along Myers Avenue from Third Street to Fifth Street. In the afternoon, the shades in the windows of the Myers Avenue cribs were usually raised to reveal scantily-clad women sitting in the windows, smoking cigarettes, and waiting for customers. In the evening, the sounds of music, laughter, and singing usually filled the air. Slumming parties often strolled along the street to see the cribs with red lights shining in the windows.

Wild and woolly images of Cripple Creek so caught the imagination of the public that one of the first popular Western "movies" was titled *Cripple Creek Bar-room*. The 1898 film, made by the Edison Company, was a minute long and was more of a tableau than a movie production. It shows five men portraying different Western characters lounging around

The pictorial boom and bust of a Western mining town:
(a) The early townsite of Fremont, which preceded Cripple Creek, Colorado, shows only a few tents and crude log buildings.
(Glenn Kinnaman Colorado and Western History Collection.)

(b) Bennett Avenue, the main street of Cripple Creek, with the town at the height of its development and a reported population of about fourteen thousand.
(Glenn Kinnaman Colorado and Western History Collection.)

(c) Cripple Creek in the 1960s had declined to a virtual ghost town with a population of only a few hundred permanent residents.

(Author's collection)

a bar, and posed rather stiffly behind a jug labeled "Red Eye." This vignette is presided over by a rather homely-looking female bartender. Female roles were often played by men in these early film productions.

The variety theaters in Cripple Creek featured eight or ten piece bands and racy burlesque shows. Among the popular places were Crapper Jack`s saloon and gambling hall, the Red Light variety theater, the Great View, the Bon Ton dance hall, and the Casino. Parlor houses, such as the Parisian, Laura Bell's, the Golden Peacock, the Mikado, and the Boston catered to a general, and often rough, clientele of miners.

The proprietor of Laura Bell's, Laura Bell McDaniel, moved east across the mountains to Colorado City in 1888, where she opened one of the fanciest brothels in town called "The Trilby." Mamie Majors ran a brothel next door in a building that still stands today. Laura Bell became the flamboyant queen of the Colorado City tenderloin district in the early 1900s and was occasionally seen riding around town in a carriage pulled by a pair of tame elk named Thunder and Buttons. They were

This photograph was been popularly, but incorrectly, attributed to a real Cripple Creek, Colorado, bar-room. It was actually part of a staged, minute-long movie (titled Cripple Creek Bar-room) made in 1898 by the Edison Company.
(Glenn Kinnaman Colorado and Western History Collection.)

owned by John "Prairie Dog" O'Byrne, who received his nickname from a pet prairie dog, who rode beside him on the seat of the carriage.

A little further to the east in the Cripple Creek red light district, only a few hundred yards from all the opulence of the Old Homestead and the other fancy parlor houses (where Myers Avenue started up the hill into Poverty Gulch), was a part of the mining town that was prone to shootings and robberies. This was the location of the lower-class dance halls, several brothels, and the poorly-furnished wooden shacks that were the cribs of French, Chinese, and Negro prostitutes. Like many frontier mining towns, Cripple Creek had a large enough Chinese population to maintain several opium dens, most of which were located in the alley behind Myers Avenue.

As with other Wild West towns, Cripple Creek had its share of eccentric characters. One was a rather overweight inhabitant of one of the cribs, who called herself Leo the Lion. One day she appeared roaring drunk and stark naked at the corner of Myers Avenue and Fourth Street at high noon and yelled at the top of her lungs, "I'm Leo the Lion, Queen of the Row!" With the typical aplomb of miners accustomed to curious events, some of the local residents took her home and let her sleep it off.

This public nudity of a prostitute was not unusual. The local newspaper in Aspen, Colorado, reported that prostitute Mary Murphy drank too much, paraded naked in the streets to do a little impromptu advertising, and was promptly arrested. The same happened in Denver when prostitutes Annie Griffin, Belle Jones, and Daisy Smith decided to dance naked on a street corner in the saloon district, and were arrested. They were able to make bail. Murphy did not do as well as the other three. She had to stay in jail because she could not pay her fine.

Cripple Creek reached its peak year of population and gold production in 1901, and after that a gradual decline set in. Water and poisonous gas in the mines, rising production costs, and a series of labor disputes between miners and mine owners accelerated Cripple Creek's decline. As the boom years passed, the district started to fade in importance. As the town's economy went down, so did the economy of its red light district. Most of the prostitutes left for other Colorado towns, such as Salida, Leadville, and Denver. The ones who stayed had to drop their prices to a dollar to stay in business.

The men of the mining district flocked to Cripple Creek for their entertainment, but most of the big mines were in the nearby town of Victor. This camp was located at 10,000 feet above sea-level at the foot of Battle Mountain and had a smaller collection of dance-halls and brothels than Cripple Creek to serve its rapidly-growing population. One of Victor's famous entertainment spots was the Union Theater on Third Street, which called itself "the hottest burlesque theater in the West." Apparently this was true. The local newspaper reported that the burlesque act called "Cleo the Egyptian Belly Dancer" was so indecent that it shocked even the audience of burly miners, and she was run out of town. Drinking, stage shows, and prostitution were the mainstays of the establishment, and brawls and shootings were common.

Chapter 11

THE WICKED WEST COAST

"The miners came in Forty-Nine,
The whores in Fifty-One,
And when they got together,
They made the native son."
(Forty-Niners' ballad)

T he emerging West Coast of the United States spawned towns and cities that exemplified much of the wild times that surrounded prostitution. Drinking, gambling, womanizing, and crime were rampant in towns from San Francisco to Seattle and beyond.

☙ THAT WICKED CITY BY THE BAY ❧

When California was annexed by the United States, two years before the gold rush of 1849, the existing Spanish town of Yerba Buena was renamed San Francisco. Over the next ten years or so, the sleepy seaport mushroomed into a bawdy, brawling city. Spurred on by the rush of Forty-Niners to the Sierra Nevada Mountains, San Francisco grew to be a flourishing city with a flourishing red light district. With the optimism and easy money generated by the gold-seekers, it developed in an almost carnival atmosphere and spawned vice of all sorts. By 1850, the year that California received statehood, the little town of San Francisco that two years before had only about 800 inhabitants had swelled to an estimated 20,000 to 25,000.

In the spring of 1849, before the gold rush was really under way, there were very few white women in San Francisco. A census in 1847 listed 138 females, which included sixty-six white women over the age of twenty, eight Indian woman, one from Hawaii, and one black woman. By the fall of 1850 the number had grown to about 2,000 women, a large number of whom were prostitutes. By the end of 1853, there were 8,000 women. In these three years, San Francisco had matured from a motley collection of tents and shacks by the waterfront into a major city. Bankers, businessman, lawyers, and doctors thronged the streets alongside miners, sailors, and merchants.

In 1849, the fastest way to California from the East was by sea. One route consisted of making a five to eight month voyage in a sailing ship down the east side of South America, around Cape Horn with its unpredictable weather, up the west side of the South American continent, and north to San Francisco. It was a mammoth journey of about 13,000 miles. Many persevered, however, and completed the journey.

Ships carrying the argonauts around Cape Horn and up the coast also brought many women from South America. Part of this influx was stimulated by food shortages in Chile and Peru, which made many women seek better circumstances among the gold miners of California. One way that prostitutes without money could make the journey was to sign a contract with the ship's captain to pay for their passage after starting work in San Francisco. In addition, speculators recruited women in South America and paid for them to make the journey. The women contracted to work to pay back their passage, plus a profit for the speculator, over a specified period of time. By the end of 1849, boats containing prostitutes were arriving almost weekly.

Early California prostitutes were given the name of "Yankedos." It was a slang name first given to Mexican prostitutes, who plied their trade among American troops during the Mexican War of 1846-47.[1] These Yankedos were intensely disliked and were persecuted by their own people. Some of the women were branded with the letters US, some had their hair shaved and their ears cut off, and some were even killed by their angry, patriotic countrymen.

When San Francisco started to boom, much of the prostitution was still carried on by women of Mexican, Spanish, and South American descent. The core of the early prostitutes were generically referred to as "Chilenos," because many of them came from Chile. Most of them in San Francisco lived near Telegraph Hill in a tawdry neighborhood called Chilecito, or Little Chile. In the 1860s, this area became a part of San Francisco's notorious red light district, "The Barbary Coast."

Like the rest of the buildings in early San Francisco, houses of prostitution consisted mostly of tents and shacks. With the housing shortage that existed in the rapidly growing city, multiple prostitutes often entertained several clients in the same tent at the same time. These women primarily worked the waterfront area, catering to sailors.

In California, 1850 and 1851 were known as the years of the "Great Whore Invasion." In the fall of 1850, the miners became ecstatic when the newspaper announced that 900 French prostitutes were being recruited in Paris to journey to San Francisco. During the first six months of 1851 alone, more than 2,000 women flocked to California from New York, New Orleans, South America, Asia, and from as far away as France and Australia.

The order of preference for women for the Forty-Niners was French, Spanish, American, English, and then Chinese. French women gained a particular reputation among the miners for being the most passionate and the most skilled and varied at love-making. The mere mention of "French love" or the "French treatment" could stir a young man's fantasies — even if he could not imagine what that might be. As a consequence, French women (or an American prostitute who could pretend that she was one) were in the highest demand and were among the highest-priced prostitutes. Other, more Victorian-minded miners frowned at hints of anything exotic and considered anything out of the ordinary to be "unnatural practices."

Even a common Paris streetwalker or an aging French whore could command a price of $400 to $600 for a night with a gullible miner, who was fresh from the diggings, flush with gold dust to spend, and a hankering for the exotic in the arts of love. As a consequence, in 1852 and 1853, hundreds of French prostitutes traveled to the Pacific coast, lured by tales of easy wealth and gullible miners. The passage from France for many of the women was paid for by French national lotteries, because the French government saw that the transportation of prostitutes to America was an excellent way to get rid of members of the population that were considered to be undesirable. French authorities used the same tactic in the 1700s, when they transported hundreds of undesirable women, pimps, thieves, and vagrants to their infant colony of Louisiana.

San Francisco, as one of the few large seaports on the West Coast and the primary outfitting point for the gold fields, naturally became a center of entertainment for the miners. Single men down from the gold camps in the hills were hungry for any kind of amusement, and so the infant city grew with an atmosphere where drinking, gambling, and all the associated diversions and vices were accepted as part of the normal way of life.

Many early mining towns were a hastily thrown-together collection of shacks and wooden houses, such as seen here in Cripple Creek in the 1890s.
(Glenn Kinnaman Colorado and Western History Collection.)

In 1853, a survey of San Francisco showed 537 saloons, including forty-eight bawdy houses, and forty-six gambling houses. As in much of the West, the distinction between the three types of establishment was often blurred, and almost any type of entertainment was freely available at all of them. The popular gambling halls and saloons were so profitable that the owners added any attractions they could think of to try and bring more customers in the doors. As an extreme example, several restaurant owners hired women to pose nude, while blasé miners ate in their dining rooms.

The primary method of bringing in men was to advertise entertainment, usually in the form of singing, stage shows, skits, and other vaudeville-type antics. To appeal to men, the shows were mostly "girlie" oriented, featuring women with bare shoulders and short skirts, both of which were quite risqué for the times. Racy theater acts might include women dancing the can-can or playing leapfrog in various stages of undress. Drinks were often served by female waiters, and sometimes the card dealers in the gambling halls were women. As would be expected, prostitution flourished in such places, usually with an arrangement for the girls to split their fees with the saloon owners.

Because of the scarcity of females and the free flow of gold from the diggings, prices for a woman in early San Francisco were high. Men, fresh from the gold-camps, were so lonely for the sight and sound of a woman that they were more than willing to part with their hard-earned gold dust for a chance to dance with a woman or spend time talking to a prostitute. During the first two years of the gold rush, the typical price for a woman to sit at the bar and talk to a lonely miner, or to share a drink with him, was an ounce of gold dust, which at the time was worth about sixteen dollars. The fee for her to spend the entire night with him ranged from $200 to $400 — and occasionally up to $600. Business was so lucrative that some of the early prostitutes made enough money to retire after only a few years.

The miners did not object to the high prices. They had certain things they wanted, and if the price was high, they accepted it as the way things were. It was not only the price of women that was high. Everything in early booming San Francisco was expensive. The price of eggs was four dollars a dozen, flour was two dollars a pound, and potatoes cost thirty dollars a bushel. When prostitution became firmly entrenched in the city, and the supply of women improved, the cost of a visit to one of the fancy parlor houses in the 1870s and 1880s had dropped to between ten and twenty dollars.

In the mid-1850s, one side of Portsmouth Square — also named The Plaza — at Kearney and Washington Streets, contained the San Francisco Post Office, the Justice's Court, the Custom House, and a horse market. The three other sides of the plaza were lined with gambling halls and the better houses of prostitution. By 1855, the area just north of Portsmouth Square was estimated to contain over one hundred houses of prostitution.

With a rapid and large influx of women, San Francisco in the 1860s became a prostitute's paradise and supported a flourishing red light district. The larger brothels were usually fairly honest with their customers, preferring that patrons hand over their money voluntarily in exchange for the pursuit of vice. In later years, the elaborate brothels, gambling houses, and cabarets of the upper Tenderloin district, where Eddy, O'Farrell, and Turk Streets meet Market Street were relatively safe. Instances of fighting or beating up a customer were rare, though occasionally fights did break out, or a visitor might lose his wallet to gangs of roving thugs. In 1869, an ordinance was passed that prohibited the employment of women in dance halls and saloons; however, there was no real effort to enforce it.

Most of the high-class parlor houses had a reputation for strict propriety, except behind closed bedroom doors. They were the more traditional parlor houses, with ornate furnishings and attractive girls. Here, the greatest danger to the visitor might be an earthquake tremor. When that happened, prominent San Franciscans might be seen hurrying out into the street in various states of undress.

By and large, bawdy San Francisco had its own ways, and the state government did not interfere. There is, however, a record of a legislative committee arriving from the state capital in Sacramento in 1878 to study the alleged wicked ways of San Francisco in order to propose the appropriate legislation. Reportedly, they made an exhaustive study of the parlor houses of the Upper Tenderloin, but no record can be found of any anti-prostitution laws enacted as a result of their efforts.

⤫· SALOONS AND SHOW BIZ ·⤫

San Francisco was legendary for some pretty tough joints. Police judged one of the toughest to be a dance-hall ominously named Hell's Kitchen, which opened in 1868. It was a three-story building with a basement, located on Pacific Street at Sullivan Alley. The basement and street levels both had a bar and dance-hall with stage entertainment consisting of singers and dancers. The real business, however, consisted of the prostitution that was transacted upstairs. The top two floors of the building were divided into a series of cubicles for women to entertain their clients. The girls were primarily French and Spanish women.

The shows downstairs began in the early evening and continued until dawn, punctuated by frequent breaks to allow the girls to coax customers to go upstairs without missing any of the show. Drinks were served by "pretty waiter girls," who were dressed provocatively for a brief time period in short red jackets, black stockings, ruffled silk garters, red slippers, and nothing else. These outfits did not last long, because the crowds became too large and unruly, and the girls complained of the cold. The women made fifteen to twenty-five dollars a week, plus commission on the liquor they hustled and half of the fee for business conducted in the upper cubicles. Just to be different, a competitive saloon and dance hall dressed its waiter-girls in short skirts and stockings, but bare on top. To counteract this tactic, the police insisted that they wear blouses. The girls complied, but retaliated by leaving them unbuttoned.

Hell's Kitchen was unusual in that the waiter-girls were required to drink hard liquor with the customers, rather than the cold tea or soft drinks discreetly served to the girls by bartenders in most other places. This practice was not without its risks for the women. If a girl drank too much and passed out, she was carried upstairs and could be had by anyone for twenty-five cents to a dollar, depending on her age and attractiveness.

Hell's Kitchen was owned and operated by hulking Ned "Bull Run" Allen, a tough character who claimed to have fought in the two Civil War battles (1861 and 1862) from which he took his nickname. A habit of drinking at his competitors' bars eventually brought him to a bad end. After a drinking bout at the Clover Club, he picked a fight with another drinker named Bart Freel. Freel was either the more sober of the two or was a better fighter, because he stabbed Allen fatally with a large clasp-knife.

Another popular and notorious establishment was a combination variety theater, saloon, and gambling house called the Bella Union, located on Portsmouth Square at Kearney and Washington Streets. It opened in 1849 and called itself the "Wickedest Place in the West." The stage shows consisted mainly of songs and risqué skits. Most were bawdy, and some were obscene, but were not reported to be as bad as some of the other shows around town. Between the stage shows, the "actresses" made the rounds of curtained boxes located around the theater, trying to cajole customers into buying them a drink. If a customer wanted to pursue any further activity, he could draw the curtains closed and strike up a bargain. The girl's fee was split with the management.

Representative of the development of the combination saloon, variety theater, and gambling hall was the El Dorado, also on Portsmouth Square. It was started in 1849 in a canvas tent, but was so profitable that within a year it moved into a wooden building, complete with ten glittering chandeliers and oil paintings of nudes on the wall behind the bar. At one end of the main hall, an orchestra entertained on a raised platform; around the sides were the usual curtained booths, where customers could receive special entertainment from short-skirted waitresses.

For those who didn't have much money to spend, the drinks were cheaper at the Olympic, the Pacific, or Gilbert's Melodeon. Miners who preferred more culture could go to the Alhambra to be entertained by a French lady violinist who performed classical compositions. Those with a taste for a minstrel show could go to the Aguila de Oro to watch a chorus of "Ethiopians," which was the contemporary euphemism for blackface entertainment.

The price of a drink at most saloons was a pinch of gold dust, which was worth about twenty-five cents. To complete the exchange, the seller pinched the purchaser's gold dust between thumb and forefinger, hence the expression: "What can you do in a pinch?" For obvious reasons, the saloon-owner preferred a bartender with extra-long fingernails. From the drinker's viewpoint, this was frowned upon. Some bartenders did quite well for themselves by running their fingers through their heavily pomaded hair before taking a pinch. Some saloons made extra profit by sweeping up the gold dust that accidentally fell into the sawdust on the floor or between the floorboards into the dirt below.

For larger transactions, a scale was used to weigh the gold dust, and a small square of carpet was often put underneath to catch any errant dust or flakes of gold. The owner of the scale burned or washed the carpet periodically to recover the gold embedded in it. Even with a scale, the transaction was not always honest. Fraudulent weights might be used, though the perpetrator risked personal violence if the deception was discovered.

Showing mankind's typical ingenuity, some miners added brass filings to their bag of gold dust to stretch it out a little further. The ones who were found out and taken to court were the lucky ones. Others were summarily shot by angry gamblers or pimps.

To be fair, not all the drinking establishments were bawdy houses and not all saloons were dives. Clayton's, the Fountainhead of Luxuries, and the Branch were all family-oriented and tried to appeal to a more genteel trade. The latter two did not serve alcoholic drinks but offered other beverages. One saloon on Montgomery Street was a stylish drinking house that allowed no gambling and only displayed decorous pictures on the walls.

⟡ THE BARBARY COAST ⟡

The toughest area around the waterfront in San Francisco was nicknamed the "Barbary Coast," after the coastal region of the same name that stretched from Tripoli to Morocco in northern Africa. The African area was notorious for its pirates, cut-throats, and dens of thieves. In San Francisco, its namesake became synonymous with tawdry saloons, evil gambling dens, vulgar variety theaters, low-class houses of prostitution, and cribs.

The Barbary Coast was just north of Portsmouth Square and was centered between Stockton and Montgomery Streets. It stretched for several blocks on either side of Pacific Street, which was locally nicknamed "Terrific Street." One section of Kearny Street that consisted of a line of saloons, brothels, and dance halls was so bad that it was nicknamed "Battle Row." One saloon on Kearny Street, where it crossed Pacific Street, was known as "The Billy Goat," because of its peculiar characteristic odor of a combination of stale beer, damp sawdust on the floor, and gamy patrons.

One contemporary described the whole area as "a sink of moral pollution, with lewd women drinking vile liquor." As a description, it was probably quite accurate. The area was a cesspool of prostitutes, murderers, cut-throats, and opium dens that offered licentiousness and debauchery of all types. The special attraction of the Boar's Head was sexual activity between a woman and a boar (a male pig). The area was also a place of squalor and misery. If a visitor didn't part willingly with his money on drink and women in the saloons, he might be hit on the head with a club in an alley and be parted from his money unwillingly.

The Barbary Coast grew and flourished because of the ships that were the primary method of long distance travel in and out of the Bay Area. Records show that over 750 ships sailed into San Francisco in 1849, as opposed to only eight in 1848, the year before the news of the gold strike spread to the rest of the country.

The shoreline by the present-day Embarcadero was from two to six city blocks further inland, as compared to today, and fronted onto the shallow bay of Yerba Buena Cove, which was the docking area. The cove was where the Ferry Building is today. Thus, originally, the brothels and saloons of the Barbary Coast were deliberately located right next to the docks, so that sailors, fresh off the boats from months at sea, could conveniently satiate their erotic daydreams and their quest for alcoholic spirits. The waterfront was Montgomery Street, named after the captain of the *USS Portsmouth*, the man who claimed possession of California for the United States. Over the course of the early years, when many ships were abandoned in port, sand and dirt were dumped over them to fill in the shallow water of the cove to create more room for the expanding city. Therefore, by default, the effect was that the Barbary Coast gradually moved several blocks inland.

Everyone on the Barbary Coast, from shopkeepers to brothel owners, looked upon the sailors as fair game. Sailors were regularly exploited, robbed, beaten, drugged, shanghaied, and murdered. When sampling the various forms of entertainment on the Barbary Coast, it was not unusual for a customer to receive drugged whiskey and to wake up in a back alley with a splitting headache and his money gone. It was also not unusual for him to be shanghaied onto a departing ship that could not legitimately attract enough hands.

The expression "shanghaied" for kidnapping sailors came from the practice of adding unwilling men to the crews of ships sailing from San Francisco to the distant port of Shanghai in China. The practice was so blatant that one saloon and boarding house on Pacific Street was even named Shanghai Kelly's. One of the owner's approaches was to give a sailor what he called a "shanghai smoke," which was a cigar loaded with opium. The drugged sailor was then hauled out to a departing ship that needed more members in its crew. One estimate placed the number of British sailors who deserted their ships in San Francisco each year in the 1890s at between 800 and 1,100. Most were immediately shanghaied back onto other departing ships. This practice became so widespread, that in 1906, Congress passed an Act to outlaw it in the United States.

Even the short boat ride from a ship anchored in the harbor to the Barbary Coast was not without its dangers. Ships usually anchored out in the bay, and the men were ferried ashore for a fee in small boats. This water-taxi service was often run by unscrupulous operators, who robbed the sailors on the way or who suddenly stopped and demanded more money to complete the trip to the dock. Some sailors were knocked on the head during the trip and shanghaied back to another ship leaving the harbor before they even reached the shore.

Similar to arrangements between brothel madams and store-owners, shady deals often existed between ship's owners or captains and local supply shops. Sailors were allowed to buy whatever they wanted on credit — at exorbitant prices — and repayment was advanced directly out of their future wages. The crooked captain and shopkeeper split the profits. Similar arrangements existed with some sailors' boardinghouses.

Fighting and murder in the saloons and brothels of the Barbary Coast were common. Some bodies were disposed of by selling them to imminently-departing ships, in the guise of shanghaied sailors who were so drunk that they had to be carried on board. By the time the captain found out that he had paid for a corpse instead of a drunk, he was usually out at sea, and, because he had accepted a known kidnapped sailor, he had no recourse to the law.

At least one dive on the Barbary Coast had a trapdoor set in the floor in front of the bar. Likely-looking victims were steered over the trapdoor and given a powerful drink of alcohol laced with opium. At the appropriate time, the bartender pulled a lever that opened the trapdoor, and the semiconscious victim later woke up to find himself back at sea on an outbound ship.

The women of the Barbary Coast tended to be coarse and dirty, often quite ugly, and were frequently riddled with disease. The problem of venereal disease became so bad in San Francisco that a proposal was made to open municipal clinics for prostitutes. Implementation of the idea was opposed on the grounds that the fear of catching the disease kept many men from visiting the brothels on the Barbary Coast.

The rapid influx of women into San Francisco led to a type of large-scale prostitution that was carried on in buildings called "cowyards" or "bullpens." A cowyard was a three or four story building with a central hallway running the length of the building on each floor. On either side of the hallway were long rows of cubicles for entertaining clients. A cowyard might have anywhere from 250 to 400 cubicles, and might have more than one shift of prostitutes per day. The largest cowyard in San Francisco was the Nymphia, a three-story building that opened in 1899 and had two shifts of girls working in 300 cribs. The builders originally planned to call the building the Hotel Nymphomania, but the police would not allow it. After a series of police and court actions, the Nymphia finally closed in 1903.

The Barbary Coast, with its wicked dives and brothels, was essentially destroyed in San Francisco's great earthquake and fire of 1906. Even though brothels and saloons continued to sell vice after this time, the Barbary Coast never returned to its wild and wicked days before the turn of the century. The entire district was finally shut down by a series of police raids in 1917.

◈ CELESTIAL FEMALES ◈

One of the attractions of early Pacific Coast towns was an abundance of Chinese prostitutes, locally called "celestial females." There was a popular, but erroneous, rumor that the genitals of Chinese women were oriented side-to-side, instead of front-to-back as in Occidental women. In what was presumably the interests of furthering scientific inquiry among interested miners and sailors, parlor houses and crib owners capitalized on this misconception by advertising that the men who wished could find out the truth for themselves. The price was twenty-five cents for a "look-ee" or fifty cents for a "feel-ee." By taking such action the patron usually became so aroused that he paid an additional twenty-five cents and proceeded with a "do-ee."

Chinese parlor houses were decorated to provide an image of what the Forty-Niners thought China should look like. The furnishings ran heavily to musk, sandalwood, and teak, with silk hangings and parchment scrolls on the walls. The smell of joss sticks wafted through the exotic furnishings.

Boatloads of Chinese women were brought from Asia to the United States to serve as prostitutes or wives. Some were kidnapped from their homes, and some were still only children, as young as eight to thirteen years old. Some were sold into slavery by their parents, a practice that was not uncommon in a society where sons were more highly regarded than daughters.

The more attractive girls were sold to wealthy Chinese residents of San Francisco, who wanted a wife or a mistress. Typical purchase prices ranged from $200 to $1,200, depending on the woman's age and beauty, with an occasional exceptional girl going for up to $3,000.

The rest of the women ended up in virtual slavery in the low-class cribs. One estimate was that low-status Chinese prostitutes charged an average of thirty-eight cents per customer, catered to seven men a day, and worked 320 days a year. They were held in such low regard that if they became too diseased or too ill to work, they were discarded like worn-out possessions. Some were allowed to "escape," in the hopes that one of the various charitable societies founded to reform wayward prostitutes would take care of them in their final hours. Some who were seriously ill were locked by themselves in a room with minimal food and water until they died of their disease or from starvation. Often they were simply abandoned to die in Cooper Alley, a back alley in Chinatown.

Not all Chinese women ended up in San Francisco, however. In 1880, fully half of the fifty-six prostitutes recorded in Helena, Montana, were Chinese.

Eventually, the traffic in Chinese women and prostitutes became such a problem that in 1874 President Grant asked Congress to do something about it. In 1875, Congress passed legislation prohibiting the importation of women into the United States for the purpose of prostitution.

⟨⟩ THE PACIFIC NORTHWEST ⟨⟩

The forests that covered the west coast of the United States in the 1820s were dense green woodlands that stretched from Canada south through much of California in a belt that was 1,200 miles long and 200 miles wide. Commercial logging started in the Northwest along the Columbia River in 1827, but it wasn't until the mass migration of people chasing gold that the demand suddenly increased for lumber for houses, mine buildings, and other structures. Ironically, the discovery of gold at Sutter's Mill in California was due to the construction of a sawmill to supply sawn lumber to the local settlers.

As a result of rapid growth, the Northwest was increasingly filled in the second half of the Nineteenth Century by single men who were loggers, mill-hands, and sailors. Like the deserts and mountains of the West, the Pacific Northwest offered adventure and challenge to those who wanted to be part of an exciting future; but like the miners, cowboys, and railroad men, the loggers also suffered from a lack of women. The ratio of women to men was about one to ten. As in any business endeavor, where there was a need, enterprising individuals sprang to fill it; so it was not long before saloon-keepers, gamblers, and prostitutes were a significant part of the Northwest`s population

The loggers around the infant lumber town of Seattle were responsible for originating and adding the expression "skid row" to the vernacular. A "skid road" was a greased road or path, often log-paved itself, down which logs were dragged by mules or oxen from where the trees were felled to the sawmill. The lubricant used was animal fat, dogfish oil, bear grease, or, if nothing else was available, rancid butter. If the contours of the land were suitable, a skid road was sometimes built on a hill in the form of a chute, so that logs could be slid downhill using gravity instead of mechanical power. An even faster way of transporting lumber was in a water-filled flume that dropped steeply downhill — in some instances for up to sixty miles — and moved logs at speeds of up to ninety miles per hour.

As with smelters in the mining communities, many a logging town started with a sawmill as its focal point. As a result, a town often grew along the skid road to the sawmill, and the term "skid road" came to refer to the brightly-lit section of town that was lined with saloons, gambling houses, dance-halls, and brothels. Eventually "skid road" was corrupted to become "skid row."

The original "Skid Row" was Yesler Way — at one time called Mill Street — in Seattle. It was used to skid trees from the forests overlooking the town to Henry Yesler's sawmill and wharf on the waterfront. The center of Seattle's red light district grew along what is today South Washington Street, between First and Third Avenues South. The area

This imposing brick building, the former Dumas Brothel in Butte, Montana, was Butte's longest-lived, lasting from 1890 to 1982. Windows from the interior corridors into the rooms allowed patrons to view an occupant before making a final choice.

(Author's collection)

included disreputable establishments, such as Billy the Mug's saloon and Lou Graham's brothel.

Similar to railroad construction camps, many sawmill towns were often only a temporary collection of small cabins in the woods. When the stands of trees in an area were exhausted, the sawmill moved on to a better location, and the girls, gamblers, and saloons moved along with it.

A sawmill sometimes paid loggers in scrip that was redeemable only at the company store. However, then as now, business was business and many madams ended up accepting scrip in payment and then shopping at the company store alongside their customers.

Because the transportation of lumber was primarily by ship, sawmills tended to be close to a river or the Pacific Ocean. To capitalize on this, one enterprising individual created a floating funhouse called "Gin Palace Polly," a boat that made regular rounds of the lumber mills to supply women and liquor. The mill operators were not too happy with the arrangement, because most of the men tended to take an unannounced day off when the boat pulled up to their dock.

In 1861, John Pennell built the first combination dance hall and brothel along the skid road in Seattle.[2] He had previous experience in selling vice on San Francisco's Barbary Coast. His place was called the Illahee, which was an Indian word roughly meaning "home away from home." The first building was a simple, unpainted frame structure with the usual bar and a dance floor with a three-piece orchestra consisting of violin, accordion, and drums. Off to one side of the main hall were small rooms, where women could entertain the lumberjacks in private. A shot of generic red-eye at the Illahee was fifty cents. The price for the girls was from two to five dollars a visit.

The population of the town of Seattle was less than 1,000, but there were an estimated 10,000 unmarried males, mostly loggers, in the surrounding area, who were in need of the Illahee's services. The girls at the Illahee were Indian, traded from their families for Hudson's Bay blankets. Unlike many of the local Indian women, who groomed themselves with highly aromatic dogfish oil, Pennell kept his girls well-washed, nicely dressed in calico, and sweet-smelling with perfume. When competition caused business to slacken off a few years later, Pennell brought a dozen white women from his old haunts in San Francisco to add to his harem of Indian girls.

In its heyday, the Illahee became so popular that it attracted loggers from all over the Northwest, and the action there was so rowdy that it was nicknamed "The Mad House." Because it was built on land filled with sawdust, it was sometimes known as "The Sawdust Pile." For obvious reasons, the girls who worked there were known as "sawdust women" and were said to be "down on the sawdust." Later, this expression grew to be a nickname for the whole red light district, because it was built on top of a former tidal flat that was back-filled with sawdust from the mills, in order to extend the waterfront area. Pennell married one of his girls, Annie Murray, in 1875 and retired to a farm in eastern Washington.

As the largest towns in the Northwest, Seattle and Portland were recreation centers for the loggers and provided every entertainment they desired. Puritan reformers claimed that by the 1890s Seattle was home to 2,500 prostitutes. This figure was probably exaggerated and more reliable estimates place the figure considerably lower.

As in other towns, vice paid its own way. Pennell's Illahee paid $1,200 a year in license fees. The professional women paid ten dollars a month to the city treasurer. One time, when the city streets needed reconstruction, the prostitutes agreed to a temporary increase in fines.

With the heroic cooperation of the local, unmarried male population of the Puget Sound area, the required $2,150 was raised in only three days.

To the saloon owners of the Northwest, any customer was fair game, and they were determined to help him leave his money with them by fair means or foul. At the Senate Saloon in Portland, when a logger came in and offered to buy a drink for a few of his fellow workers, the bartender pressed a buzzer to signal any of the girls upstairs who were unoccupied to hurry down and join them. The bartender knew that the customer would be too embarrassed to refuse to buy them a drink too.

One of the largest brothels in Portland was the Paris House, owned and operated by Duke Evans. It ran the length of a city block and had two floors of private rooms with one hundred prostitutes. The lower floor offered a wide selection of white women. If the customer's preference ran to other nationalities, he could find them on the upper floor.

One enterprising Portland madam, named Nancy Boggs, kept one jump ahead of the police and complaining reformers by operating a floating brothel on a houseboat on the Willamette River. If she was being harassed by the police on one side of the river, she simply weighed anchor and took her two dozen girls to the other river bank.

A popular place along Portland's skid row was Erickson's saloon, which had five entrances and occupied most of a city block. The bar itself was a phenomenal 684 feet long, went around all four sides of the saloon, and was staffed by fifty bartenders. As part of the entertainment used to attract clients, August "Gus" Erickson featured an eight-piece, all-girl orchestra. It became so popular that he had to install an electrified rail to keep the enthusiastic loggers and sailors away from the players. The free lunch at the bar was legendary. So were the bouncers, one of whom weighed 300 pounds. Similar to the saloons of the Barbary Coast in San Francisco, Erikson's had gaming tables, curtained booths for private entertainment, a high-kicking chorus line on the stage, and paintings of voluptuous nudes on the walls behind the bar.

An attempt by the city administration to survey vice for possible regulation backfired. When the report was published, it contained a map that showed the location of prostitutes in the city. Unauthorized reproductions of the map, along with compasses, were soon for sale for the use of men seeking female company.

In Seattle, John Considine drew enthusiastic crowds to his combination saloon, theater, and bawdy house called the "People's Theater." Admission to the theater was ten cents, but the real profits were made selling liquor. At some of the variety theaters, the same girls who served drinks and sold their favors to the customers, also had to sing and entertain on the stage. Considine, on the other hand, hired professional performers to entertain on the stage and thus attracted more customers to gamble and drink. He left the entertainment in the curtained boxes to the prostitutes.

In 1894, the city council passed an ordinance forbidding the sale of liquor in theaters, and the People's Theater was forced to close. When the Klondike Gold Rush started in 1897, Seattle was the major port of embarkation for Alaska. The city council saw that profits were to be made from the flood of gold-seekers passing through Seattle, re-considered the ordinance, and Considine re-opened his theater. To celebrate the event, he booked a performer by the name of Fahruda Manzar, who was better-

The Hotel View in Ashcroft, Colorado, had twelve sporting women to cater to more than 2,000 local miners in the early 1880s. An additional twenty saloons served to quench their thirst.

(Author's collection)

known as the belly-dancer "Little Egypt." She had created a sensation by dancing at the Chicago World's Columbian Exposition of 1893. The dance was initially intended to be a part of a cultural and educational display in the Egyptian and Algerian anthropological exhibits at the fair, but the erotic gyrations of the dancers soon attracted viewers, who were more interested in the salacious aspects of the female performers. The name belly-dance came from a literal translation of the French Danse du Ventre. It was also called the "cootch" or the "hootchy-kootchy," and was the predecessor of the strip-tease of later burlesque. As an added draw, Little Egypt had garnered a national reputation after dancing nude for a private party at a club in New York City. She later appeared on the theater circuit in Wrangell during the Klondike Gold Rush.

Aberdeen, Washington, had a street with several high-class brothels named Harvard, Columbia, and Yale. The delighted loggers rapidly came up with the nickname of "College Row." Also located in Aberdeen was the Palm Dance Hall, which was famous for its wild fights and for its forty women, all of whom were available as partners for dancing or for other more personal entertainment.

On Vancouver Island in the 1880s, an ingenious group of women set up a brothel close to one of the lumber camps. Since the lumber company's rules did not allow prostitutes in the camp, the girls called themselves magazine subscription agents. Loggers had only to walk down the road to the girls' place to pick up a copy of the latest fashion or gardening magazine, and they would receive a sales bonus that most regular magazine subscribers never dreamed of.

Similar to the Barbary Coast, some of the large lumber ports in the Northwest practiced forced induction of sailors. The ships that transported lumber around the world often found it difficult to attract sufficient crew members, so to fill this need, crooked bartenders, pimps, and prostitutes teamed up to lure men to an unpleasant fate. The men who carried out the dirty work were called "crimps." A system similar to that in San Francisco was used. A likely victim was one who had drunk too much and was not in any condition to object if he were hauled senseless out to a departing ship. If he was not drunk enough, a few drops of chloral hydrate in his drink would produce the desired effect.

One establishment that was notorious for the practice was the Bucket of Blood Saloon in Everett, Washington, which was built on stilts over the river. A convenient trapdoor dropped an unsuspecting victim into a boat or to the mud-flats below, depending on the tide, and then to the expectant hands of a crimp, who transported him to a nearby waiting lumber ship. If the victim was not needed to fill a quota of crewman, he might simply be robbed and left to drown. Similar arrangements operated in Port Townsend and Aberdeen, Washington, and Portland, Oregon. Gray's Harbor was so notorious for the practice that it was known as "The Port of Missing Men."

ᙍ· THE KLONDIKE ·ᙍ·

Further north, Alaska, during its gold rush, had much of the same vice and crime that was present in the lower forty-eight. It all started on August 14, 1896, when prospector George Washington Carmack found gold in the rich placer deposits at the junction of the Klondike and Yukon Rivers in far western Canada, close to the border between Alaska and Canada. The strike on Bonanza Creek — previously named Rabbit Creek — created the legendary gold rush to the Yukon Territory of 1897-99 and was the impetus for the founding of the town of Dawson City. By the end of 1896, the population of Dawson was 500. By June of 1897, it has swelled to 5,000.

Though Dawson and the Klondike gold rush was in the Yukon Territory of Canada and was not geographically part of the frontier of the American West, most of the would-be prospectors, merchants, gamblers, con-men, thieves, and prostitutes who flocked to the Yukon Territory were Americans hoping to repeat the great western gold rushes of 1849 and 1859. Many of them were familiar with gold rushes, because they had either previously sweated and toiled in mines or had gained direct experience in fleecing miners. Thus, the Klondike gold fever was a direct philosophical extension of the earlier gold rushes of the American West.

The Klondike strike was truly a legendary find, and the first arrivals who staked out claims made fortunes. Most, however, were disappointed. By the time would-be gold seekers reached the diggings, the best claims were staked out, and nothing remained for newcomers. Though rich, the gold district was very small, allowing a total of only about 4,000 claims. When the men arrived, the working conditions were less than ideal. Winters were so brutal that whiskey sometimes turned to slush. The temperature, even inside heated cabins, was often below freezing. The temperatures were so low that axes and other metal tools had to be kept indoors, or they became so brittle that the metal fractured when they were used. Summer days sometimes topped a humid 90°F, and the swampy country encouraged the breeding of swarms of voracious mosquitoes.

Because of the difficulty in reaching the remote gold fields, the first trickle of miners did not reach Dawson until the fall of 1897, and the real tide of gold-seekers did not arrive until the summer of 1898. By June, the population of Dawson had grown to about 28,000 people. Though the journey to reach the gold-fields was long and difficult, approximately 100,000 would-be prospector started the trek north. Probably only about 30,000 to 40,000 persevered and actually completed the journey.

Most of the men found absolutely nothing. By the time they arrived at the gold-fields a year-and-a-half after the first strikes, all the major finds had been long-since staked and claimed. Discouraged before they began, many turned around and left right away. By 1899, the population of Dawson was rapidly sinking; six or seven years later, the Klondike gold fever was all but gone. Even so, the imbalance in the sexes remained. An 1899 census of Dawson showed 3,659 men, but only 786 women. About 400 of these women were estimated to be prostitutes

In the short period while Dawson was booming, it was the same as any gold boom-town around the world. The first arrivals immediately built saloons, gambling halls, variety theaters, and brothels, all of which echoed the wild times of a young town. Women such as Klondike Kate and Diamond-Tooth Gertie (so-named for the diamond between her two front teeth) made the most of the lopsided ratio of men to women.

The Line consisted of two tightly-packed rows of cribs facing each other across identical boardwalks that were separated by frozen topsoil in the winter and a morass of mud in the summer. Most of the prostitutes were originally located in downtown Dawson on Paradise Alley, in an area bounded by First and Third Avenues from King Street to Queen Street. They were moved across the Klondike River in 1901 to Klondike City, a charming-sounding district known previously as "Lousetown," and which was located away from the respectable part of town. The area was also sometimes called "White Chapel," after the similar area in Victorian London that was made infamous by Jack the Ripper.

Most of the time the women were left alone to conduct their business. Prostitution was illegal in Canada, but the limited resources of the Northwest Mounted Police were more concerned with crimes of theft and violence than in policing morals.

In saloons on the Klondike, the only drink was often whiskey, usually of the generic variety; but plenty of it was consumed. In the

Though this is credited as the red light district at White Chapel, some historians think it may be a photo of the earlier brothels on Fourth Avenue in downtown Dawson.
(Courtesy Colorado Historical Society, Mazzulla Collection, Box 22, FF 1322, scan #10038309)

year 1898 alone, 120,00 gallons of whiskey were reportedly shipped to Dawson. For those with more exotic tastes and the money to match, champagne was available in some of the fancy parlor houses.

Because of the remoteness of the Yukon, everything during the gold rush was very expensive. Champagne cost as much as thirty dollars for a quart bottle, as opposed to the price of about five dollars in Denver. Alcohol that cost sixty dollars per gallon in bulk, when adulterated, diluted, and sold by the drink might yield $150 to $200 at the bar. A dance with a saloon girl cost a dollar instead of the twenty-five or fifty cents that it cost in the lower forty-eight states. The girls could easily make $100 a night. By contrast, wages for a common laborer were five to eight dollars a day, laundresses made five dollars a day, and the cost of living has been estimated at about six dollars a day.

Dance-hall girls and actresses, even if they were poor entertainers, could make about twenty dollars a day, plus a commission on the drinks they hustled. Prostitutes could make twice that. Thus, many women who arrived with no husband and no job prospects were easily tempted to drift into prostitution. A fifteen-minute "date" cost four ounces of gold dust, which was worth sixty-four dollars at the time. However, since many of the unscrupulous women used their own suspect scales and weights, they often made twice that amount. Prostitutes with even fewer scruples could make $250 and up a day by stealing from their clients, after getting them so drunk that they didn't know what was going on.

In the summer of 1898 Mattie Silks,[3] the famous "Queen of the Row" from Denver, took eight of her girls and joined the gold rush to Dawson. Their purpose in going to the Klondike was the same all the others who flocked to the gold fields — to make easy money. Mattie opened a combination saloon and bawdy house in Dawson and returned to Denver three months later, reportedly $38,000 richer for the summer's work. Profits were good, since each of her girls averaged fifty dollars a night. Of that, Mattie took half, plus board. In addition, there were profits for champagne at thirty dollars a bottle and from "whiskey" made from colored grain alcohol.

The end of an era: tombstones of the madams.
(a) Laura Bell McDaniel, a madam in Colorado City, is buried in Fairview Cemetery in Colorado Springs, Colorado.

(Author's collection)

(b) Pearl DeVere was proprietor of the Old Homestead in Cripple Creek, Colorado. Her original wooden marker in Cripple Creek's Mount Pisgah Cemetery is in the Cripple Creek museum.

(Author's collection)

In one novel approach, a dance-hall girl in Dawson auctioned herself off in 1897 to act as a temporary "wife" to the highest bidder for the winter. She made a quick $5,000 in gold out of the bargain. Several other dance-hall girls sold themselves for a short term "marriage" in exchange for their weight in gold – reportedly stuffing their corsets with lead buckshot before the official weighing to improve the take.

AFTERWORD

"Remember friends as you pass by
As you are now so once was I.
As I am now so you must be
Prepare for death and follow me."
(cemetery epitaph, Caribou, Colorado)

When the early 1900s arrived, and our story ends, the inevitable changes that accompany progress had taken their toll all over The West. The free-spirited mountain men and explorers were long-gone, trail-driving cowboys were a dying breed, and continuing settlement was transforming the prairies and mountains. The American Indian tribes had been relentlessly forced onto reservations, and the lands that they previously occupied had been taken over by farmers, settlers, and ranchers. The boisterous West of the early frontier and its colorful, single, male pioneers had been replaced by communities populated by families.

By 1900 the temperance movement was on the way to winning its battle over liquor and would eventually turn the West — along with the rest of America — dry. The last of the frontier saloons would succumb to the "Noble Experiment" of prohibition in 1919. By the turn of the century, railroads were providing cheap, fast transportation for goods and people traveling west. At the same time, the arrival of the steam locomotive also spelled the death knell for the era of the cowboy and the great cattle drives from Texas to Kansas.

By the turn of the century, mining had changed from the days of the independent prospector panning for gold to hard-rock mining performed by low-paid men hired by large companies that were often run by nameless, faceless absentee owners in the East or overseas. Even the short-lived booms of the Klondike and Nome gold rushes were dying away.

By 1930 the buildings of the red light district of State Street that had seen wild times when Leadville boomed were dilapidated and worn-out.
(Courtesy Denver Public Library, Western History Collection, X-6363)

As The West became more settled, saloons and brothels became targets for reformers, who had convinced themselves that family men should not frequent such establishments. Laws passed by industrious social reformers soon forced the closing of the old red light districts and changed the patterns of prostitution. Contrary to lawmakers' intentions, sex-for-sale did not stop, as indeed it has not yet today. The methods of boy-meets-girl merely shifted to different forms of advertising and assignation.

As sexual equality and sexual freedom for women increased after the turn of the Twentieth Century, prostitution diminished as an institution. During the first half of the new century, visits to prostitutes declined, particularly among middle-class males. This is not to say that premarital sex has declined since Victorian times. On the contrary, it has increased, but men have found willing female sexual partners among their social contemporaries.

Changes towards the equality of women, liberalization of attitudes towards sex, and the improved reliability of birth control appear to be dominant factors in these changing social patterns. Expanded employment opportunities for women, and a wider acceptance of divorce in the latter half of the Twentieth Century helped to release women from their previous economic dependence on men and have consequently allowed women more freedom to experiment with discovering their own sexuality. Unshackled from the fears of unwanted pregnancies and educated with modern medical information about their bodies, modern women have become equal partners in love-making, encouraging and

Obviously reflecting a popular Victorian sentiment, this gravestone stands in a cemetery near Kebler Pass, Colorado.
(Author's collection)

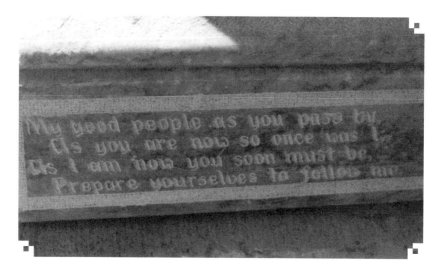

Close-up of the inscription on the base.

(Author's collection)

willing to share their husband's or boyfriend's advances, instead of denying them or sending the men to prostitutes, as was often the case with many Victorian women. Modern married couples who are sexually incompatible turn to divorce instead of to prostitution or adultery.

For all its faults, the era of the Old West was responsible for the making of American legends. From today's vantage point, the rose-colored spectacles of hindsight bathe the Old West of the last half of the Nineteenth Century with a romantic glow. It was a time of America's youthful exuberance, and the vitality of forging a new country out of a wilderness frontier.

May its memory never die.

NOTES FOR CHAPTERS

Introduction

1. One estimate made in 1849 indicated that roughly 43,000 men made the journey west, but only 5,000 women. The first census of California, performed in 1850, showed that less than eight percent of the white population consisted of women. The 1860 census of Colorado showed 32,654 males and only 1,577 females. Census data for Dodge City, Kansas, in 1875 showed that most of the residents were unmarried men in their twenties and thirties, and they outnumbered females by six to one. Such imbalances generally did not change until men traveled to the East to return with brides or until the daughters of Western immigrant families matured to a marriageable age.

2. In fairness, it must be pointed out that there were men who never visited a prostitute and, certainly, not all women in the Old West were prostitutes. Of the first 111 women who arrived at the Comstock mining area in Nevada, eighty-three lived with their husbands. As another example, the 1880 census for Caribou, Colorado, a silver mining town in the mountains west of Denver, showed that there were 138 single men and 126 married men. Of the married men, seventy-three had their families with them.

3. One possibility for connecting a would-be bride with a prospective groom was via advertising. Several businesses in the East published and circulated magazines that contained pictures and biographical information on women who wished to move out West and marry. One of the most popular of these directories was named *The Heart and Hand*, which led to the common name of "heart-and-hand women" for many prospective brides.

Chapter 1

1. Generic names for male customers, such as "john" or "trick," are still in general use today. The expression "turning a trick" is still used to describe the financial and physical transaction between a prostitute and her customer.

2. As one source, stories repeated by the author's grandparents, who

were born in the 1880s, confirm this.

3. Examples of this Victorian hypocrisy are contained in Nazarieff, Serge. *Early Erotic Photography*. Cologne: Benedikt Taschen Verlag GmbH, 1993, and Mangan, Terry W. *Colorado on Glass*. Denver: Sundance Publications Limited, 1975.

4. Sanger, *The History of Prostitution*, page 489.

5. These names are explained further in Glossary Two.

Chapter 2

1. More complete data from Sanger's study are given in Tables 1 and 2 of Appendix 1.

2. Sanger, *The History of Prostitution*, page 491.

3. Specific data from both Sanger's (1855) and Kneeland's (1912) surveys from New York City are given in Appendix 2. The majority (seventy percent) of Sanger's group were between seventeen and twenty-four, with the largest groups in the eighteen and nineteen year-old categories. The commonest age of the women in Kneeland's survey was a few years older, with the largest group (seventy percent) being between twenty and twenty-six, and the single most common age being twenty-four.

4. More complete data on the age of consent for different states are given in Table 6 of Appendix 1.

5. See data from Sanger's study in Table 5 of Appendix 1.

6. Data in Table 1 of Appendix 1 from the survey performed by Sanger shows a large proportion of milliners and seamstresses among the prostitutes he surveyed.

7. In George Kneeland's study, 88 of the 1,106 prostitutes surveyed claimed that they were involved in "theatrical work."

8. The word "cat" to describe a prostitute and the word "cathouse" to describe a brothel may have their origins in the Dutch word *kat*, which means a wanton woman. In modern times, the name "painted lady" is also used as a generic name for restored, brightly-painted, historic Victorian houses.

Chapter 3

1. A listing of these names and their derivations is contained in Glossary 1.

2. Pearl DeVere was also known in Denver as Mrs. Isabelle Martin, which appears to have been her married name. As a side note on

her professional name, "pearl" was a vulgar Victorian pornographic euphemism for the female clitoris.

3. One of the earliest guidebooks to the brothels of New York was published in 1839. It was titled *Prostitution Exposed* and was written by an author with the improbable pseudonym of Butt Ender.

4. Carbolic acid, made by distilling coal tar, is also known as phenol. This liquid can penetrate living tissue and thus forms a potent antiseptic. It is also highly poisonous and can cause dangerous burns to the skin.

5. The name "bit," as a denomination of money, came from the early practice of cutting Spanish dollar coins into eight parts, or pieces-of-eight, to make change for transactions. Each part was called a bit. Thus, a bit was worth one-eighth of a dollar, or twelve-and-one-half cents, two bits was twenty-five cents, and six bits was seventy-five cents. Though there was not an actual coin of such denominations, the names for the divided parts stuck and are still used today. The name "pieces of eight," which was usually associated with pirate loot, came about because a Spanish dollar was equal to eight *reales*. A holdover from pieces-of-eight is stock market values, which are traditionally reported in eighths of a point.

6. Indeed, the same happens today in places such as the Reeperbahn, the red light district in Hamburg, Germany, where prostitutes sit in their cribs and negotiate with customers through open windows. Tourists also drive through the Rue St. Denys in Paris to watch prostitutes waiting for and negotiating with customers.

7. Laudanum is a solution of opium in alcohol.

Chapter 4

1. During the Civil War, women in the Northern states suffered from a shortage of contraceptive sponges, because all the sponge fisheries were located in the south, in Florida.

2. Quinine, also known as Peruvian Bark, is a bitter substance derived from the bark of the *Cinchona* tree that grows in South America. Quinine is better known as a medicine to treat malaria.

3. In the late 1840s, Dr. Ignatz Semmelweis at the General Hospital of Vienna in Europe linked a high rate of deaths in obstetrical wards to doctors who performed autopsies then continued on to examine patients without washing their hands. Semmelweiss insisted that the wards be scrubbed with disinfectant, and that doctors wash their hands before examining patients. With these precautions in place, the death rate sank from about fifteen percent to less than one

percent. Unfortunately, Semmelweis' findings were not accepted by the general medical community, and he was dismissed by the hospital. He accepted another position in Budapest and published his findings in 1855, but it would be over twenty years before the germ theory was widely accepted. Semmelweis died in 1865, ironically from an infected wound acquired during an autopsy.

4. Schwimmer, Walter B., K.A. Ustay, and S.J. Behrman. (1967). "Sperm Agglutinating Antibodies and Decreased Fertility in Prostitutes." *Obstetrics and Gynecology*, 30, 192-200.

5. These estimates may be on the high side. The data reported by Sanger (1858) of the 2,000 prostitutes he surveyed in 1855 in New York City showed that 821 (forty-one percent) of them had suffered one or more attacks of syphilis or gororrhea, or both.

6. There is a theory called the "Columbian Theory," that syphilis originated in the New World and was picked up by Christopher Columbus and his men after his first voyage to America. They then took it back to Europe, where the disease appeared in soldiers two years later. It is thought that Columbus himself died from one of the disorders that results from syphilitic infection. Another theory claims that syphilis is a specific form of the disease *treponematosis* that evolved in tropical Africa. Both theories have evidence to support them.

7. Military records place the incidence of venereal disease among soldiers during the Civil War at thirty-eight percent. Similar figures exist for the British army around the same time for troops stationed in India, where between twenty and fifty percent were infected, depending on the regiment. The British army at home reported an infection rate of slightly over eighteen percent and the British navy a little over thirteen percent. In 1893, the U.S. Medical Corps reported the incidence of venereal disease in frontier troops in the West was 7.3 percent.

8. Rutter (2005) states that 3,900 prostitutes died of syphilis in New Orleans in 1900 (page eleven). In 1875, the *Times* of London reported that 5,000 prostitutes died of venereal disease each year.

9. Penicillin was discovered in 1928 by Alexander Fleming, but was not produced in quantity until 1939. Because of the need for penicillin by wounded troops, it was not commonly available to the civilian population until after the end of World War II in 1945.

Chapter 5

1. Sarsaparilla was a carbonated drink with an acrid, sweet taste. It was flavored with an extract from the dried roots of a series of climbing

vines found in tropical Central America. These roots were also used as a medicine.

2. Towards the end of the Nineteenth Century, building bars for saloons became a significant industry that employed many skilled craftsmen. Back-bars might cost as much as $500, with the counter costing as much again.

Chapter 6

1. Opium is a narcotic drug made from the dried juice of the poppy plant, *Papaver somniferum*, cultivated in the Far East. The poppy contains over twenty-five alkaloids, including morphine, that are used in medicine.

2. The name "patent medicine" came from Europe. In England, royal patents were granted for medicines, hence the name "patent medicine" was used to describe these proprietary concoctions. American "patent" medicines, however, were not patented, because, if they were, the manufacturer would have had to disclose their formulas. Instead, the American versions were proprietary drugs that had copyrighted labels and container designs, in order to protect their brand recognition.

3. This would be an astonishing eighty-eight proof (proof is twice the alcohol percentage). Most current gins, vodkas, and whiskies are eighty proof.

Chapter 7

1. The can-can was first performed in Dodge City, Kansas, in Ham Bell's Varieties dance hall and theater.

Chapter 8

1. Segregation was also not a new idea. In the late Middle Ages in Paris most prostitutes were confined to a district called *Le Clapier*, which is a French word meaning a "rabbit burrow." The Old French word *clapoir*, which means brothel, has been perpetuated in the word "clap," which is a slang term for gonorrhea.

Chapter 9

1. *Rendezvous* is a French word meaning "meeting." It came into general use via French-Canadian trappers from the northern border country.

As a matter of convenience, the month-long rendezvous was usually held in the middle of the prime beaver-trapping country, in what is now southwest Wyoming. The large annual rendezvous that attracted as many as 600 trappers at a time from all over the mountains lasted for fifteen years, from 1825 to 1840. The first one, held in Wyoming in 1825, was not considered by those attending to be a great success, because the traders from St. Louis had forgotten to bring any whiskey.

2. Census records for the North West Company's trading posts show that in 1805 there were 400 Indian wives among the traders. William and George Bent, brothers who established Bent's Fort near present-day La Junta, Colorado, both married female relatives of prominent Cheyenne Indians, and they themselves spoke several Indian dialects. Kit Carson, Jim Bridger, and Jim Beckwourth had Indian wives. Some frontiersmen had multiple wives. Beckwourth is reputed to have had eight.

3. While a certain amount of violence grew naturally out of drinking, gambling, and prostitution, contemporary accounts may have exaggerated the violence of the cowboy's rowdy celebrations. There was probably not as much bloodshed as Western lore has portrayed. Between 1870 and 1885, in the Kansas cattle towns of Caldwell, Wichita, Ellsworth, Dodge City, and Abilene there were "only" a combined total of forty-five documented killings.

4. The name "cowtown" was a somewhat derogatory name that appeared in the 1880s. The residents of these towns preferred the name "cattle town." The cowboys who herded the cattle received a nickname of "cowpoke" or "cowpuncher" from the long, metal-tipped poles they used to prod cattle as they moved them in and out of the cattle pens and railroad cars in the stockyards.

Chapter 10

1. Nevada City, a few miles downstream from Virginia City, was the home of Criterion Hall, a notorious dance hall. In 1864, a local newspaper reported that three sisters (aged one, ten, and twelve) with the last name of Canary were begging on the streets of Virginia City, while their father gambled in the Criterion. It is thought that the oldest girl was probably Martha Jane Canary, who later gained fame across the West as Calamity Jane.

2. Appendix 3 discusses the rise, fall, and change in proportion of the population of Virginia City that was typical of many mining

communities. Census data for Virginia City shows that most of the females in 1860 were aged between twenty and thirty-five. By 1870, the proportion of men to women was close to two men for every woman. Though the male population was always higher than that of women in the late 1800s, the census of 1880 shows that the percentage of females had grown to forty-two percent of the total population. By 1880, the age distribution included more females below twenty years of age and over thirty-five, with the greatest number being children less than four years old.

Chapter 11

1. The end of the Mexican War added Texas, Nevada, Utah, California, most of Arizona and New Mexico, and much of Colorado to the rest of the United States.
2. For some unknown reason, Pennell's last name is spelled in court records as Pinnell.
3. One of the last prominent survivors of the booming red light era, Mattie Silks died in Denver in 1929 at the age of eighty-three and was buried in Fairmount Cemetery.

APPENDIX 1

MISCELLANEOUS DATA RELATING TO PROSTITUTES

Table 1: Data adapted from Sanger (1858) in response to the question: "What trade or calling did you follow before you became a prostitute?"

Occupation	Number	Percent of Total
Servants and housekeepers	972	48.6
Lived with family or friends	499	24.9
Milliners, tailoresses, dress-makers, and associated trades	350	17.5
Miscellaneous trades	175	8.8
Schoolteachers and nurses	4	0.2
TOTAL	**2,000**	**100**

Table 2: Data adapted from Sanger (1858) in response to the question: "What was the cause of your becoming a prostitute?"

Reason	Number	Percent of Total
Destitution	525	26.3
Inclination	513	25.6
Seduced and abandoned	258	12.9
Drink and a desire to drink	181	9.1
Ill treatment by relatives	164	8.2
An easy life	124	6.2
The influence of bad company	84	4.2
Persuaded by a prostitute	71	3.5
Too idle to work	29	1.5
Violated	27	1.3
Seduced on board emigrant ships	16	0.8
Seduced in emigrant boarding houses	8	0.4
TOTAL	**2,000**	**100**

Table 3: Data from Kneeland (1913) asking about a prostitute's first sexual partner.

Partner	Number	Percent of Total
Stranger	420	39.3
Lover	243	22.7
Friend	208	19.5
Relative	90	8.4
Playmate	71	6.6
Acquaintance	28	2.5
Employer or teacher	8	—
TOTAL	**1,068**	**100**

Table 4: Data from Kneeland (1913) asking the reasons for 1,600 women in New York City starting in prostitution.

Reason	Number	Percent of Total
Love	768	48.0
Pay	445	27.8
Force	182	11.4
Physical predisposition	124	7.8
Moral weakness	81	5.1
TOTAL	**1,600**	**100**

Table 5: Data adapted from Sanger (1858) in response to a question about the use of alcohol by prostitutes.

Use of Alcohol	Number	Percent of Total
Do not drink	359	18
Drink moderately	647	32
Intemperate drinker	754	38
Habitual drunkard	240	12
TOTAL	**2,000**	**100**

Table 6: The age of consent in selected Western states between the years 1886 and 1895 (from Pivar, 1973).

State	1886	1889	1893	1895
Arizona Territory	—	14	18	18
California	—	10	10	14
Colorado	10	10	10	18
Montana	10	10	—	16
Nevada	—	—	14	12
Wyoming	10	14	18	18

(— not applicable)

APPENDIX 2

THE AGES OF PROSTITUTES

These two graphs show data for the ages of prostitutes from two studies in New York in 1855 and 1912, respectively. This trend was essentially the same for prostitutes in the West.

(1) The ages of 2,000 prostitutes in New York City in 1855 (from Sanger, 1858)

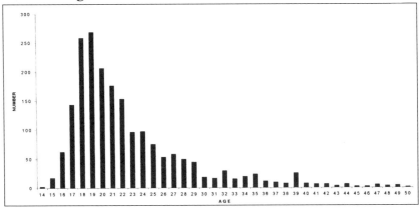

(2) The ages of 1,106 prostitutes in New York City in 1912 (from Kneeland, 1913)

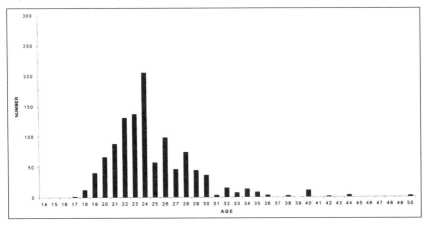

APPENDIX 3

THE RISE AND FALL OF A MINING TOWN

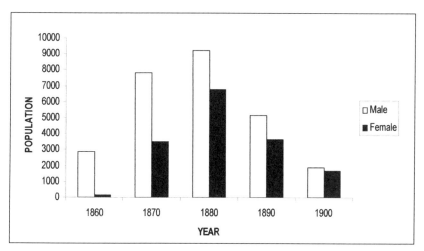

In one concise snapshot, the above graph shows the change in proportion of men to women that was typical of most early Western towns. In 1860, there were 2,857 males, as compared to only 159 females, or about eighteen males to every female. Ten years later, this had changed to two males to every female. By 1900, there were almost as many females as males.

The graph also shows an overall rise in population in this mining town between 1860 and 1880, when the mines were developing and the output of gold and silver was increasing, then a decline between 1880 and 1900 as the rich ore was worked out, the mines were closing, and miners and their families were drifting away to wherever the new strikes were being made. Similar patterns of population growth and decline, and change in ratio of men to women occurred in many mining towns in the West.

[Graph derived from data in census records for the population of Storey County, Nevada, (comprising Gold Hill, Virginia City and the surrounding gold mining area) contained in Appendix 1.1 of James and Raymond (1998)].

GLOSSARY 1

TERMS RELATING TO HOUSES OF PROSTITUTION

BAGNIO: An old English name used to describe a house of prostitution. Derived originally from the Italian name for "bath," because of the association of prostitution with public baths in ancient times.

BAWDYHOUSE: A house run by a "bawd," or woman who operates a house of prostitution.

BOARDING HOUSE: A name sometimes used as a Victorian euphemism for a brothel, because of the girls who "boarded" there.

BORDELLO: House of prostitution.

BOX HOUSE: Name sometimes given to variety theaters that had rows of private curtained boxes around the perimeter, where the actresses and waitresses were available for prostitution between stage acts.

BROTHEL General name for a house of prostitution; originally the name referred to the person rather than the place.

BULLPEN: See "cowyard."

CATHOUSE: The name for a cheap brothel, which may have had its origins in the Dutch word *kat*, meaning a wanton woman. This name became popular during World War I.

CATWAGON: A wagon that carried itinerant prostitutes from town to town, especially during the Kansas cattle drives. See also "cathouse."

COWYARD: Name used primarily in San Francisco to describe large, multistory buildings that were divided into many individual cubicles for prostitutes. Also called a "bullpen."

CRIB: A small house used for prostitution, consisting of only one or two rooms, with the primary furniture being a bed. Typically prostitutes did not live in cribs, but used them only during working hours. Sometimes several prostitutes used the same crib during different times of the day. The crib was a prominent feature of prostitution in the West and Northwest. Usually cribs were lined up along a street in a row and were thus collectively referred to as "The Row" or "The Line."

DISORDERLY HOUSE: A house of prostitution, with particular reference to many of the lower-class houses being the scene of fights, brawls, and other disorderly conduct.

FANCY HOUSE: Name for a house of prostitution, typically used for a higher-class one, such as a parlor house.

FAIRY PALACE: Name used in the nineteenth century to describe a house of prostitutes. ("fairy" was a nineteenth century name for a female prostitute).

FANDANGO HOUSE: Name for a brothel, used typically in the California gold rush days, because most of the early prostitutes were of Spanish and Mexican descent.

FEMALE BOARDING HOUSE: See "boarding house."

GOOSING RANCH: A name for a brothel; derived from the expression "goosing," which refers to a sudden prod on the backside intended to surprise the recipient.

HEIFER RANCH: Name similar to "cowyard" or "bullpen."

HELLHOLE: A name sometime applied to a brothel, because that is where self-righteous citizens claimed that the inhabitants were headed.

HOG RANCH: A Western settlement originally used as a pig farm to supply government posts with pork. Later, such pig ranches became centers of prostitution, gambling, and drinking for soldiers, and the name was generically used as a name for a house of prostitution.

HOOK-SHOP: A house of prostitution. The name is derived either from the hookers who worked there or from the name "hooking" for an act of prostitution.

HOUSE OF ASSIGNATION: House of prostitution or illicit sex, with reference to the clandestine meetings that took place there.

HOUSE OF ILL FAME/HOUSE OF ILL REPUTE: House of prostitution, with reference to the wicked reputation that some of them gained.

HURDYGURDY HOUSE: This name originally applied to a dance-hall with music supplied by a primitive hand-cranked, stringed musical instrument. Later, when many of the hurdygurdy houses degenerated into houses of prostitution, the meaning of the word changed to refer to a brothel.

LADIES BOARDING HOUSE: A name often delicately used on fire insurance maps to designate a brothel.

LINE: Originally this name referred to a row of cribs, but was later used as a generic name for a town's prostitution district. "The Line" was a very common expression for denoting the red light district of a town and prostitutes were commonly called "girls of the line."

LODGING HOUSE: See "boarding house."

PARLOR HOUSE: Expensive house of prostitution, where several high-class prostitutes lived with a madam who took care of the business affairs of the house. The customers either waited in the parlor or were entertained there by the girls with conversation, singing, or dancing before going upstairs for entertainment of a more personal nature.

RED LIGHT HOUSE: House of prostitution in the "red light district." Brothels often advertised by hanging a red light outside, by the door.

RED LIGHT DISTRICT: Area of town with the highest concentration of saloons and brothels. The name is supposed to have originated with the practice of railroad workers hanging their lighted lanterns in front of the brothel they were visiting, but the name appears to have much earlier origins.

ROW: See also "line": the red light district of a town was very commonly referred to as "The Row" or "The Line."

SKID ROW/SKID ROAD: Originally a path down which felled trees were skidded to a sawmill in the Northwest. The name came to refer to the part of a town that grew up along the skid road that was lined with saloons, honky-tonks, and brothels.

SPORTING HOUSE: House of prostitution.

TEMPLE OF VENUS: Ironic name for a house of prostitution with reference to Venus, the Roman goddess of love.

TENDERLOIN: The name appears to have originally been derived in 1876 from a police district of New York City that had a large concentration of brothels and saloons. It was roughly bordered by Fifth Avenue on the east, Eighth Avenue on the west, Twenty-third Street on the south, and Thirty-fourth Street on the north. Eventually, the use of the name was generalized to apply to the area of any town that had a large concentration of brothels. Another explanation is that tenderloin is the choicest part of a beef, therefore the choicest district to which a policeman could be assigned, if he were looking for graft and payoffs, was the red light, or tenderloin, district.

WHOREHOUSE: House of prostitution, literally meaning a house full of whores.

GLOSSARY 2

NAMES FOR PROSTITUTES

In order to appeal to Victorian sensibilities, many of the contemporary names for prostitutes were euphemisms. The culture of the era preferred to use delicate names that appeared to make a seamy profession and its participants more acceptable. Even many of today's observers of the past commonly use these terms.

Some of the terminology for prostitutes has changed over the years. For example, while modern usage of the name "fairy" is applied to male homosexuals, Victorian America used the name to describe a female prostitute. The name "gay" was similarly used for an innocent description of female prostitutes, rather than in today's homosexual usage. Contradictory to their gender, the name "jolly good fellow" was also used to describe these women.

ABANDONED WOMAN: Victorian euphemism for a prostitute, referring to the Victorian theory that a woman who entered prostitution had been seduced and then abandoned by an unscrupulous man.

BAWD: Originally a name from old English, probably derived from an earlier French word. The original usage of the name was for a male pimp, but was later applied to a woman who kept a house of prostitution. Eventually its meaning was widened to include a prostitute.

BOARDER: Refers to the practice in parlor houses of having women who lived or "boarded" there.

BRIDE OF THE MULTITUDE: Reference to a prostitute's frequent and varying sexual partners, with a sarcastic reference to marriage.

BROAD: Common slang name for a woman, making reference to a woman's hips being generally wider than a man's.

BROTHEL: House of prostitution, though originally the name referred to the person who worked there rather than the place.

CALICO CAT/CALICO QUEEN: General name for a prostitute that was used mostly by cowboys. Calico was a coarse cotton cloth commonly used by pioneer women for everything from bonnets and dresses to wallpaper, table cloths, and curtains.

CALL GIRL: A more modern name for a prostitute, referring to her mode of operation. The call girl does not have a definite place of work, but visits customers as she is called.

CAMP FOLLOWER: General name for the non-official civilians, such as laundresses and officers' wives, who were associated with army posts on the frontier. Thus, the name came to be also used as a generic name for a prostitute who catered primarily to soldiers.

CAT: A name used occasionally to describe a prostitute. It may have come from the Dutch word *kat*, which means a "wanton woman." Though it may appear so, its origins were probably not a play on the word "pussy," which is used today as common slang to describe female genitals. In the mid-1800s, the name "pussy" was often used as a name of endearment without sexual connotations, such as a father might call a daughter.

CEILING EXPERT: Sarcastic reference to the view seen by a woman making her living on her back.

CELESTIAL FEMALE Name usually reserved for Oriental prostitutes.

CHILENO: Name for the early prostitutes in San Francisco, used because many of them came from Chile and other South American countries.

CHIPPY: A name originally used for lively young women with loose morals, but also used as a generic name for a prostitute. The name was sometimes used in a derogatory fashion to describe low-class prostitutes who robbed their customers. Spelled as "chippie," the name was sometimes used for a short, knee-length dress worn by crib prostitutes, that was easy to remove when a customer arrived.

COURTESAN: Derived from the French or Italian, this name referred originally to a woman of a royal court, thus was later used to describe a high-class or high-priced prostitute.

CYPRIAN: The island of Cyprus was famed for its temples devoted to Venus, the goddess of love, thus the names "Cyprian" or "Fair Cyprian" were used as indirect names for a prostitute.

DANCE-HALL: Establishments that originally offered music and dancing, but which later degenerated into quasi-brothels or at least contact points for prostitution.

DAUGHTER OF EVE: Name for a prostitute with reference to the Biblical Eve and her sexual enticement of Adam in the Garden of Eden.

DAUGHTER OF JOY: Name for a prostitute with obvious reference to the service she provided. The name was usually reserved for Chinese prostitutes.

DEMI-MONDE: Occasional name for a prostitute, more often used to describe the prostitute's environment. The word comes from the French, literally meaning "half-world."

DOLCINEA (or DULCINEA): Used originally as a generic name for a sweetheart, but later applied to a prostitute, the reference being to the peasant girl of loose morals that Don Quixote imagined to be a lovely lady.

EASY WOMAN: A woman of loose virtue or prostitute, whose sexual favors were easy to obtain.

ERRING SISTER: Victorian euphemism for a prostitute, with reference to the girl having originally made a mistake in offering her sexual favors to someone.

FAIR, BUT FRAIL: Victorian euphemism with reference to a woman being beautiful, but not able to control her own biological urges.

FAIR CYPRIAN: See "Cyprian."

FAIRY: Nineteenth century name for a female prostitute, as opposed to the twentieth century application of the name to a male homosexual.

FALLEN ANGEL/FALLEN WOMAN: Victorian euphemism, referring to the concept that women were to be figuratively placed on a romantic pedestal. If they strayed sexually, they had then fallen off their pedestals and thus fallen from grace.

FAST WOMAN: A prostitute. "Fast" in nineteenth century usage was applied as an adjective to a lawless town or to a "fast" woman, such as a prostitute.

FILLE DE JOIE: Name derived from French to describe a prostitute, the literal translation being "daughter of joy" or "daughter of happiness."

FRAIL: Slang name for a girl or young woman.

FRAIL DENIZEN: Slang name for a woman who was a prostitute, with the Victorian idea that she was not strong enough to control her urges.

FRAIL SISTER: May derived from the name "frail" for a young woman, or may be a Victorian euphemism for a sexually straying woman being not strong enough to control her urges.

GAY WOMAN: A female prostitute, rather than being used in the sense of today's homosexual usage.

GIRL OF THE NIGHT: Name for a prostitute with reference to working hours being primarily at night. The name dates from at least the 1700s.

HARLOT: An old English name for a prostitute, this may be derived from the word "varlet," meaning a male rogue or scoundrel. It was eventually applied to a female prostitute.

HOOKER: Name for a prostitute with three possible derivations. The name may have come from the practice of streetwalkers hooking their arms through a prospective customer's arm to try and attract business. An alternate explanation is that it came from a reference to prostitutes who plied their trade among the soldiers of General Joseph Hooker's regiment during the Civil War; however, this is unlikely because use of the name pre-dates the Civil War. A more likely explanation is that the name originally came from an area of New York named "The Hook" that contained many brothels and prostitutes.

HORIZONTAL EXPERT: Refers to the prostitute's position during working hours.

HURDYGURDY GIRL: Name that originally referred to a girl who worked in a hurdygurdy house, which was a dance-hall with music provided by a hand-cranked instrument. Later, when many of the hurdygurdy houses degenerated into houses of prostitution, the meaning of the name changed to refer to a prostitute.

HUSSY: A woman of loose morals and also a generic name for a prostitute. Originally the word was a contraction of the early English word for "housewife," and was applied to women of low morals.

JEZEBEL: Name for a prostitute, with reference to the Biblical Jezebel, who was the wicked wife of Ahab, the king of Israel.

JOLLY GOOD FELLOW: Victorian American slang for an "easy" girl.

LADY OF EASY VIRTUE: Name for a prostitute with reference to loose sexual behavior.

LADY OF THE NIGHT/LADY OF THE EVENING: See "girl of the night."

LEWD WOMAN: Woman with lewd morals, e.g. a prostitute.

MADAM (occasionally spelled "madame"): Derived from the French and literally meaning "my lady." This name refers primarily to the woman who managed or owned a house of prostitution and handled the business arrangements between the customers and the girls.

MAGDALENE: General name for a prostitute, with Biblical reference. The order of St. Mary Magdalen was a religious order that accepted criminal women, and the name Magdalens was sometimes used as a generic name for reformers.

MAIDEN OF JOY: Name for a prostitute with reference to the purpose of her profession.

MARY MAGDALEN: See "Magdalene."

MISTRESS: Primarily used to describe a female sexual partner who was not a man's wife, but also occasionally used as a general name for a prostitute.

NYMPH DU PAVE: Corruption of the French name for streetwalker, literally meaning "maiden of the street." In Greek and Latin mythology, from which the name originates, nymphs were minor nature goddesses living in rivers and mountains. A more obscure interpretation of the term's origin may be that nympha, also from the Greek, is a medical name for part of the female genitals.

NYMPH DU PRAIRIE: Western version of the French name "nymph du pave" that refers to the Western prostitute's place of work being the prairie, instead of the street.

PAINTED LADY/PAINTED CAT/PAINTED WOMAN: Name for a prostitute, making reference to the fact that many prostitutes used heavy makeup, while respectable ladies and housewives did not. See also "cat." In modern times the name "painted lady" is used as a generic name for a restored, brightly-painted historic Victorian house.

PRETTY WAITER GIRL: Originally a name for a girl who worked in a dance-hall or variety theater hustling drinks. As these women started to offer sexual services as well as liquor, the name expanded to refer to prostitutes.

PROSTITUTE: A woman who sells promiscuous sexual services for money.

SCARLET LADY/SCARLET WOMAN: Name for a prostitute, with reference to the bright scarlet lip and cheek makeup used by some Victorian prostitutes.

SHADY LADY: Name for a prostitute with reference to her questionable morals.

SINGLE MEN'S WIVES: Name for prostitutes, referring to them taking the sexual place of wives for unmarried men.

SISTER OF MISFORTUNE: Name for a prostitute suggesting that a woman entered prostitution after falling on hard times.

SISTER OF THE NIGHT: Name for a prostitute, with reference to her working hours being primarily at night.

SLUT: Demeaning reference to a prostitute, probably from a fifteenth century English term meaning a "slovenly woman."

SOILED DOVE: Victorian euphemism, referring to a woman who had strayed sexually being not as pure as her virginal counterpart.

SPORTING GIRL/SPORTING WOMAN: Name for a prostitute, because a house of gambling or prostitution was sometimes called a "sporting house."

STREETWALKER: Name for a lower-class of prostitute who tried to find business by walking the streets.

STRUMPET: Very old name for a prostitute that may be derived from the French or Latin.

TART: Very old English name for a prostitute; the name has unclear origins.

TAXI-DANCER: Name for a woman who worked in dance-halls entertaining customers with dancing and drinking. Women by this name were not necessarily prostitutes.

UNFORTUNATE WOMAN: Victorian euphemism, based on the idea that a woman became a prostitute because of unfortunate circumstances.

WAITER GIRL: See "pretty waiter girl."

WENCH: Though often used to simply describe a young woman, the name was primarily used in old English to refer to a wanton woman.

WHORE: One of the oldest terms in the English language for a prostitute.

WOMAN OF THE DEMI-MONDE: A combination of French and English words that literally translated means "woman of the half-world," a reference to a prostitute's existence on the fringes of the everyday conventional world.

WOMAN OF THE TOWN: Name for a prostitute with reference to her multiple sexual partners.

WORKING GIRL: A euphemistic name for a prostitute.

YANKEDO: Name for Mexican prostitutes who plied their trade among the American troops during the Mexican War. This name was commonly used in early San Francisco, where prostitutes were primarily of Spanish-American origin.

BIBLIOGRAPHY

Acton, William. *Prostitution.* London: John Churchill & Sons, 1870.

Agnew, Jeremy. *Life of a Soldier on the Western Frontier.* Missoula: Mountain Press Publishing Company, 2008.

Anderson, Patricia. *When Passion Reigned: Sex and the Victorians.* Basic Books: New York, 1995.

Armitage, Susan H. and Elizabeth Jameson, eds. *The Women's West.* Norman: University of Oklahoma Press, 1987.

Asbury, Herbert. *Carry Nation.* New York: Alfred A. Knopf, Inc., 1929.

Asbury, Herbert. T*he Barbary Coast.* New York: Alfred A. Knopf, Inc., 1933.

Asbury, Herbert. *The French Quarter.* New York: Alfred A. Knopf, Inc., 1936.

Bancroft, Caroline. *Denver's Lively Past.* Boulder: Johnson Publishing Co., 1959.

Bancroft, Caroline. *Six Racy Madams of Colorado.* Boulder: Johnson Publishing Co., 1965.

Barclay, Stephen. *Bondage (The Slave Traffic in Women Today).* New York: Funk and Wagnalls, 1968.

Banes, Sally, Sheldon Frank, and Tem Horwitz (eds). *Our Natural Passion: 200 Years of Sex in America.* Chicago: Follett Publishing Co., 1976.

Barnhart, Jacqueline B. *The Fair but Frail: Prostitution in San Francisco 1849-1900.* Reno: University of Nevada Press, 1986.

Barsness, Larry. *Gold Camp: Alder Gulch and Virginia City, Montana.* New York: Hastings House, 1962.

Bird, Allan G. *Bordellos of Blair Street.* Pierson: Advertising, Publications & Consultants, 1993.

Black, Celeste. *The Pearl of Cripple Creek.* Colorado Springs: BlackBear Publishing, 1997.

Blair, Edward. *Leadville: Colorado's Magic City.* Boulder: Pruett Publishing Co., 1980.

Brown, Dee. *The Gentle Tamers.* New York: G.P. Putnam's Sons, 1958

Brown, Larry K. *The Hog Ranches of Wyoming.* Glendo: High Plains Press, 1995.

Brown, Robert L. *Saloons of the American West.* Silverton: Sundance Publications, Ltd., 1978.

Bruns Roger A. *Desert Honkytonk.* Golden: Fulcrum Publishing, 2000.

Bullough, Vern L. *The History of Prostitution.* New Hyde Park: University Books, 1964.

Bullough, Vern L. and Bonnie Bullough. *Prostitution: An Illustrated Social History.* New York: Crown Publishers, Inc., 1978.

Burgess, William. *The World's Social Evil.* Chicago: Saul Brothers, Publishers, 1914.

Butler, Anne M. *Daughters of Joy, Sisters of Misery.* Urbana: University of Illinois Press, 1987.

Carter, Samuel. *Cowboy Capital of the World.* Garden City: Doubleday & Co., Inc, 1973.

Chesney, Kellow. *The Victorian Underworld.* London: Penguin Books, 1970.

Couch, Jacqualine G. *Those Golden Girls of Market Street.* Fort Collins: The Old Army Press, 1974.

Crow, Duncan. *The Victorian Woman.* New York: Stein and Day, 1972.

Dary, David. *Seeking Pleasure in the Old West.* Lawrence: University Press of Kansas, 1995.

Dial, Scott. *Saloons of Denver.* Fort Collins: The Old Army Press, 1973.

Donovan, Brian. *White Slave Crusades.* Urbana: University of Illinois Press, 2006

Drago, Harry S. *Notorious Ladies of the Frontier.* New York: Dodd Mead and Co., 1969.

Dykstra, Robert R. *The Cattle Towns.* New York: Alfred A Knopf, Inc., 1968.

Ellis, Amanda M. *The Strange, Uncertain Years.* Hamden: The Shoestring Press Inc., 1959.

Erdoes, Richard. *Saloons of the Old West.* New York: Alfred Knopf, 1979.

BIBLIOGRAPHY

Faulk, Odie B. *Tombstone: Myth and Reality.* New York: Oxford University Press, Inc., 1972.

Faulk, Odie B. *Dodge City.* Oxford University Press, Inc., New York, 1977.

Feitz, Leland. *Myers Avenue.* Denver: Golden Bell Press, 1967.

Flexner, Abraham. *Prostitution in Europe.* New York: Century Press, 1920.

Furnas, J.C. *The Life and Times of the Late Demon Rum.* London: W.H. Allen, 1965.

Gentry, Curt. *The Madams of San Francisco.* Garden City: Doubleday & Company, 1964.

Gilfoyle, Timothy J. *City of Eros.* New York: W.W. Norton Company, 1992.

Gladden, Sanford C. *Ladies of the Night.* Boulder: Privately Published, 1979.

Goldman, Marion. *Gold Diggers and Silver Miners.* Ann Arbor: University of Michigan Press, 1981.

Goodstein, Phil. *The Seamy Side of Denver.* Denver: New Social Publications, 1993.

Green, Harvey. *The Light of the Home.* New York: Pantheon Books, 1983.

Harrison, Fraser. *The Dark Angel: Aspects of Victorian Sexuality.* New York, Universe Books, 1977.

Hill, Marilynn W. *Their Sister's Keepers.* Berkeley: University of California Press, 1993.

Hope, Jack. *Yukon.* Englewood Cliffs: Prentice-Hall Inc., 1976

James, Ronald M. and Elizabeth C. Raymond. *Comstock Women: The Making of a Mining Community.* Reno: University of Nevada Press, 1998.

Janney, Edward O. *The White Slave Traffic in America.* Baltimore: The Lord Baltimore Press, 1911.

Kimball, Nell. *Nell Kimball - Her Life as an American Madam.* New York: The Macmillan Publishing Company, 1970.

Kneeland, George J. *Commercialized Prostitution in New York City.* The Century Company, New York, 1913.

Lee, Mabel B. *Cripple Creek Days*. Garden City: Doubleday and Co., 1958.

Lee, Mabel B. *Back in Cripple Creek*. Garden City: Doubleday and Co., 1968.

Levy, Jo A. *They Saw the Elephant: Women in the California Gold Rush*. Hamden: Archon Books, 1990.

Longstreet, Stephen. *The Wilder Shore*. Garden City: Doubleday & Co., Inc., 1968.

Lyman, George D. *The Saga of the Comstock Lode*. New York: Charles Scribner's Sons, 1934.

MacKell, Jan. *Brothels, Bordellos, & Bad Girls*. Albuquerque: University of New Mexico Press, 2004.

Mahood, Linda. *The Magdalenes: Prostitution in the Nineteenth Century*. London: Routledge, 1990.

Martin, Cy. *Whiskey and Wild Women*. New York: Hart Publishing Co. Inc., 1974.

Mazzulla, Fred and Jo Mazzulla. *Brass Checks and Red Lights*. Denver: Published by the authors, 1966.

McDonald, Douglas. *The Legend of Julia Bulette and the Red Light Ladies of Nevada*. Las Vegas: Nevada Publications, 1980.

Miller, Max. *Holladay Street*. New York: Signet Books, 1962.

Miller, Ronald D. *Shady Ladies of the West*. Los Angeles: Westernlore Press, 1964.

Morgan, Lael. *Good Time Girls*. Kenmore: Epicenter Press, 1998.

Morgan, Murray. *Skid Road*. Seattle: University of Washington Press, 1982.

Muscatine, Doris. *Old San Francisco*. New York: G.P. Putnam's Sons, 1975.

Myers, John M. *The Last Chance: Tombstone's Early Years*. New York: E.P. Dutton & Co., 1950.

Noel, Thomas J. *The City and the Saloon: Denver, 1858-1916*. Lincoln: University of Nebraska Press, 1982.

Norman, Cathleen M. *In & Around Old Colorado City*. Lakewood: Preservation Publishing, 2001.

O'Connor, Richard. *Iron Wheels and Broken Men*. New York, G.P. Putnam's Sons, 1973.

BIBLIOGRAPHY

Parkhill, Forbes. *The Wildest of the West.* New York: Henry Holt and Company, 1951.

Pearl, Cyril. *The Girl with the Swansdown Seat.* London: Frederick Muller Ltd., 1956.

Perkin, Joan. *Victorian Women.* Washington Square: New York University Press, 1993.

Pivar, David J. Purity Crusade: *Sexual Morality and Social Control.* Westport: Greenwood Press, Inc., 1973.

Reiter, Joan S. *The Women.* Alexandria: Time-Life Books, 1978.

Rose, Al. *Storyville, New Orleans.* University: University of Alabama Press, 1974.

Rosen, Ruth. *The Lost Sisterhood: Prostitution in America.* Baltimore: The Johns Hopkins University Press, 1982.

Rothman, Sheila M. *Woman's Proper Place.* New York: Basic Books, Inc., 1978.

Rutter, Michael. *Upstairs Girls.* Helena: Farcountry Press, 2005.

Sanger, William W. *The History of Prostitution.* New York, Harper and Bros., 1858.

Seagraves, Anne. *Soiled Doves: Prostitution in the Early West.* Hayden, Wesanne Publications, 1994.

Secrest, Clark. *Hell's Belles: Denver's Brides of the Multitudes.* Aurora: Hindsight Historical Publications, 1996.

Smith, Duane A. *Rocky Mountain Mining Camps.* Lincoln: University of Nebraska Press, 1967.

Speidel, William C. *Sons of the Profits.* Seattle: Nettle Creek Publishing Company, 1967.

Steinbach, Susie. *Women in England: 1760-1914.* London: Weidenfeld & Nicolnson, 2004

Stratton, Joanna L. *Pioneer Women.* New York: Simon and Schuster, 1981.

Streeter, Floyd B. *Prairie Trails and Cow Towns.* New York: The Devin Adair Co., 1963.

Trudgill, Eric. *Madonnas and Magdalens.* New York: Holmes & Meier, 1976.

Vestal, Stanley. *Queen of Cowtowns: Dodge City.* New York: Harper and Brothers, 1952.

Walkowitz, Judith R. *Prostitution and Victorian Society.* Cambridge: Cambridge University Press, 1980.

West, Elliott. *The Saloon on the Rocky Mountain Mining Frontier.* Lincoln: University of Nebraska Press, 1976.

Williams, George. *The Red Light Ladies of Virginia City, Nevada.* Dayton: Tree by the River Publishing, 1990.

Winick, Charles and Paul M. Kinsie. *The Lively Commerce.* Chicago: Quadrangle Books, 1971.

Woolston, Howard B. *Prostitution in the United States.* New York, The Century Company, 1921.

INDEX

(Note: page references to photos are underlined)